6.95A8

**Illinois Central College
Learning Resource Center**

ARE AMERICANS EXTINCT?

JETHRO K. LIEBERMAN

ARE AMERICANS EXTINCT?

WALKER AND COMPANY

New York

Dedication

To the memory of Abraham Lieberman and Armin Hajman
Koller and to Rebecca Dumes Lieberman and Katharine
Schlesinger Koller, my grandparents, who left Europe for a
better world.

Acknowledgments

For his time and expert counsel, I gratefully acknowledge the help of Dale de Haan, aide to Senator Edward M. Kennedy. Thanks go also to Patricia Tidwell and Thomas van der Voort, legislative assistants to Senator William Proxmire, for helpful suggestions; to Congressional Quarterly, Inc., for permission to reprint Table 2 in the Appendix; to Harcourt, Brace & World, Inc., for permission to use the table on pages 89–90; to Leon Friedman, for the initial idea of a book on immigration policy; and to my wife, as always, for her forebearance during winter nights in Newport and for her help with copyediting, proofreading, and indexing. Needless to say, the responsibility for all errors of fact or judgment is mine alone.

J.K.L.

Newport, Rhode Island
May, 1968

CONTENTS

1 / *Crack in the Melting Pot*

There is a mighty land whose local provinces bear strange Indian names. The few exceptions are French, British, and Spanish, legacy of a now-faded colonialism. The natives are proud of their sparsely populated, rolling fields and precipitous mountains, and their more crowded cities. They are proud of their self-made institutions, which seem peculiar to most of the world. They are prouder still of themselves. They came from many farmlands, from the drab factories of some squalid cities, and from a host of jail cells to do their nation's work. In time they came to believe that they alone could do it. For forty years the natives of Massachusetts and Mississippi, Oregon and Ohio, New York and New Mexico, South Dakota and Illinois and Arkansas came to think they owned the land, overlooking the lease which mankind held. Like the redwood which fears the marigold will dry up its roots, Americans in the 1920's decided to seal their national borders to foreigners—or to most of them, at any rate. All men are born equal, but only some could come to the United States.

If immigration was a subject of intense national interest during the nineteenth century and the first decades of the twentieth, it is now a topic about which we all nod knowingly but inquire little. How many Americans today could identify the two nations during World War II whose immigration and naturalization policies were based on explicit racist theories? Germany, certainly, for we warred against Germany to rid the world of racism. But Japan was not the other, nor Italy, Russia, China, or France: it was the United States.

It is a commentary on the largeness of American life that our nation could so fervently embrace a war against the myth of "Aryan superiority" while insisting that because the "Nordic race" had contributed most to America, it should be given an overwhelming preference in the privilege of entering the United States to settle as citizens. It is a commentary on our institutions that it took 132 years to impose racial criteria on a broad scale and that it then took another 44 years to remove them. It is a commentary, too, on the passions and stubbornness of men, that those who proposed these criteria, those who imposed the criteria as law, and those who fought repeal of the law, denied that it did what it did.

It is part of American folklore that our nation was formed by a mixture of immigrants of all kinds from all over the world, and in a bubbling melting pot we cooked up our wonderfully creative, dynamic, progressive, and idealistic society.

There is substantial truth in this, but it is by no means the whole truth.

In fact, now that we are mending the "melting pot," we can perhaps for the first time admit that for the last forty years the pot had a very serious crack in it. The crack in the melting pot drained America of a great source of energy and dissipated a substantial reservoir of talent.

The defect in the melting pot has been the restrictive immigration laws which have belied America's faith in the common man, America's hospitality to the oppressed, and America's call to all peoples to a better world.

Now, however, after some forty years, restrictions are being removed. Not yet all, or even most. But the most blatantly evil and hypocritical restrictions are finally gone. This book is the story of how America let itself get talked into actions that denied its very soul, and how it is beginning to restore its soul to dignity.

To preserve not merely the American character, but the very "lifeblood of the United States," Congress enacted during the early 1920's a series of laws designed to restrict immigration to our shores.

During the years immediately before the first World War, and immediately after, great masses of Europeans emigrated from their native lands, arriving in droves that sometimes totaled more than one million annually. A wave of fear, which had begun in the 1850's but abated during the Civil War, was again abetted by various radical incidents and fanned by xenophobic lobbies which moved in to block the foreigners, the "new immigrants," who looked different, talked "different," and no doubt smelled different when first they docked.

The restrictive laws were based on the so-called national origins theory: each country was assigned a quota based on a ratio between that country's immigrants already here and the population of the United States. In all, a worldwide total of 150,000 entry permits was issued annually. Since nearly half the population had come in one way or another from Great Britain—either directly or as the descendants of immigrants—that country got nearly half the total, or more than 65,000 quotas yearly. Germany got nearly 26,000, Ireland, 18,000; but Greece had a paltry 307. Supporters of the national origins system justified it by noting that it was designed to be a mirror to our society: to each country according to its contribution (of people) to America, in order to preserve the "ethnic balance." But even at the start the mirror was slightly flawed: Asians and Negroes were not reflected in the national origins system at all.

America was cloaked in a vast cloth of irony. The Know-Nothing party rose to power in the mid-nineteenth century against the coming of the Irish, electing six governors and seventy-five Congressmen in 1854 and running a Presidential candidate named Millard Fillmore in 1856. In the 1840's the party required candidates for office to subscribe to this oath: "That you will not vote nor give your influence to any man for any office in the gift of the people unless he be an American-born citizen, in favor of Americans ruling America, nor if he be a Roman Catholic. You will, when elected or appointed to an official station, conferring on you the power to do so, remove all foreigners, aliens, or Roman Catholics from office or place in your gift." Abraham Lincoln after the 1856 campaign grew alarmed: "How can anyone who abhors the oppression of Negroes be in favor of degrading classes of white people? As a nation we began by declaring that 'all men are created equal.' We now practically read it, 'All men are created equal except Negroes.' When the Know-Nothings obtain control, it will read: 'All men are created equal except Negroes, foreigners, and Catholics.' When it comes to this, I shall prefer emigrating to some country where they make no pretense of loving liberty."

Despite the hatred of the Irish, some illustrious politicians of Irish ancestry were staunch supporters of national origins. Yet it was an Irish Congressman and mayor of Boston, inveighing against the temper of the times at the turn of the century, and very much aware of his origins, who transmitted the immigrant legacy to his grandsons, John, Robert, and Edward, men who in turn were to have much to do with setting America to rights during the 1960's. It was that same Boston and New England (the region that for a century had fostered the tradition we still revere—that America, as the home of immigrants, feared no man and welcomed all) that supplied the nation with not only the intellectual impetus to plead and settle for restriction but also the Congressional leaders of the movement to impose restriction.

There was the irony of government officials who sought power to defend the principles of democracy from the "alien hordes" only to assert themselves above the law and to act as arrogantly as the monarchs from whom the foreigners fled. There is the irony of the welcome extended to professional people by the Federal Government, a welcome quickly withdrawn by state governments which forbid these people from practicing their skills. There was the irony of a Congressman's attempt to prevent a three-year-old Japanese boy, adopted by American parents stationed in the Far East, from entering the country because "too many subversives" were entering our land. There was the irony of Congressmen, Senators, and private citizens, who when the situation was critical voted and shouted against America's foreign aid appropriations, but who nevertheless questioned whether America ought to permit across its borders skilled personnel from countries to which foreign aid was going.

In the minds of many, there was a more subtle irony concerning Charles Darwin and his theory. There were politicians and religious leaders aplenty who rejected the heretical thought that evolution should be taught in the schools, yet who clung to a fear that, through immigration, Americans would be "mongrelized" and perhaps even be made extinct, a fear directly traceable to the impact that the theory of evolution had made upon the nation. There was a more blatant irony in the Justice Department's attempt during World War II to imprison a concededly loyal lady, an American citizen of Japanese ancestry, more or less on the ground that America was at war with Japan and once a Japanese always a Japanese, even if never a Japanese. The Supreme Court refused to go along with this triumph of biology over law, but there was irony with no less mean a sting in the many decisions of the Supreme Court which came down on the side of what we now know (if we did not know it then) to be false science.

It is ironic that the bias in our immigration law in favor of the sons and daughters of England, *against* whose laws we rebelled, was justified in part on the grounds that from England came our language and our law. And there is irony in the fact that the southern switch in 1964 from Lyndon Johnson, who was pledged to end the national origins system, contributed to the defeat of the very system the South sought to preserve.

There was tragedy in the injustices done, the bitter hostility left when the arguments ended. But there was triumph also: Emanuel Celler, Representative from New York, who fought against the original restrictionist legislation in the House, lived to chair the Judiciary Committee when it abolished national origins forty years later. Representative John McCormack, who argued for repeal of the national origins system in 1927, two years before it went into effect, presided as Speaker of the House over its demise. And Lyndon Johnson, who voted against his party's President in 1952 on a vital immigration law, lived to be the President who, on October 3, 1965, signed into law the bill that President Truman had sought.

Withal, the fight for and against national origins—the basis of restrictive immigration laws—was a microcosm of the American scene. It touched almost every sensitive nerve in Congress and was before that legislative body in one form or another in every session from 1920 on. The courts had been wrestling with immigration problems for years preceding the time of active legislation, and they were destined to hear thousands of cases in the years to come. The Immigration and Naturalization Service, a nomadic agency now a part of the Department of Justice, bears the brunt of enforcing the 175 pages of immigration law; it is no wonder that even when it has done its best it has stirred controversy.

The difficulties which all these institutions have experienced in dealing with our immigration system stem from an inescapable fact of American life: We are an exceedingly legalistic nation. Our history is not only the story of pressure groups and passions, of minority vs. majority, of government against individual; it is inextricably the story of the laws these groups have backed or opposed and the great court battles which had preceded and followed legislation.

Behind the surface skin of the law—smooth or pockmarked as it may be—lies the bustling activity of the institutions and groups and men who have created the law to serve them. Laws —especially statutes—are merely approximations of community sentiment on the date of enactment, often agreed to with the tacit understanding that the words may cover up an ugly sore but not remove it. For all our vaunted concern with know-how, pragmatism, and getting the job done, we Americans have a preoccupation with form. Never mind that enforcement is at odds with the spirit of the law—so long as the statute is on the books. This is true in divorce and other domestic law; it is true in law regulating such personal behavior as Kinseyan sexual antics, and sometimes true, though perhaps less often, in law regulating Keynesian economic mores. It is true also of the Immigration and Nationality Act, Title 8 of the United States Code.

That Americans seem to harbor a dependence on formalisms

does not necessarily mean we are being pigheaded—only stuffy. Those who are satisfied with the law's wording may be willing to suffer others to break it. For example, the divorce laws of many states are rigid, yet in actual courtroom practice, they are easy enough to circumvent. Thus, one can fake an act of adultery (committing perjury in the process) to dissolve a marriage. The public's sense that divorce is allowable only where a spouse goes philandering is satisfied because it chooses not to examine whether those who secure divorces are in fact satisfying the law's requirements. After all it is the truth of courts, not of social scientists, that the public desires. In the face of these flexible formalisms, or fictions (call them what you will), American society remains fluid.

The power to lay down an immigration law is given absolutely and exclusively to Congress by the Constitution, and we know this is true because the Supreme Court has said so. That does not mean that courts and administrators have no voice in policymaking, for what they say the written law means is in fact what the law means, unless Congress decides to pass a new one. In drafting and enacting an "immigration law," therefore, Congress has a delicate task: It must frame a set of rules in such a way that the administrators, courts, and private citizens who daily deal with immigration problems will abide by them without excuse for change. The task is eased by the fact that representative government will usually create laws acceptable to the majority, but it is complicated by the fact that what is acceptable to the majority is not necessarily wise or workable. From a crossfire of opinions, Congress must articulate a national policy.

The failure to do so is the principal reason for statutory failure: Courts interpret the words in different ways where the meaning is ambiguous; different administrators and officials in the field read different meanings into the law, think different things, cause pain and suffering and hardship to real people, and do justice inequitably. In the formation of any national policy—where that policy must be expressed in words—the overwhelming necessity to compromise inevitably means that policy will be to some degree or other not articulate but vague and uncertain. Even the best laws—and the best laws are usually the shortest laws—can be ambiguous; justice requires a wise fathoming by courts and administrators of the policy which lies behind the words—justice, that is, requires recourse to the purpose of the law. Too often, courts are not careful in this task; where they are not, the legislature is at least as much to blame as the courts.

Two events of constitutional scope conspired to set the stage for the national origins limitation of immigration, even though they occurred some forty years before Congress chose to take full advantage of them. Under Article I, Section 8, Clause 4, the Constitution gives to Congress the power "to establish an Uniform Rule of Naturalization"; that power, together with the power to regulate foreign commerce and the power "to make all laws which shall be necessary and proper for carrying into execution the foregoing powers," encompass the related power to lay down immigration law, even though the subject is not specifically mentioned in the Constitution at all.

In 1876, with the Civil War a decade behind, with immigration beginning to accelerate, and the factory classes beginning to assemble in the cities, Congress got its first opportunity to make immigration law.

In years previous, the states (primarily New York) had skeleton systems of immigration regulations, designed to aid needy immigrants. In New York State, the Board of Commissioners of Emigration, manned by unpaid charity advocates, collected a fee from shipowners who transported immigrants, in order to help the alien when he arrived. In lieu of the fee, the master of the vessel could pay a bond on those immigrants who, according to the best guesses of the board, were most likely to become "public charges." The $1.50-per-passenger charge levied against shipowners was too much for them. It was a blatant attack on their private property rights, and they pressed a case in the Supreme Court of the United States, which obliged them in 1876. The Court declared that since Congress had the exclusive power to regulate foreign commerce, the states must desist from their unconstitutional actions. Thus, the administration of charity was thrown entirely into private hands, which sagged under the weight and shrank from the obligation. Leaders of private charities did not have a reluctance to work; but fed by burgeoning beliefs in the all-explanatory powers of the theory of evolution, they grew to have a distaste for the impoverished. Poverty, they thought, isn't made; it's inherited. Said one leader: "The hereditary character of pauperism and crime is the most fearful element with which society has to contend."

So the New York Board of Commissioners of Emigration and the New York Board of Charities joined with petitions from other seaboard states to Congress. If Congress now had the power to do what the states had previously done, it had better act. Six years later, in 1882, it did. For the first time, Congress passed an act limiting entrance into the United States: Convicts, lunatics, idiots, and persons likely to become public charges were barred. In addition, upon disembarking, each immigrant (not the shipowner) was charged fifty cents for a U.S. immigrant welfare fund. The Secretary of the Treasury was authorized to oversee the operation, but the states were delegated power to carry out the actual inspecting.

Significantly, in that same year Congress passed another restrictive law which would give rise to the second constitutional test. In 1882, the Chinese Exclusion Act became law. Henceforth, it would be illegal for citizens of China or persons of Chinese descent to enter the United States; those who did could be summarily deported. Those Chinese aliens who already had emigrated to America would be allowed to remain, but they were forever barred from citizenship. Could it be that Congress had such plenary power over entrance that a discrimination against a particular nationality and race could be imposed? Chae Chan Ping, a resident alien in California who made the mistake of leaving temporarily for China, asked that question of the Supreme Court in 1889 when U.S. immigration authorities refused to permit him to reenter. The answer was Yes. Furthermore, said the Court, when it comes to naturalization, the Congress need not treat different peoples equally, even though its power is to enact "an uniform rule of naturalization." "Uniform" means simply that the law of immigration and naturalization in

Utah must be identical to the law in Florida. Thus, an Englishman could be naturalized in any state; a Chinese in none.

Since power, once given, will sooner or later be used, immigration increasingly came under the eye of a worried Congress. As decades rolled by and immigrants rolled in, Congress eventually seized on the power to restrict in a large-scale way. At times certain Congressmen seemed almost indignant, with the special glee that comes from the possession of absolute, exclusive power. Even in 1964, Representative Michael A. Feighan, chairman of the House subcommittee that dealt with immigration matters, kept wanting to know, inquiring again and again of the parade of witnesses before his subcommittee, whether or not they agreed that Congress should retain the power over immigration which the Supreme Court in 1876 said it had. The question was rather silly, since the Supreme Court had ruled on a constitutional ground that the power was exclusive in Congress and that meant that Congress couldn't give it away if it wanted to. Congress was stuck with it, but still the thought rankled that Congress might delegate some authority to an executive agency to allocate immigration quotas among the different countries. Congress had the power, Representative Feighan seemed to be saying, and by God, Congress was going to keep it.

The power is absolute. Although the states are commanded by the 14th Amendment to be certain that the people are all guaranteed "equal protection of the laws," by historical oversight the Federal Government escaped this constitutional stricture. Not that the escape means much today where almost anything other than immigration is concerned. For recognizing that the *states* were required to integrate their schools in 1954 by virtue of the equal protection clause, Chief Justice Earl Warren in a case decided the same day noted that even though the *Federal* Government was not so directed, nevertheless by virtue of the due process clause, the Federal Government would be held to the. same standard in the District of Columbia, which is a federal city. "In view of our decision that the Constitution prohibits the states from maintaining racially segregated public schools, it would be unthinkable that the same Constitution would impose a lesser duty on the Federal Government," the Chief Justice declared for the Court. But that was 1954, and the subtle thinking that sees in clauses requiring both state and federal governments to render "due process of law" to each individual the command also to insure that each person is protected equally by the laws, was simply too advanced for the Court and the country in the decades following the Civil War. The due process clause was not held to prohibit Congress from discriminating among aliens who were seeking to come in, and from these early decisions a growing monument of precedents has preserved the power.

Indeed, restriction of the amount and quality of immigration is one of the few areas of government where through sheer force of precedent, Congress knows no bounds. The power to regulate interstate commerce may be another, but bulking large against any arbitrary use of that power is the entire "free enterprise system," with all its lobbies, and spokesmen, and the "you'd better not hurt my pocketbook" indignation they are capable of mustering. There is little to resist Congressional whims toward immigration restriction except a public aroused through the broadest-based and thus most difficult to organize pressure groups: those based on nationality, race, and religion.

In this day when racism and bigotry are cast over the Negro's just aspiration for the equality the American ideal (and laws) promise him, it may be helpful to see a broader perspective. There was vicious bigotry and racism against other minority peoples as well, and the prejudices and bitternesses still remain in many ways. But they are conquered in most part, and the Negro's fight for justice may have similar promise—all the more if the whole shameful story is known.

For the most part, this is not the story of the human emotions and efforts that brought our immigrant forefathers here and forged an America. It is rather about the inhuman efforts to deny that great and wondrous force.

We will not dwell, then, on the positive side of the immigration story. Perhaps it is enough to note here that except for the American Indian minority, we are *all* immigrant stock, and at one time or another, of *minority* stock, and that very real people—usually distressed in their homeland, fearfully braving major difficulties and dangers to stay alive and make the awesome change worthwhile, leaving loved ones behind with no practical hopes of seeing them again, coming into strange and often hostile places without education or capital or even a common language—were both the oppressed and the fore-bearers of the oppressors.

If we look in this book at the weird, ironic, and often terribly tragic history of immigration law at the level of political rhetoric, legislative victories and defeats, and court rulings, it is simply that these are the movable counters that make the "game" possible to follow. But if it is not possible to acknowledge—much less describe—the jolting disruptions, the wrenching heartbreak, the vicious injustices that came with every repressive step, you may read on with compassion and heartbreak of your own, in sad contemplation of what bigotry and greed and arrogance and ignorance could effect.

For a country whose debt to immigrants is so large, America has maintained a policy of extreme ingratitude toward them. Throughout the entire twentieth century, the United States has maintained an icy attitude toward those from outside who wanted to share in the work and the wealth. Now a thaw is beginning to appear; a time for stock-taking is at hand.

2 / *Prelude to Policy*

In the beginning, America did not have an immigration policy, except in the sense that later generations can elicit from random movement a direction shaped by history and impute a purpose to it. At least, the official organs of government had enacted no positive policy: Immigrants had always come to America, and Congress did not attempt to stop them.

Or rarely did, at any rate. There was, as everyone knows, the Alien Act, passed June 8, 1798, stipulating that dangerous aliens could be deported at the whim of the President. But the controversy that surrounded the statute and its companion, the Sedition Act, prevented anyone from actually being deported, and most of it expired on June 25, 1800. From some quarters, strong sentiment had also been voiced, at an early date, against unrestricted immigration. In 1797, a member of Congress even went so far as to argue that restriction was necessary because America was then finally fully populated. But, with one exception, America was to keep the gates wide open for ninety years.

As a result, between 1815, when the War of 1812 had been

settled, and 1860, when the Civil War began, more than five million immigrants from every part of the world settled in America. They came for a variety of reasons: famine, political and religious persecution, the spirit of adventure, boredom, desire to start life anew, the appeal of a "golden land of opportunities." They flocked in from Europe, they straggled in from Asia, and they were dragged in from Africa. Representing virtually every race, religion, and nationality, their history is tightly woven into the history of American development during that period.

It is not with these people and that development that we are concerned, however. The story of immigration restriction does not begin until Americans lost their nerve, and the middle of the nineteenth century represents the benchmark of Americans' confidence in their own institutions. America was a large land whose geographic frontier was still wide open; it needed people to build, and the belief in a historic destiny westward tempered and held in check such signs of xenophobic hatred as the Know-Nothing party. It was a time too close to the Revolutionary War for people to forget their revolutionary origins. While settlers and the Army were still fighting Indians, how could foreigners be considered not native?

The eventual restrictionist victory occurred when a variety of themes, widely divergent at their points of origin, and traveling along scattered tracks throughout the last third of the nineteenth century, finally came together. The growth of an industrial and interdependent America at the turn of the twentieth century spelled the beginning of the concerted move to keep America American. Like most large-scale historical movements, the trends which converged were social, economic, political, and intellectual: the fear of rising crime and urban decay, the financial panics and depressions which threatened labor with job loss and lower pay, the complex and daily battles for votes and the flesh-and-blood battles in war, and the new theories of evolution and human biology. All these themes, which have their own unique histories and effects, when combined, brought about the end of the great migration to America.

THE CHINESE

The first stepping-stone to general restriction was an actual, but limited case of restriction itself. Sparked by the discovery in 1848 of gold at Sutter's California mill, the Chinese began to undertake the long ocean voyage. They did not come in large numbers, as Americans measure immigration: Between 1850 and 1880 some 230,000 had arrived in America, most of them in California. At first they were welcomed, for unskilled labor was greatly needed. They worked at menial tasks such as fruit-picking and domestic service (truly "coolie labor") and were instrumental in building the western railroads, which linked to the westward-moving eastern rails to form the first continental railroad system in 1868.

The concentration of an obviously foreign people in California led locally to intense frictions. In 1860 the state legislature barred the Chinese from white schools; and they were further restricted by a law which prohibited them from testifying in court. Significantly, in the formal 1869 engraving that celebrated the joining of the continental railroad tracks, the Chinese (and the Irish) were blotted out. They performed the work; that was enough. Although Congress in 1862 outlawed the coolie trade under which thousands of Chinese had been imported to work on the railroads, feelings still were local, for six years later in the Burlingame Treaty of 1868, Chinese aliens in the United States were given most-favored-nation rights: They were entitled to the same rights and privileges of residence and travel in the United States as were aliens of the nations most favored by the United States. For the time being, they were on high ground, and for a while were at least minimally protected by the Federal Government.

In 1875, for instance, the Supreme Court struck down one of California's early attempts to restrict Chinese immigration. Chy Lung, fresh from China, had been detained in port because the California commissioner of immigration, a state official, declared her a "lewd and debauched woman," a class ineligible to land under California law. The statute was drafted to permit almost total exclusion of the Chinese. Said the Court, in ruling that the state law was unconstitutional because it conflicted with federal policy: "It is hardly possible to conceive a statute more skillfully framed, to place in the hands of a single man the power to prevent vessels engaged in a foreign trade, say with China, from carrying passengers, or to compel them to submit to systematic extortion of the grossest kind."

Significantly, however, during the same term of court, the way was cleared for the Federal Government to proceed on approximately the same basis. In the famous *Passenger Cases* in 1849, the Supreme Court struck down state regulations requiring payment of $1.50 for cabin passengers and $1 for steerage passengers, plus twenty-five cents from the ship's master for each person aboard. Immigrant passengers were said to be in "foreign commerce," and the Constitution gives exclusive power to regulate in this area to Congress. In 1876, New York State required each incoming vessel to post a $300 bond per passenger unless a $1.50 head tax were paid. The state contended that this was not a direct tax but a reasonable requirement to help the state defray the costs of paupers and others who might be unable to aid themselves. The Court denied the power: "A regulation which imposes onerous, perhaps impossible, conditions on those engaged in active commerce with foreign nations, must of necessity be national in its character. It is more than this; for it may properly be called *international.*" With the states powerless to regulate the increasing immigration, the pressure inevitably grew for Congress to act. Should Congress now care to enact a statute similar to that which the Court voided in Chy Lung's case there could be no bar, for the *Federal* Government *is* entitled to treat incoming immigrants arbitrarily. All it needed was a spark from California.

Anti-Oriental fury glowed white-hot on the West Coast in 1876. A committee of the state legislature investigated the "Oriental problem," and issued a three-hundred-page work of pure invective. Said a member who discussed the findings with a Congressional committee: "The Chinese are inferior to any race God ever made. These people have got the perfection of crimes of 4,000 years. I believe the Chinese have no souls to save, and if they have, they are not worth saving."

In the midst of the recession in 1877, this suave Christian feeling was voiced by one of the great American demagogues, Denis Kearney, himself a recently naturalized Irish immigrant, whose own former nationals on the East Coast had not yet overcome the stigma of being Irish and Catholic. He organized the Workingman's Party in order to preserve for white laborers what jobs there were. On San Francisco's west side, Kearney reveled in a series of bitter "sand-lot" speeches, which succeeded in converting even respectable people to the anti-Chinese cause. Kearney and others convinced the electorate in 1879 to adopt a new constitution, which among other things, barred the Chinese from voting, from working for any corporation or from employment on public works.

At the same time, at least in California, the Chinese found themselves ineligible to become United States citizens. The basic citizenship law, first enacted in 1790, provided for the naturalization of "free white persons." In the context of history, "white" was meant to contrast with "black," for obviously slaves should not be citizens. The Congresses following the Civil War remedied the omission: An 1870 act entitled persons of "African descent" to citizenship. Unfortunately for the Chinese, Congress did not repeal the word "white" (although it was inadvertently omitted in 1870 and not added again until 1875). Was it not possible that "white" was now to contrast with "yellow"? In 1878, Judge Lorenzo Sawyer of the Federal Circuit Court for the District of California ruled that the law provided for white and black only. Citing the fact that Senator Sumner of Massachusetts attempted to strike "white" from the law during the 1870 debates and was unsuccessful, the judge denied the naturalization petition of Ah Yup, a Chinese alien. "Neither in popular language," said Sawyer, "in literature, nor in scientific nomenclature, do we ordinarily, if ever, find the words 'white person' used in a sense so comprehensive as to include an individual of the Mongolian race. Yet, in all, color, notwithstanding its indefiniteness as a word of description, is made an important factor in the basis adopted for the distinction and classification of races."

Meanwhile, the nation had begun to take notice of the developments on the Coast, and some eastern areas themselves began to feel the sting of job competition as businessmen imported Chinese workers to break strikes in Massachusetts and Pennsylvania. An 1875 Congressional law put an end to the importation of Chinese convict and slave labor, and in 1879 Congress attempted to abandon the Burlingame Treaty of eleven years before. President Rutherford B. Hayes vetoed the bill, concerned with what might happen to the Chinese here and to American merchants and missionaries over there. But he was equally—perhaps more—concerned with the disquieting events in California, and his Administration renegotiated the treaty in 1880. Under the new terms, the United States could limit or "suspend" immigration from China when "necessary" but could not prohibit it altogether. Congress interpreted "suspension" liberally in 1882 when it passed a law forbidding Chinese immigration for twenty years. Again the bill was vetoed, this time by President Chester A. Arthur, who suggested to Congress that twenty years seemed a little long to be recognized as a "suspension." Accordingly Congress came back that year and shortened the period to ten years. This law stuck: It was renewed in 1892 for another ten years, made permanent in 1902, and not repealed until 1943.

The meaning of suspension was yet to be tested. In 1881 a Chinese laborer named Chew Heong left the United States for Honolulu and attempted to return in September, 1884. The Chinese Exclusion Act of 1882 (as amended in 1884) declared that a reentry certificate was the "only evidence permissible to establish his right of reentry." Chew did not have it and was detained on board when his vessel ported in San Francisco. He argued that by the 1880 treaty he was entitled to go and return to the United States without an entrance certificate, since the law did not then require it. The Supreme Court noted that the 1884 act excluded from its provisions Chinese laborers who resided in the United States on November 17, 1880, and

Chew did so reside on that date. The Government argued that, nevertheless, Chew remained away after the 1884 act went into effect. But since this interpretation would require a finding that Congress intended to allow Chinese to leave the country freely—*as long as they remained in the United States*—the argument failed. After all, said Justice Harlan for the Court: "*Lex non intendit aliqued impossible*—The supposition should not be indulged that Congress while professing to faithfully execute treaty stipulations, and recognizing the fact that they secured to a certain class the 'right to go from and come to the United States,' intended to make its protection depend upon the performance of conditions which it was physically impossible to perform."

The Government varied its argument four years later. In 1883, Jung Ah Lung left for China with a reentry certificate that conformed with the provisions of the 1882 act. It was stolen by pirates in Cantonese waters and he was detained when his return ship docked in San Francisco harbor. By proving that the official records showed he had been issued the certificate, that he was the person to whom it was issued, and that it had not been canceled, the federal district court permitted Jung to enter. The U.S. attorney objected: Didn't the act of 1884 say the certificate was the *exclusive* means of establishing reentry right? The Court ruled on appeal in 1888 that Jung need not have conformed with the 1884 requirements since he had a valid 1882 certificate. The 1882 act did not preclude the use of other means of proof: Under the earlier law the certificate was conclusive, but not exclusive, proof. Jung remained in the United States.

The seeds of new doctrine were sprouting, however. A three-justice dissent argued that the 1884 law should supersede the earlier act, even applied to Jung. "If appellee's certificate was forcibly taken from him by a band of pirates while he was absent, that is his misfortune," said the dissenters, in words that would be echoed by a later court commanding a majority.

The Supreme Court had been able to sustain the immigrant's right to remain because to this point, the Chinese-American treaty remained in force. Immigrants who entered the United

States under its terms were entitled to its protections. If the treaty could be abrogated, however, then perhaps returning immigrants could be permanently excluded. Congress acted on this assumption in 1888, and declared that all outstanding reentry certificates were void. The Supreme Court could find no constitutional objection, it said, in the *Chinese Exclusion Case*.

Chae Chan Ping resided in California from 1875 to 1887 when he made the unhappy mistake of leaving for China with a reentry certificate in his possession. On October 8, 1888, he landed at San Francisco, but the tax collector of the port refused him admission because, while he was enroute from Hong Kong, the new law had gone into effect annulling all certificates. The 1888 act clearly violated the terms of the Burlingame Treaty and its 1880 supplement. No matter: "The treaties were of no greater legal obligation than the act of Congress. . . . The power of exclusion of foreigners being an incident of sovereignty belonging to the Government of the United States . . . the right to its exercise at any time when, in the judgment of the Government, the interests of the country require it, cannot be granted away or restrained on behalf of anyone. . . . Whether a proper consideration by our government of its previous laws, or a proper respect for the nation whose subjects are affected by its action, ought to have qualified its inhibition and made it applicable only to persons departing from the country after the passage of the act, are not questions for judicial determination." So ruled the highest court in the land, and Chae was excluded.

Chinese could now be excluded, even if they were former residents who had departed to take a short trip. It remained only for Congress to get rid of as many Chinese *within* the United States as it could. In 1892, a federal law required Chinese aliens to possess "certificates of residence." Three Chinese aliens were accused the next year of not having such documents. Two of them, Fong Yue Ting and Wong Quan, had no certificates at all. The third, Lee Joe, had tried to obtain one, but had failed because he could produce only fellow Chinese as witnesses that he was lawfully entitled to reside in the United States—the act required "at least one credible white witness." Failure to obtain a certificate within one year of the act (May 5, 1892) was made a crime, punishable by one year at hard labor and deportation. On May 6, 1893, one year and one day after the effective date of the act, the three were arrested and remanded to the custody of the U.S. marshal who was ordered to deport them, and the appeal was taken—all on May 6. On May 10, the Supreme Court heard argument and on May 15 the Court ordered the deportation, finding the statute constitutional.

Fong and his compatriots had argued that the one-day proceedings before a U.S. judge was "in no proper sense a trial and sentence for a crime or offense." Granted, said Justice Gray for the Court: "It is simply the ascertainment, by appropriate and lawful means, of the fact whether the conditions exist upon which Congress has enacted that an alien of this class may remain within the country. The order of deportation is not a punishment for a crime. It is but a method of enforcing the return to his own country of an alien [unlawfully in the United States]."

Dissented Justice Brewer: "[The act] deprives of 'life, liberty, and property without due process of law.' It imposes punishment without a trial, and punishment cruel and severe. It places the liberty of one individual subject to the unrestrained control of another. . . . Deportation is punishment. It involves first an arrest, a deprival of liberty; and second, a removal from home, from family, from business, from property." There was no trial, without which punishment should not be dealt out, even to aliens. Furthermore, the collector of internal revenues, who issues the certificates, had absolute discretion whether or not to issue one, he continued. "In view of this enactment of the highest legislative body of the foremost Christian nation, may not the thoughtful Chinese disciple of Confucius fairly ask, Why do they send missionaries here?"

Justice Field chimed in with an equally denunciatory dissent: "Every step in the procedure provided . . . tramples upon some constitutional right." As for the white witness rule, "the law might as well have said, that unless the laborer should also produce . . . the archbishop of the state, to establish the fact of residence, he should be held to be unlawfully within the United States."

But on the Supreme Court the majority rules, and *Fong Yue Ting v. United States* fixed the principle that aliens may live in the United States at the whim of Congress, and that they need do nothing unlawful to be summarily deported. This was the high point of constitutional restriction. As we shall see later, the Government in the next few years pressed its case even harder and wound up with some significant and stinging rebukes. The Government tried the ultimate step of deporting an alien without any hearing at all; the Court blanched. That was too much. The Government tried to enforce the imprisonment and hard labor provisions of the 1892 act; they were declared unconstitutional on the grounds that no one within the United States can be made subject to criminal penalties without a trial. Nevertheless, the Government's powers were so ringingly established that the denial of due process to aliens and even to citizens continues to be a problem today.

The end of the 1880's marked the beginning of restrictionist techniques. Yet general restriction would wait forty more years. Chinese exclusion did not lead directly to that goal; the point of convergence could be reached only through the addition of other compelling forces. But that it was the beginning there can be no doubt.

The eventual restriction was to be prompted by widespread racial fears; to the long history of southern racism was now added a significant new voice. Moreover, for the first time, the fear of a nonwhite race was linked with the fact of immigration, and the easing of that fear was found to be in restriction. So the South and West stood ready to back limitations on immigration. But still they did not command a majority, nor could they command Presidents. They showed their power by aiding in the securing of a number of limited restrictions (to be discussed later on), but they needed the support of the one remaining group—the North—to write far-reaching national legislation. Rising to the challenge, the northerner supplied the nation over the course of thirty years with an intellectual theory of race, without which the all-important justification of restriction would have failed. The theory itself only became believable as the character of the nation changed.

SOCIAL CHANGE

Post Civil-War America was undergoing some startling changes: For the first time, nonfarming activities began to attract a host of workers. With railroads and telegraph beginning to link the continent, the concept of market expanded and new industrial forms appeared. Big Business started to boom. The growth in output required recruitment of workers congregated in factories, and urban populations mushroomed. Much of this change directly concerned and confronted the immigrant.

During the thirty years from the outbreak of the Civil War, from 1860 to 1890, some ten million people emigrated from Europe. This was twice the number who had come during the forty-five preceding years. Most of these ten million—contrary to a belief that was widely circulated at the turn of the century—came from England, Germany, Switzerland, the Netherlands, and the Scandinavian countries. The increase in immigration was due to a variety of factors, among them, the radical development of steam power which cut the transatlantic voyage down from one to three months to only ten days. The ships were bigger, and by standards of the day, better (although most present-day Americans no doubt would have found steerage conditions intolerable). Furthermore, costs had decreased, and competition among burgeoning steamship lines and their agents led to concessions for passengers. The new steam companies developed new routes and went to ports—in Italy and in the Baltic states—which had been ignored before.

Coupled with the more readily available means of transportation was the ever-growing desire to escape. Population pressures and the squeezing out of agrarian workers throughout Europe, together with agricultural and industrial reverses in a dozen European states, heightened the wish to go to a land of unbounded opportunities. Following the Civil War, most northwestern states, beginning with Michigan and Wisconsin, actively recruited immigrants for their farmlands, but they catered mostly to British, German, and Scandinavian newcomers.

These groups had a fairly easy time adjusting, primarily because they found much that was familiar and many communities composed of those who had preceded them. Even the Irish—long distrusted and sometimes despised—could come to communities where Irish had lived for thirty years. By contrast, Slavic and southern Europeans did not find large colonies of their own nationals, primarily because the countries in which these people were born drastically restricted the outflow of their nationals until the 1870's. The Austro-Hungarian Empire did not officially recognize the right of emigration until 1867, and the government remained hostile to the departure of subjects for another ten years. The Russian-Turkish War, which concluded in 1877, ended Turkish domination in Bosnia, Bulgaria, Herzegovina, Montenegro, and Serbia, and for the first time allowed this large mass of Slavs to leave. Though Italians may have had an easier legal time of it, the reason for leaving did not become pressing until the 1880's when the local fruit and wine economies collapsed, due to increased Florida and California production and French tariffs.

By the time these people were ready to come, farmland—on the scale that it had previously existed—was running out. Indeed, the Census Bureau in 1890 listed that year as the end of the American frontier. By this time, northern European immigrants were, as a rule, relatively more affluent than were the middle and southern Europeans, many of whom were destitute. Then, as now, one did not just go out and farm; money was required. With farmland becoming scarce, and with their own capital even scarcer, the newer immigrants flocked to the cities. So, too, did immigrants from Germany, Great Britain, and Scandinavia. It is misleading to suggest that the immigrants representing new nationalities were failures because they went to cities, while the "older" type immigrants were successes in the noble occupation of farming. *Everyone* was going to the cities. Native sons of native Americans were leaving the farms (that's when it all started), and in 1910 the proportion of "older" type immigrants living in cities was 68.3 percent, compared with the "newer" immigrants' 78.6 percent, hardly a difference overwhelming enough to be explained by the supposed difference in disposition between the two types. Moreover (what was difficult for the solid citizen of the time to understand) a large part of America's lure was the very opportunity to participate in industry. Had not the centuries of farming in Europe only brought these newcomers to ruin?

After 1890, a significant change did occur. During the twenty-four years between the start of the last decade of the nineteenth century and the outbreak of the First World War, fifteen million immigrants—a number equal to the total who had come since 1815—swarmed, or so it seemed, across the Atlantic. It was in this period that the northern and western Europeans were outnumbered by southern and eastern European immigrants, principally from Austria-Hungary, Greece, Italy, Romania, Russia, Poland, and Turkey.

Immigrants from the western European heartlands had fled during the late 1840's and 1850's from the persecution they feared would follow the political revolutions that had convulsed many nations. The immigrants from eastern and southern Europe were fleeing from a different kind of persecution, less political, more religious and even racial. It began on a large scale in 1882, when persecution of the Jews became the official policy of Russia. Following in the wake of Tsar Alexander II's assassination in 1881, the May Laws clamped down ruthlessly on the Jews' right to exist: They were restricted in worship, in practice of profession, denied the right to hold office and to be educated in the state schools. Reports of Pogroms in 1881–1882, 1891, and 1905–1906 exposed the slaughter of thousands to a sometimes indignant world. On June 22, 1906, Congress even adopted a resolution to express its disapproval: "*Resolved*, etc., That the people of the United States are horrified by the report of the massacre of Hebrews in Russia on account of their race and religion, and that those bereaved thereby have the hearty sympathy of this country." So the Jews came to America from Russia, Latvia, and Lithuania in ever-increasing numbers: from 5,000 in 1880 to 258,000 in 1907. Between 1900 and 1914, 1,200,000 Jews sailed across the ocean; altogether, the total from eastern Europe exceeded two million.

The Jews were not alone in the hapless fate of persecution. The Armenian massacres in the mid-1890's started a stream of Christian immigration from that country. Syrians, too, expatriated by the Turks, left their homeland by the hundreds of thousands; although they tended to go first to Egypt, India, and South America, by the 1890's the United States became a fourth welcoming place.

The peasant classes from Italy, Greece, and Austria-Hungary were driven here less from persecution than from hunger. U.S. tariff policies, plus local economic conditions, including the enormously wide-scale subdivision of once large estates, transformed the peasant farmer into an urban laborer. Compared with European prospects, workers *would* find a golden opportunity in America.

If it is untrue that the third great wave of immigrants came out of motives alien to those who had preceded them (a commonly held theory at the time), it was nevertheless true that the conditions they faced when they arrived were different and that the people who were to greet and grieve with them in the New World did find differences which today we call cultural. Poor and unable to speak the language, they found it difficult to escape from the coast to the interior farmlands. Many—perhaps most—never considered it; the frontier was closed and they began to cluster in large urban centers, not only New York City, but also in Massachusetts, Rhode Island, Connecticut, New Jersey, Pennsylvania, Ohio, Illinois, and Missouri. As they accumulated in the cities, settlements became virtual ghettos; the homes, such as they were, were wracked by dirt, disease, and wretched poverty. The plight of these immigrants is evocatively traced in Oscar Handlin's *The Uprooted.*

Because they tended to cluster together—where else could they live so cheaply and who else would have them?—because they spoke different tongues, performed the most menial labor, and wondrously retained their ethnic backgrounds through their own churches, schools, and newspapers (although their children struggled to escape it and largely succeeded), many solid Americans, themselves children and grandchildren of immigrants who in their time had spoken different tongues and clung together, began to wonder whether these "new" immigrants could ever be assimilated into the American culture of the United States. It was from these observations and with these thoughts that a new and startling idea began to take hold of the American imagination.

THE CONCEPT OF RACE

In human affairs, it is the idea that counts. Any set of facts, any number of statistics, any type of conditions will be endured or modified or destroyed, depending upon the mental gloss that people impose on them. In the area of immigration policy, Americans viewed the rainbow of the world's peoples through the tinted spectacles of racism.

It was not a racism that existed full-blown in the revolutionary spirit; it was a racism that took decades to develop, that did not come fully of age until the twentieth century. But in the history of its development can be seen the steady pull toward restriction. Without justification, legislation is nearly impossible; with reasons—however, good or bad—legislation is almost impossible to stop, and it was a peculiar theory of race, which a large segment of Americans came to embrace, that justified the law.

To be sure, there had always been a certain antipathy toward foreigners. Perhaps it was inevitable that in a country of so many diverse nationalities and cultures conflicts would erupt. Incivility toward those slightly different from oneself dates far back in American history, long before there was any consciousness of American nationhood. Though most states would have profited from censure in this regard, Massachusetts early established itself as a bastion of intolerance, due primarily to the particularly rigid orthodoxy of the Puritans, whose beliefs were regarded in England as heterodox and caused their persecution there. So the slaves became the tyrants: In a famous episode in the late seventeenth century, the colony expelled Anne Hutchison because she could not fully adhere to the elders' religious beliefs.

From a pattern of thought habituated to the emotional feeling that what was different was bad and should not be communicated, the road to dislike and distrust of foreigners was probably a natural one. To a large extent, this xenophobia manifested itself in contempt and at times extreme hatred for the Irish. Derision of the Irish was in part due to the common stereotype that the Hibernian was a hard-drinking, rowdy, roustabout; in part to the fear that as the Irish clustered in urban areas, patterns of life would change and jobs disappear; and in part to the fact that the Irish were Catholic. Protestant America has always been fearful of the Pope.

Too, there had always been suspicion of the Jew, and in the late nineteenth century, a fear of the "international Jewish bankers." In turn the Germans, the Italians, the Greeks, and to a lesser extent (because of their relative lateness in arriving) the Slavs, all found that the mind of the settled white Anglo-Saxon Protestant had erected stereotypes for each. These stereotypes, which linger today, were muddled; their common themes were linked with a bristling condescension. Other peoples were obviously inferior because they were poor, congregated in cities, drank too much (or didn't drink enough), were not serious enough (or were too serious), and did not assimilate. Over the years, only the Scandinavians managed to escape most (though not all) of the ridicule that fell on everyone else. Nevertheless, the outstanding fact of the mid-century was an absence of a racial ideology toward immigrants. It was not until the 1880's and 1890's, when large numbers of "newer" immigrants began to arrive and when Darwinian theories had sunk to common consciousness, that something new began to emerge in the American intellect.

Not that the concept of race was unknown; it was obviously very much a part of the American experience, from the first awareness of the American Indian as other than European, "having little of Humanitie but shape," from the first importation of the African slave, and from the first glimmering of understanding that the Chinese who competed for your job could easily be attacked because he was racially different. Race-thinking was not un-American, but only in the 1870's was the link between race and nationality, between racial character-istics and immigration, beginning to be fashioned.

To those who had early thought it out, the greatness of Anglo-Saxon culture was only a partial explanation for the greatness of America. Indeed, many people believed that in America was being created a new people, a fusion of the British culture with the best that the vast world had to offer. Assimilation through the "melting pot" (a term which did not come into popular vogue until after the turn of the century, when its underlying philosophy was increasingly under attack)— this was what distinguished America from any other nation at any other period in history.

The comfortable thought that with the guidance of Anglo-Saxon culture the diverse nationalities that made up the United States would actually improve America was buoyed by the impact of *The Origin of Species* in 1849.* In broadest outline, the theory of evolution holds that a species owes its existence to its successes in the struggle for survival against a harsh environment. Through a weeding-out of the unfit members, the species is purified and strengthened. For a while, the theory, as stated in its most simplistic form, was heart-warming, for did not the continued survival of the Anglo-Saxon amid ever-better circumstances indicate that he was winning the struggle? And if the survival of the fittest meant survival of the best (what else could it mean?), then it was obvious that the best, the Anglo-Saxons, were justified in their belief and in the com-forts, which were the evidence of their belief, that they were superior to the newcomers. And it was also obvious that the immigrants were the best of the lot from Europe. Herbert Spen-

* This is not the place for a history of the thought of Charles Darwin and his contemporary evolutionist thinkers, most notably, Herbert Spencer. "Darwin" is here used simply as a convenient shorthand with which any educated person today is familiar. The reader must forego the pleasures of the debate over the propriety of attributing the evolutionary movement to Darwin alone; happily, there is a vast literature on the subject to which the reader can repair.

cer himself in 1882 affirmed that the fusion of these best peoples from throughout the world would result in an American man better than the world had ever known.

Furthermore, by its emphasis on adaptation to environment, the theory lent itself to the belief that a changing environment could shape character; to cure social ills, therefore, one must alter the environment. In the early years of the theory, before it could gnaw away at the kernel of religious faith which opposed it, Christian thinking (where practiced) contributed to the conventional wisdom that "men are created equal." All men came from God, and were equally precious in His eyes.

But the theory of evolution, like most great scientific hypotheses, was politically neutral. It could equally be used by many men to support a host of propositions. One of the earliest was not political at all, but religious: If man evolved from lower forms of life and was not in fact created by God on the sixth day, why then man was merely another animal and, what is more, different men might represent different stages of animal development. Some men might in fact be *biologically* inferior to others.

This line of thinking, not necessitated by the theory, began a trend of doctrine that has continued to plague us to this day. If man is an animal then he must be subject to the same laws of biology as other animals. If biology is a science, these laws can be studied and catalogued, as can the different races of man. Paradoxically, the fundamentalists who outwardly rejected the theory, denying that man descended from the ape (which belief biologists today tell us is erroneous anyway), were among those who clung strongly to the beliefs that the logic of the science seemed to necessitate. Tennessee could enact a law forbidding the teaching of evolution in the public schools; yet many in Tennessee could believe that the white man was necessarily superior to the black.

The truth is, of course, that man is not an animal. Many biologists, even today, continue to be trapped by the erroneous and unnecessary tack taken at the close of the nineteenth century. Man not an animal? He is no more an animal than a fish is a conglomerate of inert substances found in primordial seawater. True, the fish evolved from that primeval substance; true, man evolved from animals. But that they are equivalent is simply erroneous, as erroneous as saying that because both man and mud will fall when dropped from a height, man must be mud.

The excitement of discovering that biology, which had long been more a system of classification than anything else, could be made a science like physics through the discovery of "laws" led the intellectuals astray. The laws of heredity, rediscovered from the pioneering work of Gregor Mendel, proved so intellectually satisfying—a palliative to the previously nagging question, "What mechanism caused the transmission of characteristics from ancestor to descendant?"—that scientists turned toward heredity and away from environment, neglecting for an instant in history what was known before and after, that the human species obeys special laws of its own, that environment is at least as important as heredity in man, the "animal" without refined instincts. Alas, Sigmund Freud was just beginning to explore these questions in the 1890's, and still in trouble, or perhaps these truths would have been learned (or remembered) far earlier. For Freud developed a mechanism of environment (however erroneous in detail it may be held today) that would have given pause to those who thought that the only possible "laws" were hereditary.

The possibilities of a rigid biological scientism made their first appeal when during the 1870's the American of older stock began to look around to find his former political and social dominance threatened. It was in New England, the region of the staunchest defenders of America's noblest ideals, that the new theories were born. It may seem surprising that the old patrician society would provide the intellectual link between race fear and immigration, but the shock will be lessened when it is recalled that the "Boston Brahmins" had ruled for years in the secure knowledge that they were obviously superior and in control. As the Irish and other populations of Boston grew to political power, the "native" stock grew apprehensive. Perhaps something was wrong if the best was not always on top.

Characteristic of the mounting fear and the Darwinian influence were Henry Cabot Lodge's denunciations of unrestricted immigration, which he delivered ringingly on the Senate floor in 1896. Quoting Gustave le Bon's *The Psychology of Peoples,* which Lodge had read while summering in France the year before, the upright Senator pleaded for a literacy test to cut down immigration; otherwise, he argued, America's inherited character would be "bred out." It fell to Francis A. Walker, second president of the Massachusetts Institute of Technology, and a leading economist of his day, to reconcile the fear of extinction with the earlier optimism of the belief in the survival of the fittest.

Walker was born to a liberal Massachusetts family that decried slavery and believed in the rights of all individuals. Walker struggled for twenty years, against his own instincts, against the idea that immigrants were lazy, slovenly, and inferior. In Walker's own struggle was mirrored society's: Only as the evidence of slums became more prominent, as the Irish ascended to political power around Boston, as labor unrest became more pronounced during the industrialization of those decades, did Walker slowly, with anguish, succumb to a fear and dislike of the foreign element in America. He became a nativist.

To the proposition that the best of Europe was emigrating from its homeland, Walker countered with just the reverse. By 1890, the steady stream of Europeans caused in him such anxiety that he concluded that only the least fit emigrate. To Walker, the economist, the least fit were the poorest, hence the reduction in time and cost of steamship travel allowed "the very lowest stage of degradation" to cross the ocean. The immigrants, he declared, "are beaten men from beaten races; representing the worst failures in the struggle for existence. They have none of the ideas and aptitudes which belong to those who are descended from the tribes that met under the oak trees of old Germany to make laws and choose chieftains." In 1891 Walker followed up these sentiments with what he took to be the clinching proof that America was in danger. He had been the chief of the Bureau of Statistics in 1870 and presided over the federal census that year. For the first time, the statistics showed that the national population growth was declining. For many years he believed the slackening off was a response to pressures of industrialization and the tendency toward urbanization. Upon analyzing the figures twenty years later, Walker concluded that the decline in the birthrate was a fact only for the native stock; immigrants continued to maintain an increasing rate of reproduction. Why? Because the natives were refusing to compete with cheap labor. Rather than bringing up large families who would bid down the wage, native Americans were contenting themselves with small families. They "shrank from the industrial competition"; they were "even more unwilling to bring sons and daughters into the world to enter into that competition."

For ten years this kind of speculation simmered, as many began to adopt its basic tenets. In 1894 a number of young men founded the Immigration Restriction League of Boston. Most of the founders had taken seminars at Harvard under the direction of professors who brooded over the ending of Anglo-Saxon dominance. The League was to gain national prominence, enlisting in its cause after 1910 such eminent men as Harvard's president, A. Lawrence Lowell (who in the 1920's saw the need for a "Jewish quota" at Harvard), and the University of Wisconsin economics professor John R. Commons. The League was a common meeting ground for many Boston intellectuals, members of old New England families, now out of touch with the sense of noblesse oblige that earlier members of such families as the Adamses had felt. The League was seriously concerned and through the frequent discussions of its well-educated members proved a significant breeding ground for the racist idea.

As the 1890's progressed, the earlier cold fear of immigration tempered; America had taken up the white man's burden in a war against Spain. With the rise in nationalist fervor came a decline in the dread that native Americans would be squeezed out. After all, had not America decisively defeated a weaker people, and weren't Americans strong enough to assimilate the different races in Hawaii, the Philippines, and Puerto Rico? But it was during this time that the link between immigration and the idea of distinctive "races" began to crystallize.

Although virulent racist philosophies had been developed in Europe throughout the century by Count Joseph Arthur de Gobineau and Houston Stewart Chamberlain (whose epic has been described as "the most foolish book ever written"), their impact in the United States was negligible. America awaited the development of the anthropological sciences, which, typically, began their intellectual journey as a system of classifications. In 1899, an M.I.T. economist, William Z. Ripley, published *The Races of Europe,* a book destined to bring the question of race into sharp focus. Readers learned that Mongoloid, Negroid, and Caucasian were not the only races. Ripley discerned in the European Caucasians three distinct races: the Teutonics (tall, blond men from the north with a low cephalic index; i.e., long skulls), the Alpines (stocky, brown-haired people from central Europe with a higher cephalic index), and Mediterraneans (slim southerners of darker complexion and an apparently lower cephalic index than the Alpines). These three groups came to be taken as "races" in the same sense that the Chinese and former slaves were taken as belonging to distinct types.

This classification system fit in well with the statistics of immigrants since 1890. It became apparent that the "newer" immigrants from middle and southern Europe, whom many had always thought somewhat different, really were different, racially different. Ripley himself was not a racist in the modern sense of the word; he deplored the term "Aryan race" and showed that it lacked any scientific basis. He believed that environmental factors played a large role in shaping man's character. But he had laid the basis for a "scientific" discussion of race, and that was a start.

Meanwhile, a new kind of biology was emerging from the early descriptive aspects of the theory of evolution. This was the science of eugenics, a branch of biology concerned with the improvement of the species by proper breeding. The understanding that the child's characteristics are inherited from the parents through a genetic mechanism at last gave birth to the concept that a person's characteristics can be passed from one generation to the next without any environmental intervention.

Sir Francis Galton, the famous English biologist and cousin of Darwin, published in 1869 his *Hereditary Genius,* purporting to show on the basis of historical analysis that greatness tends to accumulate in families. He investigated records of "eminent" families and determined that they tended to produce eminent sons and daughters in a higher incidence than were produced by lower-class families. The reason he ascribed to biological heredity, completely overlooking or rejecting the possibility that "eminence" came from the far greater opportunity enjoyed by the rich and the educated to realize the human potential. Galton's "facts" could have proved precisely the opposite of what he assumed they proved. Nevertheless, from his investigation, Galton reached eugenics: "The science of improving stock, which is by no means confined to questions of judicious mating but which, especially in the case of man, takes cognizance of all influences that tend in however remote a degree to give to the more suitable races or strains of blood a better chance of prevailing speedily over the less suitable than they otherwise would have had."

The less than logically drawn conclusions of Galton's investigations seemed to be borne out at the lower end of the ladder by R. L. Dugdale's study of the Jukes family in 1875 and H. H. Goddard's study of the Kallikaks in 1912. These were pseudonyms for families founded during the American Revolution and before. The founders, Max and "Old Horror," managed to produce during the course of two centuries 79 criminals, 161 prostitutes and otherwise immoral people, 143 feeble-minded unfortunates, 200 paupers, 24 alcoholics, and 26 illegitimate children out of a combined total of 1,189 descendants analyzed. That their misfortunes could have been due to severe environmental handicaps, compounded by the neglect of generations of indolent parents, was ignored by the public.

At the beginning of the twentieth century, Galton began pushing the eugenics movement in earnest. Although he had initiated his research as early as 1865, the social significance of his science awaited a public concerned with controlling the human species. America in the new century was.

The rough idea of eugenics was to breed the best men and women only, so as to produce the best offspring possible and reduce reproduction among the dregs of society. Unfortunately for the movement in the long run, the practical methods of eugenics as far as humans were concerned were never clearly delineated; pure theory was never converted into engineering specifications. There was long and learned debate about exactly how to tell who was best, but in the end it came down to what we might have guessed all along: The Anglo-Saxon and Teutonic "races"—the "Nordics" as they were later to be called when the Germans lost favor in the heat of war—were the best and should be given the most encouragement. Since they were falling behind in the battle to produce children (hadn't Walker shown that the newer immigrants were demonstrating far greater fecundity?), the newer immigration ought to be restricted. During the early years of the century, as these beliefs caught hold, civic reformers found their own notions of the efficacy of education and social services under increasingly heavy attack. For if crime, insanity, and poverty were inherited characteristics—which they surely must be—all the efforts of all the do-gooders in the world could not defeat the laws of biology.

The leader of the American eugenics movement was the zoologist Charles B. Davenport, whose father traced his lineage back through almost 900 years of English history. Financed by Mrs. E. H. Harriman, he established a eugenics record office, and through the compilation of statistics hoped to become a sort of eugenics consultant to the multitudes. He was also a leader of the American Breeders' Association, whose name alone provides a clue to the bold new science of the day. Its first concern was with plants and animals; four years after the association's founding in 1903 it brought human eugenics within its fold. Davenport came to believe that immigrants should be allowed to enter only if the quality of their "germ plasm" was up to snuff. One way of making such a determination was to check the family background of Europeans who desired to emigrate, an undertaking of such difficulty that it was not until the late 1940's and early 1950's that American immigration law could require, and attempt, a thorough screening of all refugees streaming out from behind the Iron Curtain.

Now the strands were coming together in the popular mind. In 1901, a Wisconsin colleague of Professor Commons, Edward A. Ross, suggested in an address to the learned American Academy of Political and Social Science that a people who fail to reproduce as quickly as lower races in their midst are committing "race suicide." The term caught on. President Theodore

Roosevelt began to urge more children on American women. Scores of magazine articles and books picked up the cry, darkly warning that Americans would become an extinct race unless proper steps were taken.

William Ripley reentered the scene in 1908 when he suggested why it was that "bad blood" drove out the good. Biological experiments had shown that when two different kinds of plants or animals were cross-bréd, it sometimes happened that a characteristic which neither of the parents possessed was passed on to the offspring, and it was demonstrated that this "latent" characteristic was possessed by a remote ancestor. This, the theory of "reversion," was said to explain how the mixing of the pure blood of Anglo-Saxons with "degenerate breeding stock" could "mongrelize" the species. Never mind that it might equally presuppose the uplifting of the lower race; it was scientific.

The man who absorbed all these trends and connected the strands into a thoroughgoing racist theory was Madison Grant, neither a Harvard man nor a New Englander. He was a New York bachelor-lawyer, Yale, class of 1889. In 1916, shortly before America's entrance into the war, Grant published *The Passing of the Great Race*, a book so gibberish-ridden that it compelled belief. It was the epitome of nearly four decades of race-thinking. In a nutshell, Grant's thesis was that blood does not mix. The laws of genetics obviously demonstrate this fact: When two races are cross-bred, the result is "a race reverting to the more ancient, generalized, and lower type."

Grant, the patrician whose forebears predated the Revolution, was panicked about the menace of unrestricted European immigration; Negroes and Orientals he could afford to ignore. He was not soft and compromising; he saw no need to be politic; he felt no compassion for the plight of the "lower races." His worst enemy was the Jew: "The cross between any of the three European races and a Jew is a Jew." Again, "these immigrants [Polish Jews] adopt the language of the native American; they wear his clothes; they steal his name; and they are beginning to take his women, but they seldom adopt his religion or understand his ideals."

How to tell the superior from the inferior race? There are

a number of methods: Examine the cephalic index, for example. Thus the "Nordic" (Grant's term for Ripley's possibly more constricted category "Teutonic") is dolichocephalic. Q.E.D. Should that argument fail to satisfy, it is worth noting that the Nordic has light-colored eyes and blond hair, as well as a fair complexion and a propensity to tallness. Who can argue against such overpowering proof as this? Democracy, concluded Grant, is a fraud and worse, a danger to true Americans; for only if the superior Nordics are allowed to control, which cannot happen if the influx of Alpines and Mediterraneans continues, will America maintain its ideals and save itself from extinction. As he said elsewhere, summing up his position: "The backbone of western civilization is racially Nordic. . . . If this great race, with its capacity for leadership and fighting, should ultimately pass, with it would pass that which we call civilization. It would be succeeded by an unstable and bastardized population, where worth and merit would have no inherent right to leadership and among which a newer and darker age would blot out our racial inheritance. Such a catastrophe cannot threaten if the Nordic race will gather itself together in time . . . and reassert the pride of race and the right of merit to rule. . . . Democratic ideals among an homogeneous population of Nordic blood, as in England and America, is one thing, but it is quite another for the white man to share his blood with, or entrust his ideals to brown, yellow, black, or red men. This is suicide pure and simple."

If it is difficult to imagine how such blatant *ipse dixits* could sway the populace toward restriction, it should be noted that when *The Passing of the Great Race* first appeared it did not produce an immediate effect. The ultimate victory was still five years away. Throughout the period until America's entrance into World War I, progressivism held the upper hand. Racist theories of immigration were boiling, but on the back burner. It remained for the war and its aftermath to provide the final push.

The importance of the intellectual conceptions cannot be gainsaid, however. As usual in human history, it was false science that raised prejudice to respectability, even necessity. Eugenics— founded on an alliance between Darwinism and the discoveries of Mendel—came to rule the day. It was thought that man inherits all his characteristics, that each race inherited separate race characteristics, and that the influence of environment on man was a negligible factor in determining his beliefs and behavior. In making such assumptions—which oddly enough were accepted by so many whose religious and democratic instincts should have led rather to rejection, the eugenicists and restrictionists were guilty of serious mistakes.

First, insistence on "breeding" as the answer to human development led them to ignore the obvious fact that only insofar as man is an animal does inheritance play a role in determining the individual's character. Fundamentalists of the day, and a few social scientists many decades later, could have told the right-thinking scientists that man in significant respects—perhaps largely—is not an animal, and that there are other forces at work in the shaping of man's character; environment must be counted at least as important as heredity. Scientific discovery led to excess. An interesting idea—survival of the fittest—was taken as an entire solution, before the whole problem was bared.

Second, the borrowing of some rudimentary concepts from anthropology, then a science in its merest infancy, led to wholly erroneous concepts of "race." That some people were different from others was obvious enough without a science; the classifications of mankind that developed were based on inadequate statistics and deficient assumptions.

Third, the reliance on the theory of reversion without the science of biochemistry added to the fallacy of premature "breeding" of scientific knowledge. The eugenicists would have done far better to heed the words of Charles Darwin, writing in 1875: "As man advances in civilization, and small tribes are united into larger communities, the simplest reason would tell each individual that he ought to extend his social instincts and sympathies to all the members of the same nation, though personally unknown to him. This point being once reached, there is only an artificial barrier to prevent his sympathies extending to the men of all nations and races."

Sadly, many eminent scientists made many unwarranted assertions, deserting caution to support political views. Sadder still, significant questions were not even asked, for the new biology was too exciting to denigrate by casting doubt on its applicability to man. Why limit that which can be extended to prove so much? Yet it never proved anything; it merely provided an explanation, convincing those who for other reasons wished to be convinced. Saddest of all, from the point of waste, the assumptions once taken as proofs have been found to be false—neither as assumptions nor as conclusions do they hold.

SOME RADICAL INCIDENTS

The chronicles of violence and more subtle expressions of hatred toward people who are different would fill more than one book. From the earliest days of colonization, American settlers made it clear many times that they distrusted those who were different. The American Indian discovered it; the slave found it out also, and sometimes, but rarely, did a little rebelling of his own. The immigrant was in no different situation. The Irish, the Chinese, the German, and the Jew were provided some dramatic excuses for enraged hostility, and even they do not compose the entire list.

The Irish: Philadelphia, 1844. One year before, a Catholic bishop received permission from the Philadelphia public school authorities for Catholic children to read the Douai instead of the King James Bible in the schools; in addition, the children were permitted to forego the Protestant instruction then taught (and which today would be plainly unconstitutional). This policy awoke a torrent of nativist opinion which decried the meddling of a "foreign prelate" in school affairs. The result: a riot. In May, 1844, a group of Protestants marched into an Irish neighborhood and was met by a more pugnacious townspeople who forced them to retreat. The call went out for reinforcements, and the tumult that resulted May 6, 1844, led to one death and many injuries. For three days the riot continued; block after block of Irish houses and two Catholic churches were burned. Quiet then prevailed until the unwise decision to celebrate the Fourth of July as a memorial to the riot's dead. The parade of 70,000 led to further incitement the next day when fighting began anew.

Now they attacked the St. Philip de Neri Church, where it was rumored, truthfully, that guns had been stored. The ugliness of the crowd compelled the governor of Pennsylvania to send in the militia, which set up cannons to guard the church. Rioters like to fight, and the militia opened fire. Days later, the net result: 13 dead, more than 50 wounded, and an exodus of thousands of Catholics.

The riots quelled for a time what from the mid-thirties on had seemed might become a national preoccupation, the baiting of Irish Catholics. The public would not condone this kind of fighting, although it was receptive to anti-Catholic publications. One of the most enduring anti-Catholic books was that work of classic horror, *Maria Monk's Awful Disclosures of the Hotel Dieu Convent of Montreal, or the Secrets of Black Nunnery Revealed,* first published in 1836 (and reissued in 1960). Ostensibly written by a novitiate, the book described the education of a nun, revealing the necessity "to live in the practice of criminal intercourse" with the priests. Maria Monk, the author, was not fictitious, but she was never a nun; she was in fact apparently a prostitute, but this fact did not affect the success of the book, which became notorious and went into its twentieth printing. The venom of such works as this caused the credulous to believe and stoked the fires of anti-foreign sentiment.

The Germans, Chicago, 1886. For more than a decade, the most rabid xenophobes were convinced that the labor movement was inspired by foreign hordes intent on subverting America. Perhaps the link with immigrants was necessary because of the difficulty in explaining why "native" Americans would react with strikes and other demonstrations against the increasing might of big business. Chicago provided the setting for an outburst against immigrants which has continued down to this day.

In 1886, labor leaders throughout the country had called for an eight-hour "general strike." For weeks, the newspapers of the workingmen had been preaching the necessity of anarchy and violence. Chief among them was the *Arbeiter Zeitung,* a German language newspaper which urged dynamite as an adequate weapon and explained how nitroglycerin and a gas pipe could make an efficacious bomb. On May 5, political radicals, anarchists, and plain laborers congregated in Chicago's Haymarket Square to mark the strike. Just as the otherwise peaceful crowd, ringed by more than a hundred policemen, began dispersing, a bomb exploded, killing and injuring many. The "Haymarket Affair" touched off a widespread fear of foreigners, of anarchists, of immigrants. Since the anarchists in Chicago (the only city where anarchists then flourished) were immigrants, immigrants were obviously anarchists, and the cry went up against the importation of people who could only ruin America.

Chicago itself reacted by sentencing six immigrants to death, one to an extended stay in prison (these seven were German), and one native to death. The men were editors of the *Arbeiter Zeitung* and their friends; the proof that they had planted the bomb was simple. Iron fragments found in Haymarket Square seemed like what would have been found had the nitroglycerin bomb, described in the newspaper, been constructed and detonated. Furthermore, one of these editors had been known to stand on the Indiana side of Lake Michigan on Sundays, and with friends, toss bombs in the lake, pretending they were directed at various capitalists.

Editorial writers responded with reserved aplomb: "The enemy forces are not American [but] ragtag and bobtail cutthroats of Beelzebub from the Rhine, the Danube, the Vistula, and the Elbe." Again, "these people are not Americans, but the very scum and offal of Europe." "Long-haired, wild-eyed, badsmelling, atheistic reckless foreign wretches, who never did an honest hour's work in their lives." "There is no such thing as an American anarchist." All this, despite the fact that most of the immigrant press quickly condemned anarchy and violence. These images would reappear after World War I when continued anarchist incidents led to the final fear that brought victory to the restrictionists.

The Italians, New Orleans, 1891. Lynching of Italians seemed a popular sport in the 1890's, each time because a public, convinced that Italian equals Mafia, knew that a suspected son of Italy was a guilty man. The most dramatic episode took place in New Orleans, where the superintendent of police was murdered in 1891. Massive arrests were prompted by the suspicion that the Italian populace was behind the killing. "We must teach these people a lesson that they will not forget for all time," said the mayor. Incredibly, however, at the trial the jury did not convict. Local citizens thereafter carried out the state's function themselves, hanging eleven Italians implicated in the killing.

A chain reaction began with Italy's formal request that United States officials right the wrong committed in Louisiana. The Secretary of State, James G. Blaine (who lost the Presidential election in 1884, it is said, on his failure to repudiate the xenophobic slogan, "Rum, Romanism, and Rebellion"), had not been much converted to the plight of other nationalities in America, and he brushed aside Italy's diplomatic request. "I do not recognize the right of any government to tell the United States what it shall do," he said. "We have never received orders from any foreign power and shall not begin now. It is a matter of indifference what persons in Italy think of our institutions. I cannot change them, still less violate them." Italy recalled her minister, and in short order a fear gripped Americans throughout the country that Italy would make war on the United States (although the affair was eventually settled peacefully). Wild rumors sprang up across the land: Italians in America were actively preparing for the day the Italian warships would steam toward America. The cry for immigration restriction, to protect the nation against the shipment of foreign criminals, gained credence.

The Jews, Atlanta, 1914. The Leo Frank incident is not surprising, for all its brutality, and the reader will readily guess its denouement. Frank had the misfortune of being a well-to-do pencil factory manager; when Mary Phagan, the poor working girl, was found murdered, unfounded talk of a sex crime led to Frank, and he was easily convicted. This was too much for the clergy and journalists of Atlanta, but the more they protested and the more northern Jews determined to support Frank's continued legal fight financially, the more outraged the citizenry became. Tom Watson, a Georgia zealot who made anti-Catholicism a consuming mission, found a new enemy, the Jew.

The particular Jew was murdered shortly after the Georgia governor commuted his sentence to life. Mary Phagan's avengers broke into the jail, and after a 175-mile trip, slaughtered Leo Frank. Tom Watson thundered: "It is a peculiar . . . thing that one race of men—*and one only*—should be able to convulse the world, by a system of newspaper *agitation and suppression,* when a member of that race is convicted of a capital crime against another race. . . . From all over the world, the Children of Israel are flocking to this country, and plans are on foot to move them from Europe *en masse* . . . to empty upon our shores the very scum and dregs of the *Parasite race.*" Prior to 1914, Russian and Polish Jews had come to America in excess of 100,000 annually.

THE SCOPE OF LEGISLATION BEFORE WORLD WAR I

If the mounting viciousness explains the trend toward restriction, it throws little light on the reasons for the mildness of the restriction. The optimistic belief in America's ability to assimilate and grow with the immigrants far outweighed the tension and discontent. Optimism was shared by native and second- and third-generation Americans; the growing political power of the immigrants themselves was often a persuasive reminder to Congressmen who might otherwise have strayed from the conventional belief. Indeed, it was significant that in the same year as the Haymarket Affair, the Statue of Liberty was formally dedicated with Emma Lazarus's celebrated poem inscribed on its base. The battle lines were being drawn, but the official position of the United States was still on the side of the "tired and poor," the "wretched refuse," the "huddled masses yearning to breathe free."

Aside from a relatively minor enactment in 1819 concerning compilation of limited immigration statistics, the Federal Government shied away from lawmaking after the expiration of the Alien Act in 1800. The first major governmental action came in 1849, not from Congress but from the Supreme Court, which ruled in the *Passenger Cases* that immigrants came to America in the stream of foreign commerce and could be regulated only by the Federal Government. This was simply an affirmation of the open-door policy.

In 1862, Congress made its first real move, outlawing slave labor from the Orient. In the same year, taking advantage of the fact that southern opposition had absented itself from Congress altogether, Congress passed the Homestead Act, which put citizens and aliens on a par in the settling of public lands. Two years later Congress enacted a law to encourage immigrants and to establish a bureau of immigration to aid the new arrivals. This bureau was abolished in 1868, at the same time that the Burlingame Treaty for the admission of Chinese immigrants was signed. In 1870 Congress permitted the naturalization of Negroes; and in 1876, in the *Henderson* case (involving the immigrant head tax) the Supreme Court completed its rout of state laws regulating immigrant admissions. The year before, however, Congress banned two more classes of immigrants: prostitutes and foreign convicts. This last was in response to pressures exerted by those who feared that America would become a dumping ground for the criminals of the world; it was believed that some countries were releasing prisoners from jail on condition that they emigrate to the United States.

By the 1880's, the tide had turned; the legislation which followed began to compile lists of certain "excludables." In addition to the Chinese Exclusion Act of 1882, that year saw Congress' answer to the Court's decision that the Federal Government, not the states, must have the ultimate regulatory authority. Not only was a beginning effort established under the Secretary of the Treasury, but to the list of excludables were added idiots, lunatics, and people likely to become public charges. The list was further expanded in 1885 with the passage of the Foran Act, forbidding anyone from assisting or encouraging "the importation or migration of aliens . . . under contract or agreement . . . to perform labor or service of any kind in the United States." The contract labor provision did not apply to skilled workers or to artists, singers, lecturers, actors, or domestic servants. Behind this prohibition lay organized labor, which testified that it was being subjected to cheap competition and the strike-breaking tactics of businessmen. Making the comparison with the already-prohibited coolie trade, labor helped nudge Congress along. Thus began one of the first great ironies of immigration law, for in the revised statutes decades later, it was illegal to enter the country *unless* the immigrant could prove he had a job waiting.

In 1891 Congress put still more classes of people on its "little list": polygamists, paupers, people suffering from contagious, dangerous, or loathsome diseases, those convicted of crimes involving "moral turpitude" (adulterers were later to get themselves in trouble because of emanations from this concept), and those whose voyage had been paid by another (unless friends or relatives). The 1891 law incorporated a new feature into immigration law: Illegal entrants could be deported if they were caught within a year of their arrival.

These laws were not coherent attempts to close the gates generally. For the most part, in fact, they were simply single responses to what were considered separate problems. A backer of the Foran Act went so far as to say that "this bill in no measure seeks to restrict free immigration; such a proposition would be odious, and justly so, to the American people."

Beginning in the late 1890's, however, concerted efforts did begin in Congress to restrict immigration. The first device tried was a literacy test that would bar those unable to read and write in either English or a native language.

Congress, seizing on the literacy test as a means of cutting down on eastern and southern European immigration, passed such a bill in 1897, requiring literacy for immigrants more than fourteen years old. During the depression in 1894, the Democrats were ousted from control, and the Republican Congress at the close of the term of the Democratic President, Grover Cleveland, overwhelmingly passed the bill. The Immigration Restriction League stirred public sentiment in favor of the test, and the two houses of Congress voted two separate bills—guided by two Massachusetts legislators, Senator Henry Cabot Lodge and Representative Samuel Walker McCall. The Congressional conference committee reconciled the conflicting versions of the bill by tightening up even further. The conference bill was passed by both houses (though the Senate majority was drastically cut), and sent to the President. Cleveland vetoed it. The President noted in his message to Congress that the bill heralded too great a change from the national policy that had so long existed.

Illiteracy points to the lack of opportunity abroad, not to criminality or disease at home, he said. Furthermore, the dislike of the newer immigrants was unwarranted, since others before had heard the same cries. And in any event, he concluded, the literacy test was a misplaced device for doing away with the perceived evil. The House mustered a two-thirds majority to override the veto, but the bill lay dead in the Senate.

In 1903, partly in response to the assassination of President McKinley by the anarchist Leon Czolgosz, Congress extended its list of undesirables: anarchists, beggars, epileptics, those who had been afflicted with insanity, and the importers of prostitutes. Four years later, tubercular patients, imbeciles, people with feeble minds and with defects which might hinder their ability to earn a livelihood became similarly unwanted.

The head tax was doubled to $4 in 1907 by an act passed only after an intense struggle. The forces which wanted the literacy test were subdued almost single-handedly by the iron will of Speaker Joe Cannon, a Republican who feared the party's loss of immigrant support. The debate coincided with another period of agitation against Orientals in California—this time against the Japanese. President Roosevelt, fearing the national consequences of the West Coast incidents, urged Senator Lodge to withdraw the literacy test in return for restriction of the Japanese. Lodge conceded and the bill passed. Under the compromise, the President was given authority to make executive agreements with foreign powers limiting immigration; Roosevelt entered into the so-called Gentleman's Agreement with the Japanese to cut down on an outflow of laborers from that country. Of the Japanese problem, generally, there was more to come.

That same year an immigration commission was established to make a thorough investigation of every aspect of the subject matter under its jurisdiction. Four years later, the commission (popularly known as the Dillingham Commission) issued its report: More than forty volumes concluded generally from a welter of statistics and comparisons that the "new" immigration was radically different from the "old." Whether through deliberate subterfuge or an honest failure to appreciate the subtleties of statistical comparisons, the commission's "findings" confirmed old suspicions and created new alarms, which restrictionists picked up and hurled at the public for decades.

Fundamentally, the commission's mistakes were two: It indiscriminately mixed groups together for purposes of comparison, and it ignored the time span of the immigrants' lives in America. As pointed out a half-century later: "Had specific groups of immigrants been considered individually, instead of being lumped together in two arbitrarily chosen categories, a very different picture would have emerged. It was undeniable that Italian and Slavic immigrants, for instance, were predominantly male, unskilled, illiterate, and transient. But there were larger percentages of males among German, Scandinavian, and English immigrants than there were among Jewish, Bohemian, and Portuguese; Bohemians, Moravians, and Finns had lower percentages of illiteracy than had the Irish and Germans; Englishmen, Germans, and Scandinavians showed a greater tendency to return to Europe than did Armenians, Dalmatians, Jews, and Portuguese; Jews had a higher percentage of skilled laborers than any group except the Scots, and the Irish had a smaller percentage than the Italians." Furthermore, had the "new" immigrants been compared with the "old" immigrants at their comparable state of assimilation—that is to say, had the commission compared the siuation of the "new" immigrant in the early 1900's with that of the "old" in the 1870's, instead of the early 1900's, as was actually done—the call for a literacy test might not have been heard. Of the "old" immigrants in the 1870's, 22.9 percent were skilled; of the "new" immigrants in the 1900's, 18.1 percent were skilled, a closeness even more remarkable when it is considered that the "newer" immigrants were subjects of generally more repressive and less economically developed monarchies than their earlier-arriving brethren.

The Dillingham Report, together with the streams of race-consciousness that were clouding thought, brought to life the literacy test movement once again, and again it was defeated by Presidential veto after having passed both houses. The campaign of 1912, a three-way fight among Taft, Roosevelt, and Wilson, led each candidate to seek the immigrant vote; Congress delayed action until after the election, when it voted anew for the test. Owing to the peculiarity in the Constitution that continued an old Congress and a defeated President well into the spring beyond the November election day, Taft, like Cleveland before him, had to decide whether to consent to the act shortly before departing the White House. He vetoed it, for reasons similar to Cleveland's. The Senate mustered the necessary two thirds to override, but five votes in the House provided the margin and the line held.

Two years later, Congress ran through the verse again, passing a literacy test once the 1915 elections were safely by. Now it was President Wilson's turn to veto. The law was so stringent that it would keep out even those illiterates fleeing from political persecution (notably Russian Jews), and Wilson responded that it "seeks to all but close entirely the gates of asylum which have always been open to those who could find nowhere else the right and opportunity of constitutional agitation for what they conceived to be the natural and inalienable rights of men." The vote in the House to override failed this time by a margin of four. The pattern was as it had been in the past: The South and West were strongly for the test, and its defeat came from holdouts in the North.

For nearly twenty years, the swelling chorus of xenophobes was unable to choke off immigration. Despite the serious concern —evidenced by the fact that on three separate occasions nearly two thirds of Congress assembled thought it proper to implant the literacy test in national policy—more traditional notions of American policy prevailed. Partly, the old beliefs survived because two defeated and outgoing Presidents could shuck off politics and express their personal beliefs. Partly, it was because it was good politics to side with the immigrants, as Wilson came to see. The immigrants now constituted large numbers of urban voters as they became naturalized; if extremists feared the "foreign bloc vote," every politician had at least to be wary of it. Sadly, in a very few years, the greatest political and social catalyst of all—war—brought all the bubbling forces to full boil.

WAR AND AFTERMATH

The war to make the world safe for democracy had chilling effects on democracy at home. The German-American community contributed to the quagmire into which America fell by protesting, through their organization, the German-American Alliance, United States policies which seemed to favor Britain at the war's start. Within months, the "Teutonic race," which had been praised almost universally as a bulwark of the American character, suffered a severe reverse. Germans were suspected of sabotage and treason everywhere; by the time the United States formally declared war on Germany the public was hysterically determined to root out German culture. In different ways and with different styles, but with the same end in mind, Theodore Roosevelt and President Wilson led the cry for "100 percent Americanism" against that most damned of all human creatures, the "hyphenated American." To tool up the nation for war, absolute loyalty was demanded: A war as complex, as large, and as far away as now was faced could not be won by a divided nation. So rather than allow national energy to be drained by deviant behavior it was drained by exhausting efforts to compel uniformity. In state after state, even the teaching of German in public schools was outlawed. Roosevelt actually went so far as to advocate killing "disloyal" German-Americans.

The people could be denied no longer. In 1917, Congress for the fourth time enacted the literacy test into law, and this time it bludgeoned its way into the statute books over Wilson's veto. Although immigration had fallen off during the war years, the law's proponents had pointed to the days of peace to come. Only if one member of the family was literate, or the immigrant was a refugee from religious persecution, was he exempt from the requirement that he must be able to read and write at an elementary level. The list of excludables had just about reached its outer limits with the new additions: Hindus and Asiatics other than Chinese (but not the Japanese), stowaways, chronic alcoholics, vagrants, and to show that science had made firm strides, persons of "constitutional psychopathic inferiority."

More insidious were the Espionage Act of 1917 and the Sedition Act of 1918, the successor statutes of which are today being slowly whittled away as unconstitutional by the Supreme Court. In essence, they provided that disloyal *opinions* were punishable by sentences of up to twenty years in the federal penitentiary. These laws gave rise to Justice Oliver Wendell Holmes's ringing statement that "the most stringent protection of free speech would not protect a man in falsely shouting fire in a theater, and causing a panic." From this case arose the doctrine that the Government may restrict speech and the press if there is a "clear and present danger" of "substantive evils that Congress has a right to prevent." Ironically, the cases which spelled out this attack on the 1st Amendment involved not Germans, but Russian socialists who advocated draft resistance because they feared that Wilson's order of troops to the Russian front following the October Revolution meant the end of the socialist state.

Germans were taken care of in a more summary fashion. The Departments of Justice and Labor by virtue of the 1917 and 1918 acts were empowered to deport aliens on a variety of grounds, the deadliest of which were the expression of radical beliefs and mere membership in organizations which advocated the overthrow of the Government by violence. Statutes of limitation did not apply; a man could be deported for committing the "crime" years before his arrest. Under recent Supreme Court decisions, mere membership cannot constitutionally be the basis for a crime. Except for the fact that a unique doctrine holds (perhaps still today) that being an alien is worse than committing a crime (as we shall later see), deportations under the 1917 and 1918 acts would be suspect by today's standards. But niceties do not inhibit even democratic governments during war, and the departments plunged ahead, even to the extent of authorizing *private* groups to hunt for subversives. The American Protective League, supported by the Department of Justice, grew to 250,000 members determined to track down secret subversives, and either reform them, turn them in, or tar and feather them. Until the end of the war, few deportations were actually carried out, however.

Armistice brought jubilation and the Big Red Scare. Strikes convulsed the nation in 1919; labor unrest spread as America unwound from wartime restrictions. Radical movements on behalf of the Russian Revolution picked up tempo. In April, a mad bomber precipitated the crisis. More than thirty packages containing a Gimbel's Department Store label and a bomb inside were found in a New York post office, about to be sent to prominent addressees. The search began when one bomb exploded in the hands of the maid of the chairman of the Senate Immigration Committee. Cabinet officials, judges, and financiers were marked for death; the public knew the Communists to be at the bottom of it; though, as in Haymarket Square twenty-three years before, the bomber's identity was never discovered. In June, a bomb smashed the front of the Attorney General's home in Washington, killing the carrier who had failed to get out of the way. Nearby were found copies of a pamphlet advocating the death of public officials. It was time to save the country.

A. Mitchell Palmer, just appointed Attorney General by Wilson three months before, began his preparations. Moving young J. Edgar Hoover from the Enemy Alien registration section of the department to the General Intelligence Division, Palmer encouraged the compilation of files on more than 60,000 suspected persons. Yet for five months, Palmer hesitated, not knowing exactly how far he could or should go. In October, the Senate passed a resolution censuring the Attorney General for inactivity; newspapers and private groups throughout the country had poured out a torrent of shrill cries that dozens of institutions were Communist-dominated. By November, Palmer was ready. Thinking back on it the next year, he wrote: "Like a prairie fire, the blaze of revolution was sweeping over every institution of law and order. . . . It was eating its way into the homes of the American workman, its sharp tongues of revolutionary heat were licking the altars of the churches, leaping into the belfry of the school bell, crawling into the sacred corners of American homes, seeking to replace marriage vows with libertine law, burning up the foundations of society." For this man with Presidential ambitions, the solution was obvious: Deport the radical aliens.

The first raids began November 7, 1919, in New York at the Russian People's House, where 200 men (and boys) were attending night classes. Without warrants, federal agents created havoc inside by searching quickly and recklessly. Finding no weapons, they beat many of the students with blackjacks and took them away. Nine other cities witnessed similar raids that same night; by morning 450 people had been arrested and half released as innocent. Many who were detained soon discovered that they were outside the bounds of normal legal procedures. Because aliens have no vested right to remain in the country, an administrative hearing could determine whether a law had been violated (such as reading an anarchist pamphlet); court trials were unnecessary. In December some 250 Russians and other aliens were removed to Ellis Island in New York and deported to Russia aboard an Army transport that was quickly nicknamed the "Soviet Ark."

January, 1920, saw the beginning of more massive raids. An Acting Secretary of Labor changed the administrative rules at Palmer's request; no longer did the arresting officers need to inform suspects of their right to counsel or the charge on which they were booked. On January 2, an initial 5,000 people were picked up in thirty-three cities, 2,000 of whom were subsequently released. *The New York Times* thought the results were "far-reaching and beneficial."

But with all good things come the spoilers. Inquiries by concerned citizens and groups revealed that hundreds of arrests were made utterly without foundation. One arresting officer in Newark, New Jersey, picked up a man because "he looked like a radical." A certain Detroit diner delivered all its occupants that night to the police, and across town an entire orchestra was taken into custody. It turned out that one man was held because agents did not know that the dangerous-looking drawings in his home were plans for a phonograph. The circumstances of the imprisonment came into the open and revealed an unusual severity: hundreds cramped into tiny rooms, lack of heat and food made up for by an abundance of thrashings.

Investigations showed that Palmer had flagrantly violated the Constitution, even as it was then construed. Only 3,000 warrants were issued to cover 5,000 arrests. Convictions were obtained without witnesses. Defendants were not allowed counsel, even of their own choice and even if paid from their own pockets. Confessions were extracted physically. When the Acting Secretary of Labor who had gone along with Palmer in a relaxation of the rules left in March, the new Acting Secretary tightened up. More than 4,000 were finally released, and of the 2,720 prisoners whom Palmer had promised would be deported, only 556 actually went. Palmer panicked, accusing the Acting Secretary of Labor of being a Communist sympathizer, urging a Congressional impeachment. Instead, Congress decided to investigate Palmer, though nothing came of it. When he predicted uprisings in May and on the Fourth of July and they failed to materialize, Palmer and the scare were on the decline.

The fear of radicalism as the gravest menace gave way once more to racism, as antipathy toward the European reached new heights. European commentators began criticizing American materialism and spiritual defects; Rudyard Kipling was incensed at America's demands at Versailles. The hissing of American tourists in Paris was given wide and exaggerated circulation by the press; and the country came to believe that "America is hated by every European country." Within three years, America was transformed in European eyes from "savior of civilization" to "Uncle Shylock." The reversal of attitude soured many Americans who felt their participation and efforts in the war merited better.

Other problems came in a rush. Depression hit the United States at the same time that the influx of Europeans resumed its prewar dimensions. Prohibition exacerbated the nativists' relations with the alien urban drinker, who above all seemed to resist the conformity required by the Eighteenth Amendment. The requirements of 100 percent Americanism changed focus but not intensity. Xenophobia was reaching its climax. For too long had America endured disloyalty, nonconformity, riots, unlawfulness, labor unrest, arson, and murder. The prelude to policy had ended—a firm national policy against immigration was taking shape.

3 / *Policy Round 1: Victory in the Twenties*

For forty years, public opinion had been shifting direction. It was impossible for Congress, the "Grand Inquest of the Nation," to ignore the drift. For many years, Congress had been responsive to the desire for change, and by 1920 the time had come for the world's greatest legislative body to mirror more precisely its constituents' demands. Now the ponderous and heavy-handed efforts of the past would bear fruit.

An engine of the status quo, Congress is built to go slowly. As even a junior officer aboard a great warship knows, it is difficult to alter course; the great weight of the vessel and the inconsistency of the water dictate that the prudent captain order a steady "right" or "left" rudder to prevent it from jamming. The captain must also bear in mind that once the ship begins to turn, it will continue to swing; opposite rudder must be applied well before the ship has swung onto the proper course, in order to forestall overshooting the mark. These things are well known to captains, and a few simple orders to the helmsman will prevent serious mishap. In Congress it is not so easy.

For the most part, Congress had avoided turning too quickly; when too drastic a change in national policy is called for by some elements within its halls, Congress will jam and cease to function, and other pressing matters will inevitably force the legislators to find a way around the impasse. In the past, cries for general restriction had never resulted in paralysis. Now these cries were so insistent that attempts to silence them might have.

The turn in 1917 showed the way: Even a recalcitrant President could be overridden, and Congress assumed control of the wheel. To the knowledge that restriction was feasible was added this sobering fact: Between 1918 and 1921, 1,487,000 immigrants came into the United States, but only 6,142 were excluded for failing the literacy test. The device that was to keep out undesirables did not work at all. That so many immigrants met the standards of literacy did not make them any more desirable; the belief that between five and twenty-five million more were waiting to come intensified the fear.

ESTABLISHING NATIONAL ORIGINS

In 1920, proposals were revived for some kind of percentage plan that would limit total immigration. Such plans had been advocated by, among others, the Dillingham Commission in 1911. Support came from the rapidly growing Ku Klux Klan (which claimed three million adherents in forty-five states by 1923), a revival of the older post-bellum Klan that now engaged in anti-Negro, anti-Catholic, and anti-Semitic crusades. Henry Ford chimed in with his rabidly anti-Semitic *Dearborn Independent*. Americanization efforts in certain areas had paid off: Nineteen states required both public and private schools to use only the English language for instruction. Oregon required the foreign-language press to publish simultaneous and adjacent translations; Oregon also outlawed private elementary schools, including religious schools. California required adult aliens to pay a head tax. These last two laws were voided by the Supreme

Court. Other reformers during the decade past who had been trying to Americanize resident aliens grew disenchanted when they found their less than legislative but nevertheless best efforts to no avail. These funny people from other lands seemed to prefer their old ways; maybe the nativist theory that their ways were inborn was correct. Organized labor joined in, afraid that as they believed had happened in the past, an influx of foreigners would depress the wage. Samuel Gompers and his allies in the American Federation of Labor had fallen under the spell of the wartime desire for 100 percent Americanism. And in every community, editorialists and citizens demanded an end to the "bestial hordes." Even some of the immigrant groups joined the call, for if you were against others you must be for America.

In the House, the Committee on Immigration under the leadership of Albert Johnson of Washington pressed for a two-year suspension of all immigration. Relying on the innuendo that the bulk of immigration was Jewish, a most "dangerous" race, the House put its seal of approval on the bill. The Senate was more cautious, relying as it did on the protestations of American businessmen, the only significant group that opposed the extreme demands of outright suspension. If immigration were stopped, where would cheap labor come from?

Senator William P. Dillingham of Vermont, who had introduced percentage bills before the war, came forward with a new proposal. If the number of immigrants each year were limited to 5 percent of the number of foreign-born of each nationality as determined by the 1910 census, immigration would be cut while allowing northern Europeans to enter. The House concurred, reducing the percentage to 3. When the bill was sent to President Wilson for his signature during the last week of February, 1921, he refused to sign it. The "pocket veto" was successful because there was no time left to override: On March 4 a new Congress and a new President prepared to guide the United States to victory.

One of the first acts of the man who had urged the nation to return with him to "normalcy" was a call for something the country never yet had, a general restriction law. The new

Chief Executive, Warren G. Harding, called for an early session of Congress in April. Within eleven days the House had passed another restriction bill, and less than three weeks later the Senate acted also. Because Representative Johnson decided not to press for his own suspension bill, but agreed to go along with the Dillingham proposal, the differences were minor and they were quickly ironed out. On May 19, 1921, President Harding signed it, and the national immigration policy had taken a new course.

The 1921 plan, based on the 1910 census, was explicitly temporary. Its proponents had passed it in a hurry to provide a level of protection while they sat back to think things out more clearly. In 1922 the law was further extended until 1924. The new law was simple in conception: 3 percent of each national group, measured by the number of persons born outside the United States, would equal the quotas assigned each nation in Europe. The total worked out to 356,995. Of this theoretical maximum, 77,342 could come from Great Britain, 68,059 from Germany, 42,057 from Italy, 34,284 from the Soviet Union, 25,827 from Poland, 20,042 from Sweden, 14,282 from Czechoslovakia. Even Greece, which later was to receive a quota of 308, could send up to 3,294 of its citizens each year. The relatively high figures for some countries (though, to be sure, a drastic reduction over past years) were due to the decision to base them on the number of foreign-born immigrants in the United States; millions from eastern and southern Europe who had arrived by 1910 were still alive.

During operation of the 1910 census plan, the racial ideas of Madison Grant were fully aired. The *Saturday Evening Post*, in a series of articles, popularized the notion that the superior Nordics must be made safe from inferior breeds of the east and south. To prevent the final deterioration of the species, Representative Johnson and his committee formulated a plan based on the 1890 census. The sense of using the 1890 figures was clear: It was only at this time that the geographic nature of immigration began to change. A system based on the older figures would therefore guarantee a preeminent place to Nordic immigrants in the future.

For a time, justification proved a more difficult problem. It was one thing to propose a legislative scheme which everyone knew was aimed at racial classification; it was still another, even in 1920, for Congress solemnly to memorialize such a scheme into law when the only excuse was that some races were better than others. It is the ambivalence of America that though you can say such a thing, you are hesitant in voting for it if there is any other way out. There was.

To the committee now came one Captain John B. Trevor, an Army officer in charge of the military intelligence service in New York City from the end of 1918 until June, 1919. His work in ferreting out subversives in Manhattan led him to an intense interest in the subject of immigration. With Madison Grant he was a trustee of the American Museum of Natural History and he thus had firsthand exposure to the thinking of the times. Trevor was rich, and he had the spare time to develop statistics which clinched Johnson's case and then went far beyond it.

It was not difficult for Trevor to compile tables which showed that the 1890 census was in fact fairer than the 1910 census, if you knew what your purpose in using them was. Trevor assumed with Johnson that a legislative scheme that would permit into the country a racially-balanced group similar to the racial mix that actually existed would have no trouble in passing. Since the thinking then was to allocate quotas on the basis of living Americans who were foreign born, the nearer one came to the present, the more quotas that would necessarily be allocated to the undesirables. In fact, since by 1896 northwestern European immigrants for the first time were in the minority, the use of a 1910 census gave almost as many quotas to the southern and eastern European as the northwestern. Clearly this was untenable, for if one considered the *entire* population, native born and foreign born, then it was plain that northwestern stock predominated. Trevor's tables gave the offensive to Johnson, who now could justify the obvious racial bias in using the 1890 census figures. It was not a question of giving a larger percentage of quotas to the foreign-born Nordics, Johnson said; it was rather a question of giving a percentage of quotas equivalent to the proportion that the particular racial stock bore to the population as a whole. Trevor showed that, whereas the Alpines and Mediterraneans made up 12 percent of the population, the 1910 census gave them 44 percent of the quotas. The 1890 census figures would reduce their quotas to 15 percent, which was still higher than they deserved. But why quibble over 3 percent? Johnson could afford to be generous. The House quickly passed the Johnson bill.

The Senate was still not quite so sure. Its immigration subcommittee recommended retaining the 1910 census, but reducing the percentage from 3 to 2. The stumbling block was still the matter of justification: No matter how you phrased it, the mere fact that the House had had to reach back to a census thirty years old meant discrimination.

Senator David A. Reed of Pennsylvania now took charge. It occurred to him also that the real objective was to maintain the racial mix, and he saw that the percentage plan that depended on the number of foreign *born* was merely an artifice. There might be another way to reach the same result, and the solution led directly from Captain Trevor's study. Senator Reed's plan was the "national origins system": Compute the ratio of each racial (now called nationality) group, regardless of whether foreign or native born, to the total U.S. population, and carve out from an absolute maximum quotas that reflected each of these ratios. Thus, to take a simple example, since nearly half of all Americans derived from British immigrants during the past three centuries, nearly half the quotas would go to immigrants from Great Britain. The best part of the scheme was that it demanded use of the 1920 census; it could not be fairer.

Senator Reed's amendment to the pending immigration bill was made so quickly and with so little fanfare that historians are still not sure whether the idea came from Reed or Trevor. That Reed and Trevor were closely allied there can be no doubt. Trevor's March 5 report to the House contained a column that showed what the quotas would be if the national origins system were used; on March 6 Reed announced his intention to move an amendment. With almost no discussion (except for a favorable word from the Senate's venerable immigration guru, Henry Cabot Lodge), and amidst debate on a host of other issues, the Senate adopted it with a temporary compromise: Until 1927, the foreign-born plan based on the 1890 census would go into effect. The House, however, rejected a national origins amendment to Johnson's bill.

Debate in the House during 1923 and 1924 had focused to a large extent on the question of restricting the Japanese. Since it was a foregone conclusion that some sort of general restriction would be laid against Europeans, the question of most intense interest, prompted by western Congressmen, was whether the Japanese would be added to the list of already-barred Chinese and other Asians.

The Gentleman's Agreement of 1907 was the result of a diplomatic compromise between Roosevelt and the Japanese Government. Rather than bar the Japanese altogether (which might have been internationally unwise, since Japan was a growing military power), the agreement resulted in Japan's drastically curbing the number of visas it authorized to Japanese laborers. Immigrants entering America dropped to an average annual rate of slightly more than 3,000, off from a 1906–1907 high of 30,000. From 1908 to 1911, the number of Japanese leaving America exceeded those entering. After the war, however, charges from the West Coast that immigration was again on the upswing, coupled with the fear of "picture brides" who were being ordered from Japan, led to a desire for complete exclusion.

The exclusion provision received wide attention. Cried Representative MacLafferty: "For God's sake, you men who know what the colored problem means, not only to the white man but to the colored man, stand with us in this. We will not forget if you do." Mr. Miller of Washington summed it up: "The Japanese cannot be made Americans. The native-born are Japanese heart, blood, and soul. They never yield to the American idea of things. In their hearts they owe a superior allegiance to the Mikado. Their national sentiment is fixed, their faith is pledged. There is no such thing in truth as an American-Japanese; he is a Japanese, simon-pure, every inch of his body, every drop of his blood.

"Aside from an intense national spirit and attachment for his ancestral and blood home, he, like all other races or nationals, responds to another philosophy at once basic and fundamental. Scientists tell us that the older the racial or national customs, the older the character without change or modification, the more difficult it is to change the mental, moral, and temperamental makeup of a people. Oriental blood is the oldest blood in the world today unchanged by environment. Oriental customs, characters, and temperaments are the oldest of all. Japan for 2,000 years lived under one dynasty; her people, cycle in and cycle out, lived with their strict and unbending customs, institutions, habits, and thoughts. The national ideal was fixed. The very lives of the people were trained in one channel, and thus they made the character molded to one standard of the purposes of life. Only within the memory of men now living has [sic] her institutions become changed. Japan's modernization is not yet fifty years old, and some of her institutions are not yet changed.

"Is it any wonder, therefore, that the individual Japanese character cannot fit into our modern and democratic ways and customs. His nation has not had the rejuvenation that always follows the infusion of new or other blood of the same race. His blood is unchanged in thousands of years—marriages of his nationals within the national blood. It is not to be wondered at that his character is fixed, his customs unchangeable, his ideas and purposes of life permanent. When he comes to our country or is born here, in either case, the blood is unchanged and he remains as a true Oriental, a Japanese, as if his foot had never touched American soil. He remains a Japanese in heart and soul and blood—as unchangeable as the stars."

To this Mr. Gilbert added his more general declamation on the day the 1890 plan passed the House: "Let this tolerance of these national and racial differences grow and it will be but a little while until it will be permissible in this Congress for some member to address this House in German, in French, in Yiddish, or in whatever particular language the colonists speak from which this particular representative may happen to come. . . . No greater curse could ever have been inflicted upon a people than the importation of Negro slaves into this country when their subsequent elevation to equal rights and privileges shall have in fact been consummated. We in the South are not so sensitive to its viciousness yet, for there a healthful social sentiment takes the place of law and a proper distinction has served to prevent its evils, yet so gradual is its effacement that we are callous to its ever-increasing encroachments until some outstanding occasion awakens us from our lethargy. The other day one of this race, with thick lips, curly hair, was entered into a beauty contest with white girls in one of our northern cities. Under the policies hitherto pursued a race of yet another color, the yellow man, the Japanese, has begun his encroachments in the West, causing the same results as caused by the Negro in the South."

The atmosphere was all the more charged as a result of contemporary Supreme Court decisions concerning the right of the Japanese to be naturalized. Following lower court precedents in Chinese cases, the Court rejected the possibility of citizenship for Japanese aliens, on a statutory, not constitutional, basis. Takao Ozawa, born in Japan, applied for naturalization to the United States District Court for the Territory of Hawaii. He had studied for three years at the University of California, his family had been educated in American schools, spoke English, and attended a Christian church. It was conceded that he was *fit* for citizenship. But would it be lawful?

Ozawa argued that a 1906 statute had implicitly repealed the phrase "free white" in the naturalization law, since new conditions were set in which the phrase was not mentioned. He argued further that "white" meant "not Negro," and that the use of "free" underscored the point; the Japanese were never slaves. The Court rejected these arguments. Never mind that the drafters of the first naturalization statute in 1790 had in mind African slaves and had not considered the Japanese— what would they have done had they considered them?

Ozawa had a reserve argument: In any case, the Japanese are "white." The Court was ready for this one, too. "White" means "Caucasian," said Justice Sutherland. Although there are borderline cases, this appellant "is clearly of a race which is not Caucasian and therefore belongs entirely outside the zone on the negative side. . . . Of course, there is not implied— either in the legislation or in our interpretation of it—any suggestion of individual unworthiness or racial inferiority. These considerations are in no manner involved."

That same day the Court told how serious it took the law to be. In another case, a Washington state court had refused to compel the Secretary of State to file articles of incorporation for the Japanese Real Estate Holding Company. Under Washington law, aliens ineligible for citizenship could not form such a corporation; and even though the plaintiffs in the suit showed that they had *in fact been naturalized* by a court before they sought to form their company, nevertheless they lost. The Supreme Court affirmed the decision. Since the court which naturalized them knew they were Japanese it had no jurisdiction and therefore its naturalization decree was void.

The ultimate racial distinction found judicial approval in 1923. A high-caste Hindu, Bhagat Singh Thind, born in Punjab and a resident of the United States, applied for and received a certificate of citizenship from the United States District Court for the District of Oregon. The Government brought suit to cancel; the District Court dismissed the suit and the Court of Appeals for the Ninth Circuit was confused, certifying two questions to the Supreme Court. Only the first was considered: Whether such an East Indian was "white" within the meaning of the law. Clearly, argued Thind's counsel, he was neither Mongoloid nor Negro. Furthermore, Thind was related by a common ancestral group to the Aryan linguistic groups of Europe and entitled therefore to the epithet Caucasian.

Justice Sutherland was equal to the task. As for language groups, slaves learned to speak English and that didn't make them white. Citing the *Encyclopedia Britannica,* the Justice noted that "Caucasian" includes, according to some "ethnologists," not only Hindu but Maori, Tahitian, Samoan, and Hawaiian, and even the "Hamites of Africa, upon the ground of the Caucasic cast of their features, though in color they range from brown to black. We venture to think that the average well-informed white American would learn with some degree of astonishment that the race to which he belongs is made up of such heterogeneous elements." No doubt. And, as the law professors would say, query whether the *Encyclopedia Britannica* was entitled to judicial notice.

Anyway, Hindus are not white even if Caucasian: "It cannot be doubted that the children born in this country of Hindu parents would retain indefinitely the clear evidence of their ancestry. It is very far from our thought to suggest the slightest question of racial superiority or inferiority. What we suggest is merely racial difference, and it is of such character and extent that the great body of our people instinctively recognize it and reject the thought of assimilation." Characteristic of Sutherland's judicial opinions was his cloaking of ambiguous phrases in moral certainty. He rejected the thought of assimilation precisely because he feared it would happen. To top it off, the justice noted that the act of 1917 forbade Indian immigration. Even though it was after the fact, "it is not likely Congress would be willing to accept as citizens a class of persons whom it rejects as immigrants."

This was a curious conclusion, and it caused tensions later on, for the *children* of these nonassimilable, racially unalterable people *were* citizens. The Court had decided this on a constitutional plane a quarter-century before. In 1894 Wong Kim Ark left California on a trip to China; on his return in the later summer of 1895, he was refused permission to land. He was born in San Francisco in 1873, the son of permanent-resident Chinese aliens who had returned to China in 1890. He had successfully made a previous trip in that year.

After an extensive review of ancient law bearing on citizenship and allegiance, the Court came to the point in Wong's appeal. The Civil Rights Act of 1886 declared that "all persons born in the United States, and not subject to any foreign power, excluding Indians not taxed, are citizens of the United States." Unwilling to let the matter rest there, Congress proposed the 14th Amendment to the Constitution, ratified in 1868: "All persons born or naturalized in the United States, and subject to the jurisdiction thereof, are citizens of the United States."

So, concluded the Court in 1898, "The 14th Amendment

affirms the ancient and fundamental rule of citizenship by birth within the territory, in the allegiance and under the protection of the country, including all children here born of resident aliens, with the exception or qualifications (as old as the rule itself) of children of foreign sovereigns or their ministers, or born on foreign public ships, or of enemies within and during a hostile occupation of part of our territory, and with the single additional exception of children of members of the Indian tribes owing direct allegiance to their several tribes. The Amendment, in clear words and in manifest intent, includes the children born, within the territory of the United States, of all other persons, of whatever race or color, domiciled within the United States. . . . The power of naturalization, vested in Congress by the Constitution, is a power to confer citizenship, not a power to take it away."

(The curious exception to the rule that the children of all ethnic groups born in the United States are citizens was justified in 1884 when an Indian who claimed he had separated himself voluntarily from his tribe was refused registration as a Nebraska voter. The Court declared that the Indian tribe is "an alien though dependent power" and that Indians are not "subject to the jurisdiction of the United States" at birth. To whom they were subject, if not to the United States on whom they were "dependent," was never made clear.)

The implications of the fact that Japanese aliens ineligible for citizenship could spawn children who would be citizens went unconsidered in the 1920's by Congress, as well as the Court. The reaction of Congress to the *Ozawa* case was simple: If the Japanese cannot be naturalized, why should they be allowed to emigrate at all?

Against the impassioned allegations of Congressmen who hated Orientals, and the restrictive decrees of the Supreme Court, opponents of both the 1890 plan and the national origins system (some of whom might have gone along with the 1921 law then in effect) could effectively resist neither. Before the House initially passed the 1890 census plan, Representative Emanuel Celler of New York told his fellow legislators: "Let us at least be truthful. In fact, deception is futile. It is clear as the sun that the majority of the Immigration Committee and most proponents of this measure like the gentleman from Kansas [Mr. Tincher], who blurted out his true feelings while talking on the bill, do not want the 'wops,' 'dagoes,' 'Hebrews,' 'hunkies,' 'bulls,' and others known by similar epithets. Just so, in 1840, 1850, and 1860, you did not want the 'beery Germans' and 'dirty Irish.' The Germans and Irish were mongrels, self-seekers, disreputable, and would not assimilate. We know now how good a citizenry they have become."

The Senate was not expected to pass the anti-Japanese provision which succeeded in the House, despite the fierce debate, since the annual quota would have amounted to only 146. But a statement on the American immigration debates made in the Japanese Diet in February of 1924 inflamed sentiment in the Senate. Said the Japanese Ambassador: "If this bill is enacted by the United States it would lead to grave consequences. I do not mean to say by that that the Empire will go to war with the United States over this question. But what I do mean to say is that, if the Japanese people are to be classified by the United States as an inferior race, that action would seriously destroy the present desire of the Japanese people to cooperate with the other signatory nations in supporting the nine-power treaty and to observe the letter and spirit of that treaty in resolving our issues with China. If this bill becomes law, no one can foresee where that will end." Incensed that the Japanese seemed to be threatening the United States with "grave consequences," the Senate retaliated by passing the exclusion section.

Throughout the debate, the national origins system escaped censure and probably eluded understanding. When the time came for the Senate and House plans to be reconciled, the conference committee simply opted for the full Senate scheme. Submitted to the House for the final vote, it became apparent that it didn't much matter what form the general restriction law took. Complained Representative Dickstein of New York: "Mr. Speaker, it seems to me that the only interest taken so far by the members on this floor is in the Japanese question. They do not care much about what was inserted in the provisions of the conference report after the bill left this House."

But the arguments of a small number of scrappy Congressmen—Celler, Dickstein, and LaGuardia of New York, Sabath of Illinois, Mooney of Ohio—were to no avail. Neither rationality nor ridicule could steady Congress on its course. That body was determined to alter policy beyond its 1921 dimensions and by May had completed its work. The House (322–71) and Senate (62–6) agreed on the conference report, which dictated that until 1927 a 2 percent quota based on the foreign-born within the country in 1890 would apply and thereafter the national origins system would be ushered in as America's final solution to its immigration problem.

On May 26, 1924, Calvin Coolidge signed the bill into law. If America paused to celebrate or contemplate the occasion, it did not reflect long on the new national origins system. Victor Herbert, America's leading composer of light opera, died that day. Senator Carter Glass announced that if the soldiers bonus bill were passed over a Presidential veto, he would resign. The House passed a bill providing for a general reduction in taxes by 25 percent. A 37-year-old male stenographer ingeniously committed suicide by starting his car and sealing the exhaust gases in the garage. A newly discovered Babylonian record fixed Noah's age at 64,800 years. All these items were front-page headlines in *The New York Times*; and that newspaper's coverage of the immigration law dealt in the main with the Japanese exclusion, which *The Times* called "unnecessary and deplorable." When President Coolidge proclaimed the 1890-based quotas in effect on June 30, 1924, there was even less contemplation. For on that day Albert B. Fall, Harry F. Sinclair, and others were indicted in the first round of the Teapot Dome scandal, and William G. McAdoo of California led Alfred E. Smith of New York on the fifteenth ballot of the Democratic National Convention.

IMPLEMENTING THE SYSTEM

At the heart of the new national origins system were sections 11 (b) and (d) of Public Law 68–139:

Sec. 11 (b): "The annual quota of any nationality for the fiscal year beginning July 1, 1927, and for each fiscal year thereafter, shall be a number which bears the same ratio to 150,000 as the number of inhabitants in continental United States in 1920 having that national origin bears to the number of inhabitants in continental United States in 1920, but the minimum quota of any nationality shall be 100."

Sec. 11 (d): "For the purpose of subdivisions (b) and (c) the term 'inhabitants in the continental United States in 1920' does not include (1) immigrants from the geographical areas specified in subdivision (c) of section 4 or their descendants [Central and South American immigrants], (2) aliens ineligible to citizenship or their descendants, (3) the descendants of slave immigrants, or (4) the descendants of American aborigines."

The reader who refuses to let the turgidity of law discourage him will discover five important objectives of the new law and one commonly employed lawyers' trick:

1. The law placed an absolute limitation on the number of immigrants who could enter annually from the Eastern Hemisphere. No longer would the hordes inundate America. The number was fixed at 150,000 but the actual number entering each year could be somewhat larger, because excluded from the quota provisions were wives, husbands, and unmarried minor children of American citizens. If you went abroad and were married and after a few years decided to return home, you could bring your spouse and children, without regard to the quota of any nation. Also included in this quota-free group were ministers and professors.

2. Immigrants from the Western Hemisphere were not restricted by the quota system. These were the immigrants specified in sub-subsection (1). The policy considerations of the State Department, along with the friendly persuasion of business interests in the border states which did not want to see this source of migrant labor dry up, prevailed over the logic of the day. It was to be a sore point forty years later.

3. Since most Asians were ineligible for citizenship, most Asians were excluded from emigrating. This was a polite, lawyerlike way of saying, "people of yellow skin not wanted." Even the original statutes which made certain Orientals ineligible for citizenship spelled it out by specifying that people

from delineated latitudes and longitudes were ineligible, not by specifying nations or races.

4. Immigrants from Africa were excluded outright. The wording in this subsection was obscure because inverse. The principal language allowed a certain percentage of foreigners whose nationals lived in the "continental United States." The subsection then specified that Negroes—"descendants of slave immigrants"—were not to be considered inhabitants for the purposes of the immigration laws. Of the 105,000,000 people in the United States at the time of the 1920 census, only 94,000,-000 were counted in national origins. The missing persons were mostly Negro, thus further undermining the national origins logic, and extending the vast racial inconsistency of our laws. By the act of 1870, people of "African descent" were given the right of naturalization and by the *Wong Kim Ark* decision in 1898 the Supreme Court had determined once and for all that people actually born within the United States (except Indians) were citizens. Yet now Africans could not emigrate.

5. Most curious of all, "the descendants of American aborigines" were barred from emigrating. But these included the Indians, and they were already here! Stranger still, the 1924 act permitted the naturalization of American Indians for the first time. So Indians (unlike Africans) could become citizens but they could not emigrate. The only real effect was on South American Indians, Alaskan Eskimos and other natives of American territories; not until 1940 did Congress put the imprimatur of trustworthiness on "races indigenous to the Western Hemisphere."

The trick employed is not so readily apparent in the law as enacted in 1924. It lies in the separation of the phrase "inhabitants in continental United States" from its definition. For in later years it was a simple enough matter to drop the definition and substitute such words as "as heretofore defined." So in later years the "national origins system" was to take on a glow of equity and even-handedness which it clearly does not have on initial reading.

Only one stumbling block remained. No one really knew what the national origins of the U.S. population in 1920 were,

Trevor's tables to the contrary notwithstanding. The 1850 census gave guidance to the foreign-born then living in the United States, but there were no prior censuses with information like that. Because a determination of origins dating back to the early seventeenth century would have to be made, the 1924 law provided that the 1890 census plan would have to be used until 1927, at which time it was hoped the new data would be ready. The facts were to be scientifically determined: "Such determination," the law read, "shall not be made by tracing the ancestors or descendants of particular individuals but shall be based upon statistics of immigration and emigration, together with rates of increase of population as shown by successive decennial United States censuses, and such other data as may be found to be reliable." From this sentence stemmed most of the opposition that was to follow, an opposition doomed to fail because it was comprised, not of the liberal Congressmen who had wished to maintain the open door, but of those Congressmen who wished to retain the 1890 plan permanently.

As the spirit of the twenties soared, and the nation turned to an investigation of Teapot Dome and other things which made the decade famous, the energy for restriction which previously existed began to flag. There were enough hard-core supporters to ensure that the national origins system would not be overturned, but it took five years and two additional delays before the national origins quotas were finally promulgated in 1929. By that time even the President of the United States was once again on record as against such restrictions. And try as they could, proponents of restricting Western Hemisphere immigration, which rose during the twenties to match the numbers allowed in from Europe, were unable to impose their desire on Congress. Attempt after attempt failed.

To determine the national origins basis of the United States, a commission of six experts was appointed under the joint authorities of the Secretaries of State, Commerce, and Labor. It was headed by a statistics expert, the assistant director of the census, Dr. Joseph A. Hill, who had been with the bureau since 1899. For four years the statisticians compiled their figures, each year confident that with another year of work their results would be more viable. In 1927 Congress delayed the beginning of the national origins system one more year; in 1928 it repeated this maneuver, while opponents tried to kill it altogether.

A brief exchange between Senator Reed and Congressman John McCormack, the future Speaker of the House, points out the difficulty in the liberal opposition's position. Representative McCormack was discussing a fact which to him seemed salient: The records on immigration before the twentieth century were notoriously bad.

> REPRESENTATIVE McCORMACK. We have no record prior to 1790. The records of the ports of entry from 1820 on are very uncertain; in fact, the records, as I understand it, in the City of New York were burned at the Ellis Island fire of 1896. Many of the early records were destroyed when the British occupied the city of Washington, all the data necessary was lacking or not kept; and Doctor Hill and his committee faced a tremendous task, and to the best of their ability tried to perform it, but the whole thing is impossible of human performance or ascertainment, without being offensive.
>
> SENATOR REED. May I interrupt you with a question?
>
> REPRESENTATIVE McCORMACK. I would be glad to have you do so.
>
> SENATOR REED. Have you read the entire statement of the American Legion?
>
> REPRESENTATIVE McCORMACK. Yes, I have.
>
> SENATOR REED. Do you think there is no force in their argument that 53 percent of the foreign-born who were called in the draft claimed exemption on account of alienage?
>
> REPRESENTATIVE McCORMACK. Not on this question; no, I do not.
>
> SENATOR REED. Do you think we ought to base our quotas on a group of which 53 percent declined to serve the country in time of war and ignore all the native-born Americans?
>
> REPRESENTATIVE McCORMACK. As I said before, the

argument in my opinion, advanced by the representative
of the American Legion is an inflammatory, emotional,
and irrelevant argument.

It was all these things, of course, and insofar as it was
inflammatory, emotional, and irrelevant, it stood its best chance
of succeeding. For the actual accomplishments of the statistics
committee made sensible minds somewhat gloomy. The essence
of the charge against its work was that its conclusions were
mostly guesswork: Few actual records were available to the
committee and the assessment of nationalities in the early records
was made almost solely on the basis of names. The implications
of this charge come starkly through the report of Senator Henrik
Shipstead of Minnesota in hearings before the Senate Immigration Committee in February, 1929, quoted at length in the pages
that follow.

> Under the law it seems plain that the committee is
> confined to the report of the commission. It, therefore, be-
> comes important to learn what is the foundation of the
> commission's report.
> Therefore, I call the committee's attention to the testi-
> mony of the chairman of the commission's "experts" whose
> duty it is to report to the commission of three Cabinet offi-
> cials in order that we may learn upon what their report
> is founded.

[The 1928 testimony before the same committee follows.]

> SENATOR SHIPSTEAD. Doctor, upon reading the report
> I got the idea that the census of 1790 plays a very important
> part in your report.
> DOCTOR HILL. Yes; that is true.
> SENATOR SHIPSTEAD. It is almost a foundation for the
> entire report, as I read it.
> DOCTOR HILL. Well, you are talking now about the
> census records, not about the Century of Population Growth
> [a report published by the Census Bureau in 1909].
> SENATOR SHIPSTEAD. I am talking about the census

record, and the Century of Population Growth is based, as I understand it, upon the census of 1790?

DOCTOR HILL. Yes.

SENATOR SHIPSTEAD. So the census of 1790 becomes the key to the arch of the whole basis of calculation as I understand the report. I wanted to know if that is your idea.

DOCTOR HILL. Yes; for that part of the population which we call the original native stock, representing about 45 percent of the total.

SENATOR SHIPSTEAD. Can you tell us how many or what percentage of the statistics gathered in that report were destroyed when the British burned the Capitol here?

DOCTOR HILL. Well, the records for New Jersey, Delaware, Georgia, Kentucky, and Tennessee. These records have been lost, but it is not altogether certain that they were destroyed when the British burned the Capitol, although that is the tradition.

SENATOR SHIPSTEAD. It was given at one time as something like six or seven states of which the statistics were burned at that time, so given by one of the commissioners of immigration.

SENATOR COPELAND. Does the Senator mean that the records relating to those states were burned?

SENATOR SHIPSTEAD. Yes. . . . It will be seen from the [1924 law] that the most important element in this determination is "statistics of immigration and emigration." The next important element is "rates of increase of population as shown by successive decennial United States censuses." As reliable statistics of immigration and emigration are not in existence the whole plan fails and leaves the determination to mere guesswork or conjecture.

SENATOR REED. In the absence of statistics, you say?

SENATOR SHIPSTEAD. Yes. I say "reliable statistics" are not available. According to the best authorities, there are no reliable statistics of immigration for the first 213 years of this country's history. I believe you stated in the debate upon this proposition that there were none until 1820?

SENATOR REED. Yes.

SENATOR SHIPSTEAD. I am quoting from your statement. "There was no official governmental record of immigration commenced until the year 1820."

Dr. Edward McSweeney, former assistant commissioner of immigration, has made a statement on that . . . He said [reading]:

"In 1819 a law was passed making it necessary for the captains of all incoming ships bringing passengers to the United States to file a manifest of the passengers, but except to give the number of the passengers to the Government it was never other than perfunctory and almost never used. These accumulated manifests were burned in the Ellis Island fire of 1896. The first real attempt to gather immigration statistics was after the Immigration Bureau was established in the early nineties."

In 1906 Congress passed a law providing that the Director of the Census be authorized and directed to publish in permanent form, by counties and minor subdivisions, the names of the families returned at the first census of the United States in 1790.

Speaking of the difficulties in this work, William S. Rossiter, then chief clerk of the Census Bureau, stated, "The break in official records is one of the marks of the teeth of the British lion, these papers and many others having been destroyed during the occupation of Washington in the War of 1812."

Mr. Rossiter also states:

"Vagaries of size, shape, paper, ruling, chirography, and language could easily be forgiven, if, however, thereby we could restore the missing schedules for Delaware, Georgia, Kentucky, New Jersey, Tennessee, and Virginia, another reminder of the British, for they were also destroyed during the occupation of Washington."

Mr. Rossiter estimates that one fourth of the enumeration is now lacking and that it would be very difficult to comply with the law of 1906.

Director of the Census North was not seemingly deterred by the fact that such a large part of the records was missing, and proceeded in 1909 to make a voluminous report which not only used the partial records but gave meticulous percentages of the racial divisions in the country based solely on names, the same as the late Senator Lodge has done in his "Distribution of Ability" in 1896. Well, certainly the recklessness of that would be apparent; for instance, here is a man by the name of Murphy; suppose he marries a girl of German descent. What would the children be? If you go by name of course they would be called Irish; the German would be wiped out. If an Irish girl should marry a man with a German name, a Scotch name, or Scandinavian name, the Irish descent would be wiped out.

These fragmentary statistics of immigration and emigration are, therefore, admitted by the chairman of "experts" to be the foundation of their report. One half of the records of the census of 1790 were destroyed more than one hundred years before the commission began its work. In the census of 1790 the only information gathered by the census-takers was the name and age of the individual. No information was gathered to determine their national origin. The only manner in which the national origin could be determined of the population of 1790 would be from the remaining records of the seven remaining states. Six are gone, and the only manner in which the national origin of the remainder can be determined is by tracing the national origin of each individual of the population at that time by spelling or sound of his name. This is "tracing the ancestors of descendants of particular individuals," but the law creating the committee of experts says, "such determination shall *NOT* be made by tracing the ancestors or descendants of particular individuals but shall be based upon statistics of emigration and immigration . . . "

It seems plain and must be patent to the committee that the census of 1790 is specifically eliminated from consideration in this work by specific provision of the law. It is plain, in view of the statement of Doctor Hill that the census of 1790 is the foundation of his report that this evidence places the report in an indefensible position. . . . The immigration statistics up until the early nineties were "perfunctory and almost never used," and what there was of them were destroyed by the Ellis Island fire in 1896. The immigration statistics are therefore eliminated not only by the provisions of the law on account of unreliability but also by the fire.

Doctor, have we got the returns for 1800?

DOCTOR HILL. Have we got them?

SENATOR SHIPSTEAD. Yes.

DOCTOR HILL. There are some states missing still. States for which the 1800 census records are missing include Georgia, Kentucky, Mississippi, New Jersey, Tennessee, and Virginia, and certain limited areas in some other states; also Indiana Territory and Northwest Territory.

SENATOR SHIPSTEAD. There were six or seven missing out of 1790.

SENATOR WILLIS. I was wondering whether or not that might not be a check worth while. Our committees made these computations on the basis of the census of 1790. Suppose they should start an entirely independent inquiry, taking the census of 1800 and 1810 and see where they come out. It would be a pretty useful check, would it?

SENATOR COPELAND. Up as far as 1830 it would be, Doctor Hill. That would be a very large undertaking, a very large task, especially as we would have to work with manuscript records. We haven't printed these schedules as we have those of 1790.

SENATOR WILLIS. You say you have not any printed record for the census for the earlier periods?

DOCTOR HILL. I mean by that, the original records. Of course, we have census reports giving statistics.

SENATOR WILLIS. 1790 was printed; 1800 was not or 1810?

DOCTOR HILL. No; nor has any later census been printed.

SENATOR SHIPSTEAD. Can you tell me the first census

we took in which we undertook to find out what country these people came from?

DOCTOR HILL. 1850.

SENATOR SHIPSTEAD. There was nothing done up until that time by our [investigators] to determine where these people came from in Europe?

DOCTOR HILL. That is true.

SENATOR COPELAND. In 1850 did they go back further than the immediate parents?

DOCTOR HILL. It did not go back as far as that; simply their own birthplace, whether foreign-born, and in what countries.

SENATOR COPELAND. When did they begin to ask anything about the parents?

DOCTOR HILL. They made a beginning in 1880, but, as I stated a while ago, that was not a complete classification. The first complete classification made of parents was in 1890.

SENATOR SHIPSTEAD. Then until 1850 there was nothing to show except by assuming from the names?

DOCTOR HILL. Well, we have the figures, you know.

SENATOR SHIPSTEAD. Were there any other immigration figures other than those required by the Government to be filed by the officers of incoming ships with the immigration officers, the number of passengers, and that the passengers landed were accredited to the flag carried by the ship?

DOCTOR HILL. I think you are right about that. I am not familiar with the immigration regulations of those days [an astonishing admission!].

SENATOR SHIPSTEAD. So, if the ship came in carrying passengers from all over Europe, assume she had 1,000 passengers, the officer would file with the immigration department a manifest showing that 1,000 came here, and that [it was] a German ship and immigration officials would accredit those immigrants to Germany; is that right?

SENATOR REED. I doubt whether there was any ship of that capacity at that time.

SENATOR SHIPSTEAD. Of course, the figures I assumed

merely for the purpose of illustration. For instance, an English ship coming in under the English flag carrying passengers from all over Europe, the passengers would be accredited to England?

SENATOR WILLIS. The way they handled ships in those days that would not be a bad guess, because they did not have tramp vessels gathering up cargo. A ship was laden, and went to a certain port.

SENATOR REED. Your conclusions upon that were checked, were they not, by statistics of emigrants from various countries?

DOCTOR HILL. So far as we could get them.

SENATOR SHIPSTEAD. . . . The only excuse for basing the quotas on the census of 1790 and the only scientific thing about it is that they determine the national origin of the population of 1790 by tracing or by guessing the national origins of the individual, using his name as a basis. This method was considered so unscientific at the time of the passage of the immigration act that the Congress specifically prohibited this method from being used. Therefore, up until 1890, we find there was no complete classification made of the national origins of the parents of the American population by the Census Bureau. This is an admission of Doctor Hill in the hearings conducted by your committee. It seems to me, therefore, that the record as well as the law rules out the "Rate of increase as shown by successive decennial United States censuses."

There remains, then, "such other data as may be found to be reliable." . . . I find on reading the report of the committee of experts that they have arbitrarily divided the American population into two classes, the native American stock and the immigrant stock. The native American stock is held by the committee of experts to be composed of those whose ancestors were here before 1790, and that part of our population whose ancestors came here after 1790 are designated as immigrants and the children of immigrants. This arbitrary classification is the foundation of the report of the committee. I would like to know how this committee of "experts" discovered that the population of the United States prior to 1790 were not immigrants or children of immigrants. That is a new theory that I nominate to stand on par with Doctor Einstein's fourth and fifth dimensions, interesting for speculative purposes but surely not to be relied on to form the foundation of an American immigration policy. I know of no provision of law nor do I desire any such that may prohibit those whose ancestors were here before 1790 from purchasing for themselves championship belts for the purpose of designating to the world that they are the only "simon-pure" Americans . . . It must be evident and apparent to the committee that [on the basis of the foregoing analysis] the sources enumerated in the law [which made these sources the exclusive methods of determining national origins] have been searched and found wanting.

Shipstead's blistering attack had little effect. The chairman's laconic comment with which he closed the 1929 hearings was: "I am also reminded that the Society of 1812 wishes its name placed in the record as being in favor of the national origins."

A week earlier Dr. Hill testified to the committee about one other assumption made which did not seem to perturb the committee members but which surely would have made Francis A. Walker shudder. The assumption: "that the natural increase of these various national stocks . . . was the same." When asked to repeat his statement about the rate of fecundity, he replied:

DOCTOR HILL. That is the assumption that we made. We assumed that the natural increase was the same. We assumed that the Irish stock increased the same as the German, that the German stock increased the same as the English, that is at the same rate. Most people would say that that is not in accordance with the facts. They would say, "Why look at the French Canadians, look at the Irish, and look at the Germans. How much more rapidly they breed than the English stock does." There is a decided difference at the present time for about one generation, and then, when you get to the second generation, the difference has largely disappeared.

SENATOR COPELAND. Have they become Americanized?

DOCTOR HILL. When you get to the third generation, I do not believe you will find any difference in the natural increase, they have become Americanized in that respect. There are some figures that indicate that. We have the figures that show the second generation of any stock does not have as many children as the first generation. So I would say that there is no material error in the assumption of equal rates of increase.

This was the final irony before national origins went into effect. It was the contrary of this very assumption that enabled Walker to prove that America might be bred into extinction: The inferior races outbreed the superior ones. How else, it was asked, could the superior races be beaten? And yet, when the time came for an honest application of the assumptions that underlay the victory, they were discarded. Only a cynic would say that in so doing the inferior races could be denied their fair share of quotas. It is far more likely that Dr. Hill was right.

"VICTORY"

Time had run out. When Herbert Hoover accepted the Republican nomination for the Presidency in 1928, he stated his opposition to national origins; quotas could not be determined "accurately and without hardship," he said. He was not talking idly, for as Secretary of Commerce, he shared responsibility for preparing the national origins quotas. But for the most part he kept silent on the issue during the campaign. (Both the Democratic and Republican campaign platforms expressed approval of the law about to go into effect; the Democratic platform did criticize one provision which by allocating a lower priority to alien wives and children of resident aliens—the "second preference"—made it difficult and in some cases impossible for a recent immigrant to bring his family.)

Following Hoover's victory, many groups apparently thought that the battle *against* the national origins system had been won; the number of petitions sent to Congress in 1929 diminished noticeably, and at the same time, the restrictionists substantially increased the vigor of their activities in order to block any last move to delay national origins. Coordinating the efforts of the various groups was the Immigration Conference Committee, headed by John Trevor.

On March 3, 1929, the day before the inauguration of President-elect Hoover, the House passed another postponement resolution, but it was too late for the Senate opponents of national origins to pass the resolution also. So the new President, on record against national origins, had the duty (mandatory, ruled his new Attorney General) to proclaim the quotas. Said Hoover of the quotas to become effective July 1: "While I am strongly in favor of the restricted and selected immigration, I have opposed the national origins basis. I therefore naturally dislike the duty of issuing and installing the new bases but the President of the United States must be the first to obey the law."

On July 1, 1929, Hoover made it official. But the victory had been won long ago, and the country contemplated bigger things. First in the news that day: Bobby Jones had just taken the U.S. Open Golfing Championship, beating Al Espinosa in the playoff, 141 to 164. It was also front-page news that John Coolidge, son of the former President, would take the six-week summer course in public utilities at the Harvard School of Business Administration, but a spokesman for the New York–New Haven–Hartford Railroad, his employer, declined to say whether young John would be promoted as a result.

The new quotas had the desired effect: They cut even more rigidly into the reduction in immigration which had been effected during the preceding ten years. The 1920's welcomed four million immigrants, less than half the number who had come to the United States between 1900 and 1909. From 1930 to 1939, the number dropped overwhelmingly, to just below 700,000, a reduction of more than 80 percent over a decade which was itself a reduction by 50 percent of the period twenty years before. Russian, German, and Italian dictators who forbade their countrymen from leaving could not alone account for such a slack.

Table 1 in the Appendix gives the original quota numbers

established by President Hoover. It is enough here to show a few components of the annual total:

GREAT BRITAIN	65,721
GERMANY	25,957
IRELAND	17,853
POLAND	6,524
ITALY	5,802
FRANCE	3,086
USSR	2,784
ALL ASIA	1,323
GREECE	307

The peoples of eastern and southern Europe had at last been kept in their places.

Since the law specified that unused quotas could not be distributed to other countries, the unwanted British, German, and Irish quotas were barred to other foreign nationals. That there were unused quotas in the big three was in later years to prove one of the system's grave defects.

In the 1920's an answer to the problems in the cities was found: Cut out all the immigration. By stopping the flow of unwashed newcomers from foreign shores, dirt, crime, and moral decline would surely halt. That it did not does not disprove the theory, for as we shall see, the law that was passed didn't quite work out the way it was supposed to. But the restrictionists did win a notable victory, heeding the words of a Chicago resident made famous by Peter Finley Dunne: As "a Pilgrim father that missed the first boats," Mr. Dooley learned that he must "raise me claryon voice agin' th' invasion iv this fair land be th' paupers an' arnychists—ye bet I must—because I'm here first."

4 / National Origins Theory

Imposing the national origins quota system on our immigration law is like kicking the conductor when the train is late. Obvious alternatives were rejected out of hand, most with the lack of respect that is characteristically accorded ideas ahead of their time.

If the principal problem was too great an influx, a far less abrasive method of limiting the number of immigrants could have been adopted by establishing an annual immigrant ceiling determined on a first-come first-served basis. If the problem was crime, Prohibition was a good way not to go about it. From start to finish, it was an ignoble social experiment—once having established sobriety as a national policy, Congress consistently refused to vote adequate funds to police the nation. And criminal acts committed by the duly constituted authorities in the states were legion. If the problem was urban congestion, slums, and decay, reform and rebuilding were technically possible; even federal assistance was not entirely out of the question. Congress had already passed the Maternity Act of 1921, establishing a program of federal financial assistance to protect the health of newborn children. A lady (known to a generation of lawyers only as Mrs. Frothingham) and the Commonwealth of Massachusetts were enraged; surely it was unconstitutional for Washington to spend taxpayers' money in such a manner. (If the Government can meddle in the affairs of health, who knows but that it might start interfering in far more serious matters, even affairs of state.) The Supreme Court permitted the Maternity Act to stand, sidestepping the issue: The interest of the lady and the state "in the moneys of the Treasury—partly realized from taxation and partly from other sources—is shared with millions of others; is comparatively minute and indeterminable; and the effect upon future taxation of any payment out of the funds so remote, fluctuating, and uncertain that no basis is afforded for an appeal to the preventive powers of a court." Since the Court would refuse to entertain suits by protesting taxpayers, the way was opened. Congress plainly did not welcome the opportunity; the most serious problem facing the nation was still thought to be the foreign menace.

The method that would solve the country's ills was premised on one of the wildest "scientific" theories ever to be accepted by a mass of literate people. To be a qualified national origins theorist, you did not need a Ph.D., although as anywhere else in life it might help. The most important qualification was conviction and an unyielding certitude in your moral and genetic superiority over other forms of humanity. The second most important qualification was sheer pertinacity: The longer and louder you yelled the righter you were. So well suited are the techniques to the theory that neither have yet perished in the struggle for survival.

With the general outlines of the theory, the reader is familiar; but because the theory was to assume among some groups so exalted a position in our national life that it was said to be second only to the Constitution in importance, it behooves us to take a closer look at this theory of social science which through legislative afterthought became enshrined in law.

RACE AND NATIONALITY

The most obvious fact about the theory is that it masquerades under an assumed name. The entire justification for the theory is grounded in beliefs about *race,* not nationality. Although first-class theorists could show that racial qualities of mankind vary with national borders, no systematic part of the theory explained how quotas could logically be determined from postwar European geography. Perhaps this was merely the inconvenient reality of the world; no one really believed that the races of mankind changed with the political determination that a country's boundaries should be altered. As a practical matter, it was somewhat awkward to determine Czechoslovakia's quotas, for instance, when the country had not even existed as such during the heyday of emigration. Still, the exigencies of politics, it is well known, cause social events to lag behind science.

The national origin was only one of many groups from which to choose the fortunate few. Religion is an obvious example of another group, but this one carries two insurmountable problems. In the first place, the nation has a tradition of religious freedom. Though the 1st Amendment probably does not preclude Congress from enacting laws excluding the immigration of people of particular religious faiths, it would have been inexpedient to rile that body of Christians which believes in what it preaches. Secondly, religious groups are too broad to permit fine-tuned selection. Most Americans are Christian, either Protestant or Catholic, and so not surprisingly are most Europeans. It would be impossible to administer a quota system based on religious affiliation, therefore, not only because it is difficult to deny that a person is of the faith he says he is, but because many different sects in Europe have no exact equivalent in America.

Occupation was another possible method of selection, but again the difficulties were probably insurmountable. There are so many occupations that the administrative scheme would have been unworkable. The problem of definition was immense. How broad should each category be? Should the categories be agricultural, industrial, managerial, and other, or should they consist of such groups as automobile mechanic, mortician, and linguist? Still, there is some sense in an occupational quota, for surely contributions to America can be measured by the occupations of those who performed them. The remaining flaw was simply that occupational quotas would not eliminate the perceived difficulty:

There would be no way to keep out the Italian farmer if you let the British one in.

No matter what facet of man's makeup is catalogued, one alone was paramount: the sum. For it was the contention, implicit at least, that America was not being arbitrary or selfish in settling on any one component of the mystery of man; it was settling on all. The beliefs, the aspirations, the intelligence, the assimilability—all must be considered, and the most efficient way to do it was by national boundary. National origins solved the administrative problem because it was easy enough to determine whether a man came from Germany, Hungary, or Turkey (although it was not quite as easy to determine country of birth, which is what the law required). National origins solved the definitional problem because the categories were neither too broad nor too limited; they were precise and easily ascertainable. It solved the political problem because no single feature of personality was taken into account and thus there was no discrimination. Admission into the United States would depend on the whole man.

Of course, there are unfair people in the world, and there were to be many who chastised the authors of national origins theory for being discriminatory. Legislators and advocates of the plan have been stung by this charge for years. It is not true, they insist, because it is the very basis of legislation to classify and discriminate. Doesn't the internal revenue code discriminate between rich and poor? Under a graduated, progressive tax, the rich pay proportionately more. Don't zoning ordinances discriminate by establishing some areas in the city for houses and others for industrial uses? Yet the Supreme Court of the United States has upheld progressive taxation against due process claims and zoning laws against attacks that they violate the principle of "equal protection." The Supreme Court has said on many occasions that in itself discrimination does not violate that great principle; what does violate it is *arbitrary, unreasonable* discrimination.

It is, for instance, entirely reasonable to discriminate between those who obey posted speed limits and those who do not. Even though the act of speeding may have done no harm in and of itself, it does present a danger to the community and as long as the punishments for speeding are not overly restrictive (such as unduly long prison sentences) the good that results outweighs the loss in liberty to travel as fast as you like. So speeding laws are reasonable.

The racial theories that underlie national origins theory support what was purported to be an eminently reasonable classification. The basic assumption is twin-edged: that members of a common race behave similarly; that members of different races, to the extent that they are different, behave differently. A secondary assumption was that, given the administrative difficulties of admitting on the basis of race, nations are a close approximation of the world's myriad racial groupings. Since it is also reasonable to maintain the basic behavior of Americans in general, members of different nations (races) should be admitted to America in proportion to the strength of the members already here. With that purpose in mind, the classification is surely reasonable, and the law is not unconstitutionally discriminatory.

The twin-edged assumption bears investigation, for in its truth or falsity lies the answer to the charge that supporters of the theory are bigots.

RACE AND THE QUALITY OF MAN

From the North Pole to the South Pole, all mankind belongs to one species, biologically named *Homo sapiens*. Living men of a different biological species have never been found. So much was not denied by turn-of-the-century anthropologists. They meant by this, as we mean today, that mankind is a "genetically open system"; men and women from every part of the world can and do interbreed. Creatures of different species rarely mate and when they do, their offspring are normally sterile. Thus the horse and the donkey can produce a mule, but the mule can produce nothing. The offspring of any human mating, no matter what the parents' ancestry, will (barring accidents) be fully capable of reproduction in his or her turn. The differences among men are of a slighter nature than the gulf that separates species.

These differences have been said to constitute different *races* of men, and it is at this point that agreement ends.

Surprisingly enough, in view of the racial hostilities that have flared up during the past century, not until the late nineteenth century did biological racism become a significant factor in man's dealing with man. Obvious differences in coloration and hair texture having been noted, most men throughout most of history explained the inferiority of everyone else by reference to the false gods believed in or the manifest inferiority of the artifacts of culture. The notion that "blood will tell," in its application to whole societies, is a modern invention.

Using the texture of hair and pigmentation, one classification in 1900 discerned six major races with a total of twenty-nine subdivisions:

A. Woolly hair, broad nose:

   Yellow skin, steatopygous—Bushmen
   Dark skin—Negrito, Negro, Melanesian

B. Curly or wavy hair:

   Dark skin—Ethiopian, Australian, Dravidian
   Tawny white skin—Assyroid

C. Wavy brown or black hair, dark eyes:

   Clear brown skin—Indo-Afghan
   Tawny white skin—Arab or Semite, Berber, Littoral
      European, Ibero-Insular
   Dull white skin—Western European, Adriatic

D. Fair, wavy or straight hair:

   Reddish-white skin—Northern European, Eastern European

E. Straight or wavy hair, dark, black eyes:

   Light brown skin—Ainu
   Yellow skin—Polynesian, Indonesian, South American

F. Straight hair:

Warm yellow skin—North American, Central American,
  Patagonian
Brownish-yellow skin—Eskimo
Yellowish-white skin—Lapp, Ugrian, Turkish, or Turco-
  Tatar
Pale yellow skin—Mongol

As we have already seen, Ripley and others like him catalogued
the races of man in part according to the skull shape, a concept
derived from G. M. Retzius, a Swedish student of anatomy who
in 1856 discerned dolichocephalic, brachycephalic, prognathous,
and orthognathous people.

But none of these concepts will work because it is never
stated for what purpose the classification is made. For instance,
there *is* a difference among the blood types of individuals but
it does not depend upon the pigmentation of skin or the length
of the skull. Though it is true that the frequency of Types A,
B, O, and AB blood is different in different parts of the world's
population, it is not true that the color of the person in whom
the blood is found will change the nature of the blood. Type A
blood from a person of Chinese descent is the equivalent of
Type A found in the royal families of northwestern Europe.
This fact did not prevent the Red Cross from segregating black
blood from white during World War II, nor did it deter the state
of Louisiana in 1958 from requiring segregated blood for trans-
fusions, pursuant to recommendations of its Joint Legislative
Committee on Segregation.

The plain fact is that there are no "pure" races in the
world; during the course of thousands of years genetic transfer
among all peoples has worked its awesome work. That a person
is the child of his parents is tautological; that a person is therefore a descendant of a particular race is a leap too great to take.
It has been estimated that less than one percent of the human
complement of genes is required to mark an individual of one
race or another; parents can easily transmit to the child genetic
combinations gathered from a variety of human stocks that
neither parent has individually.

Because the races are not pure, it becomes a matter of

guesswork to determine by looking whether an individual belongs to the "Nordic" or "Alpine" or "Mediterranean" race; the secondary assumption—the equivalence of national and racial groups—is necessarily a fallacy also. As the distinguished Harvard anthropologist Clyde Kluckhohn has pointed out:

> To speak of the "Italian race" is nonsense, for there is every reason to assume that the Italians of Piedmont share more ancestors with persons who are French or Swiss than they do with their fellow Italians of Sicily. . . . The existence of physical stereotypes for human groups that live in the same area or speak the same language or practice the same religion is probably to be traced to the preconception that organisms that resemble each other in action ought to resemble each other in physique. In any such group there *are* large numbers of individuals who are closely related biologically and who approximate a certain physical norm. The lay observer focuses his attention on these similar persons and either fails even to notice the others or dismisses them as exceptions. We thus get the persistent stereotype of the Swede as blond and blue-eyed. Dark Swedes are commented upon with surprise though, in fact, blond individuals are distinctly in a minority in a number of districts in Sweden. . . . If a man and a woman whom ten competent physical anthropologists classify as "pure Mediterranean" marry, their ten children may approach in varying degrees the Mediterranean, Alpine, and Atlanto-Mediterranean types.

The extreme dependence on physical differences to mark human behavioral differences that endure for all time—the uneducated raving of Madison Grant, that is—has been shown unequivocally false. But that there are noticeable differences among men is not false, and many self-described "moderate" racists have maintained that while perhaps it is going a bit too far to find in every somewhat different man an unaltered racial inheritance, nevertheless it is clear that whites and blacks and browns and reds and yellows are different. That races may be impure, they say, does not invalidate the theory on which national origins is based: People more or less alike behave more or less alike; people more or less different behave more or less differently.

From this point on, the science of mechanism disappears and only the science of description and correlation is left. Those who believe that black is inferior to white have never explained scientifically why. Such "facts" as that in the Negro, "cranial sutures unite very early in life, [checking] the development of the brain long before that takes place in other races, and this fact accounts to some extent for the more or less sudden stunting of the Ethiopian intellect shortly after arriving at puberty" have been shown to be utterly false.

Those who believe that others are inferior have been reduced to pointing out in which ways. The only hope for the proponent of national origins is to conclude that, for whatever reasons (as yet unknown), people of different racial stocks simply *are* different, some superior and some inferior. During World War I, much was made of the fact that on intelligence tests conducted by the American Army, immigrant groups scored lower than native Americans. This fact was taken as convincing proof that Nordics are natively more intelligent than the lower "races" of Europe. Of course the conclusion drawn was simply unwarranted: The tests measured literacy, achievement, and test-taking ability, all of which in humans are learned responses. The most the tests proved was that immigrants had had less opportunity, a fact few would have disputed anyway. The tests did, however, give the lie to the supposed racial superiority of whites: Negroes from Ohio and Indiana outscored whites from Kentucky and Mississippi.

If intelligence is not the measure, then perhaps, argued the undissuadable theorists, the superiority lies in the achievements of Nordics. Again, the evidence does not warrant the assertion. Unless the measure of the greatness of Nordic civilization—whatever that is—is Nordic civilization itself, there is simply no way to show the superiority of northwestern European civilization. If Great Britain—and by extension America—represent for Madison Grant the highest reach of mankind, how explain the fact that nearly two thousand years before, Roman legions found a "race of barbarians" living in the British Isles? How explain the development of democracy in Greece, a country that was granted only 308 quotas under the 1929 Presidential proclamation? How explain the geometry of the Egyptians, the algebra of the Arabs, the poetry of the Hebrews, the paper and printing of the Chinese? How explain that Christ Himself was born a Semite?

Ah, national origins theorists say, those are easy to answer: People have changed; they have deteriorated. Then how explain the rapid industrialization and modernization of Japan after World War II (a people whose old blood, Representative Mac-Lafferty pointed out, made them "unchangeable as the stars")? They changed. And would the theorists concede that between the 1500's and the 1800's, no migrations into Great Britain changed the nature of the British "race," yet as the great anthropologist Franz Boas has noted, the society changed from "the boisterous joy of life of Elizabethan England" to "the prudery of the Victorian age." No doubt they would concede it, and with the concession collapses their entire case.

The only possible explanation left is that differences in men are due to differences in their surroundings, their circumstances, their patterns of belief, and their physical environment. This is not to deny the great importance of genetic inheritance in the propensities of any given individual; it probably is true that a baby inherits certain capacities which can be developed more highly than the same capacities of the baby in the next hospital crib. But the differences do not depend on race, and the crucial element is in the child's development. No one is born speaking any language; a normal youngster of any race is capable of speaking any language that exists, provided he is raised by parents who use it. So with his aspirations and dreams, his capacity to endure boredom and to tolerate bad working conditions, his desire to better himself, his belief in human freedom and the right of self-determination.

In short, racial differences insofar as they exist, are purely physical and of a minor sort, genetically speaking. They determine nothing about the quality of the man. Because they did not know enough and because they did not know better, race theorists confused individual genetic differences with general types of genetic differences. No one has ever shown—though many have tried—that a specific "type" difference or a combination of them causes a difference in capacity, creativity, or culture.

That there are cultural differences among the many nations of the world is not gainsaid, but the national origins theorists who insisted that the different nationals are bound to their different cultures simply were mistaken. The proof is overwhelming that second- and third-generation Americans, of no matter what national origin, are almost always fully "assimilated." Since it is unproved that "race" determines behavior, the purpose for the classification of immigrants by national groups dissolves, and the resulting classification must necessarily be unreasonable.

Unfortunately for the history of our immigration laws, in this one instance of national policy, to be arbitrary and unreasonable in classification was not at the same time to be unconstitutional. On this point, as we have already seen, the Supreme Court had early taken its stand. The Constitution of the United States extends (except in rare instances) but to the geographical borders of the country. Since restrictive immigration legislation sets up a scheme to determine which aliens *outside* the nation shall enter, the Constitution's requirement that the Federal Government render "due process" is inapposite.

Even had the constitutional doctrine not been so clearly laid down, 1924 was the wrong time for anyone to challenge the lawfulness of national origins. The far more blatant treatment of native-born citizens whose ancestors had unwillingly come to the United States more than a century before stood the test of constitutionality. In the mid 1890's, when one "scientific" definition of a Negro was a white man with one eighth "African blood," a man named Plessy was arrested for violating a Louisiana statute that forbade him from sitting in a "white only" coach. In 1896, the Supreme Court upheld the law on the grounds that there was another car for Plessy to sit in. "We consider," the Court said, "the underlying fallacy of [Plessy's] argument to consist in the assumption that the enforced separation of the two races stamps the colored race with a badge of inferiority. If this be so, it is not by reason of anything found in the act, but solely because the colored race chooses to put that construction upon it." Very similar feelings were piously expressed by Congressmen in 1924; the law did not stamp anyone with a badge of inferiority—it simply recognized an existing social situation, that different races are represented in America in different proportions.

Of course, the Court in 1896 could very simply have come to the opposite conclusion by noting that under the Louisiana law, a person of one eighth "Caucasian blood" would not be considered a white man. Obviously, therefore, the racial classification was inconsistent and did not meet the equal protection test. Legal minds may find that way out too glib; for them there is always the tack the Court finally did take in 1954 when it recognized that the "separate" accommodations were not in fact "equal."

So the Court could have found, if the right case had been presented to it in the proper way, that even National Origins was an unconstitutional legislative act. Immigration legislation was commonly considered by observing its effects on foreigners; in so doing, it was insulated from judicial review. But suppose we think rather of its effects on our own citizens. One of the most important functions of an immigration statute which imposes an annual limit is to provide ground rules for the admission of families of those who are already in America. If it can be shown that the existing law consistently discriminates along racial lines against certain groups of American citizens by making it burdensome for them to be reunited with families because of the length of waiting lists in oversubscribed countries, then it is not a great jump to the conclusion that their liberty to associate with their families in America on the same terms as other people has been denied without due process of law. Denied, that is, because the classification system was arbitrary and unreasonable.

The argument was never made to the Court, but it is not inconceivable that had Congress not abolished national origins when it did, the Court would soon have acted in its place. In light of the recent *Loving* case, in which miscegenation laws were ruled unconstitutional, it may even have been probable. In the 1967 case, a white man and his Negro wife were convicted in Virginia, which, with fifteen other states, outlawed racially mixed marriages. They were convicted despite the fact that they had been married in Washington, D.C., and sentence was suspended on condition that they remain outside Virginia for twenty-five years. The Virginia Supreme Court in 1955 had upheld the law by noting that its purposes were "to preserve the racial integrity of its citizens," to prevent "the corruption of the blood" and a "mongrel breed of citizens." A Virginia circuit court judge of Caroline County upheld the Lovings' convictions against the argument that those convictions violated the equal protection clause. He said that the law provided equal punishments for white and black. Furthermore, he said, "Almighty God created the races white, black, yellow, Malay and red, and he placed them on separate continents. And but for the interference with his arrangement there would be no cause for such marriages. The fact that he separated the races shows that he did not intend for the races to mix." The only exception to the ban on mixed marriages was in the case of persons with one-sixteenth or less "blood of American Indian." According to the registrar of the Virginia Bureau of Vital Statistics, "the desire of all to recognize as an integral and honored part of the white race the descendants of John Rolfe and Pocahontas," gave these minimal Indians high status and showed how slippery the concept was. This entire lunacy was finally tossed out in 1967. Said Chief Justice Warren for a unanimous Court: "[There was] patently no legitimate overriding purpose independent of invidious racial discrimination which justifies this classification. . . . We have consistently denied the constitutionality of measures which restrict the rights of citizens on account of race." National origins could well have fallen by the same judicial logic.

INTERNAL INCONSISTENCIES

From a scientific point of view, shorn of emotionalism, the only possible justification for national origins is the cultural differences among societies. That the cultural differences among the score of European nations are not great enough to warrant a rigid geographical legislation is at least arguable (and was largely not argued because of the insistence that the difference was due to race). Accepting the justification, however, it becomes apparent that national origins did not discriminate enough!

The quota for each country was determined by lumping together the "foreign-born" and those whose ancestors had at some point come from the same country. From this sum came the total of that nationality represented in America. Who says, however, that a descendant of a British emigrant circa 1695 is anything like the British emigrant circa 1925 or 1965? Though in some sense they are both "British-American" the sense is highly artificial. It is happenstance whether the descendant—whose family may have warred against the British in 1776—feels any ties to the newly arrived son of England. And if there are similarities between the ways in which the eighteenth-century and twentieth-century British immigrants would react to America, the similarities would be far less true for nations which have not kept such close pace with American development. Does 1820 German culture represent 1920 German culture? Czechoslovakia? Italy? Greece? Ireland? These are questions not even asked in the 1920's. National origins theory claimed it properly balanced the nations in terms of their contributions to America, but it is clear that it did not even begin to assess the different contributions which different generations have made.

Another grave defect in the theory as legislated was the fact that unused quotas in the countries with large numbers could not be distributed to countries with small quotas. The argument against redistribution was obvious: If no one from Great Britain decided to come in any given year, 65,000 quotas might be given to Italians and the racial mix would be woefully distorted. (Imagine the damage that 65,000 Italians could perpetrate on 105,000,000 Americans!) Yet without redistribution, the same thing would happen: In 1964, for instance, only 31,265 people came from England and only 6,256 of the 17,756 Irish quotas were used. The small quota countries had been oversubscribed for years and their quotas were completely used. Thus, in proportion to the number of British who entered, the racial mix was still distorted (though concededly less than it would have been had there been redistribution). The fact remains that the situation did not square with the theory. The solution, to peg the quotas of small-quota countries on the actual admissions from the largest quota country, would have been administratively unworkable.

Still another defect in the administration of the system—though not in the theory—was that over the years a myriad of special laws were passed to overcome rigidities in a policy that had become politically intolerable. Refugees and other hardship cases had to be accommodated. By the 1960's, as we shall see, the national origins system was shot as full of holes as was the theory which nurtured it.

And, finally, the national origins argument focused on the "contribution" of the various nationalities; by "contribution" was generally meant the degree of conformity, the efficiency of the melting pot process. There was never any stress, rarely any thought, given to the fact that diversity is equally important in maintaining freedom in a land such as ours. It would have been subversive.

At the hearings in the winter of 1929, the secretary-general of the Sons of the American Revolution countered the opposition charge that national origins was discriminatory by saying: "The temporary 1890 'foreign-born' census harshly discriminates against the native-born descendants of those distinguished patriots which it is the function of our society to commemorate." It must have come as a shock to some members of our society to discover what their function was; one wonders whether the likes of Thomas Paine, who stirred the deepest passions both for his cause and against himself, were to be included in the commemoration. The secretary-general apparently had never read, or much disliked, the sentiments of the ancient biographer Plutarch, a southern European: "It is indeed a desirable thing to be well descended, but the glory belongs to our ancestors."

5 / *Policy Round 2: The Battle of Substance and Form*

During the thirty-nine years of its operations, national origins grew progressively weaker as an administrative system, though the fervor which its principle generated remained undamped in many quarters. The Depression, which began soon after President Hoover's proclamation of the national origin quotas, quickly turned the nation's attention from the immigration debate. During the next ten years, there were minor changes in the immigration and naturalization laws, but the national origins system remained untouched. In fact, it withstood an impressive attack in 1939.

That May the *St. Louis* sailed from Germany to Cuba, bringing 936 refugees, 930 of whom were Jewish and 734 of whom planned eventually to come to the United States and had been cleared by immigration officials. They had to disembark in Cuba only because the quota backlog did not permit immediate entry, but they were all assured of entering at least by 1942. Unhappily, Cuba reneged on its promise to let them land, and they were forced to return across the Atlantic. (Through the efforts of the Joint Distribution Committee, they were all resettled outside Germany, although this was of little comfort to most when Germany the next year conquered all their new homelands but Britain. In vain did the committee request permission for immediate landing of the 734 who held U.S. quota positions. Tampering with the national origins system, after all, is a serious matter, said the State Department; the 734 would alter the immutable culture of America, since they would arrive ahead of their mathematically calculated time.

This was the disheartening aftermath of an effort by Senator Robert Wagner of New York and Representative Edith Rogers of Massachusetts to liberalize the law a bit: Their Child Refugee Bill would have permitted 10,000 refugee children per year for two years to enter the United States outside the regular quota system. The legislation was killed by a formidable array of patriotic groups, such as the American Legion, the Veterans of Foreign Wars, chapters of the Daughters of the American Revolution, and even such immigrant groups as the Society of Mayflower Descendants. Their principal theme was the dangerous effect that children under fourteen years would have on our internal security: Were not these "thousands of motherless, embittered, persecuted children of undesirable foreigners" the "potential leaders of a revolt against our American form of government"? (The American Legion's national executive committee was softer; it opposed the legislation because it would tend to break up families.) By the time the *St. Louis* had reached Havana, the Wagner-Rogers bill was all but dead. By June 2, President Roosevelt had refused to support the bill; he was afraid, he had earlier written in a letter to a prominent supporter of the legislation, Eddie Cantor, "there is a very real feeling that if this question is too prominently raised in the Congress during the present session we might get more restrictive rather than more liberal immigration laws and practices." At the end of June, the Senate Immigration Committee finished its work on the bill, amending it so that the 20,000 children would mortgage the German quota numbers in that amount. Senator Wagner, seeing that this change would save children at the expense of adults, could have none of it; the bill was withdrawn, and national origins had survived the attack.

Significantly, it was President Hoover in 1930 who inaugurated another trend in immigration policy, one destined to become a wedge cutting into national origins, though begun with somewhat different intentions. The 1924 legislation permitted unlimited immigration from the Western Hemisphere, but a severe Depression encouraged the executive branch to discover some way to limit what alarmists feared would be great waves of people from Mexico and other southern nations. President Hoover authorized the American consul in these countries to construe strictly the "public charge" provisions of the law. Mexicans could emigrate without regard to the number of their fellow immigrants, but *only* if they met the many other restrictive elements of the laws, one of which required a finding by the consul that they were not likely to become a public charge. Language of this type in a statute places almost unfettered discretion in the hands of administrators, and during the days of a depression it was relatively easy to find the vast majority of eager immigrants "likely to become public charges." They were stopped at the border.

The policy of strict enforcement began as an economic measure, but its wider implications became quickly apparent. Other provisions in the law forbade the "subversive"; in times of increasing danger from abroad, and an isolationist mood at home, it made sense to instruct American consulates in Europe to keep a vigilant eye on visa applicants. By the end of the decade, the executive branch was firmly in control of immigration policy (within the broad outlines enacted by Congress) by rigorously and over-strictly reading the laws it was charged with administering.

The executive branch's growing predominance in immigration policy led to tragedy in the initial phase. Between 1933 and 1943, 1,244,850 quota numbers went unfilled, and because they could not be redistributed, were lost altogether; 341,567, or more than a third, were earmarked for German-occupied or German-dominated nations. Franklin D. Roosevelt, though on record against the excesses of the immigration laws, never made a concerted effort to mitigate their evil effects; it was one of his greatest failures.

Nevertheless, the increasing willingness of the executive

branch to deal with immigration tended more and more to shift the focus from nativism to internationalism. As long as restrictionists could maintain the cry that we must think above all of America—by that, meaning we must preserve what was taken to be American culture and mores—it was all too easy to promote concepts like national origins. But the Chief Executive, as he deals with immigration, thinks beyond the national boundaries; he necessarily must see the immigrant cast in an international light. Immigration became a matter of foreign affairs, within the President's special competence. From this perspective and with the decline of isolationism, a new battle could take shape. This was the battle of substance and form.

As with most types of substantial legislation enacted after many years and fierce debate, reform cannot come immediately. There must be a shift in the mood of the electorate (as well as a change in the composition of Congress), and there must be a change in the situation which prompted the legislation. The best way to attack is to scuttle indirectly; a head-on clash will usually bring only a repetition of the earlier debate. So it was with immigration restriction. The Depression caused a very perceptible shift of mood; the rising totalitarian governments in Europe did likewise. When the Japanese brought the United States into the Second World War, the isolationist majority received a blow from which it never recovered. America would become an international power in peace and in war, hot and cold. We would be aware of our past mistakes in ignoring the importance of world opinion.

Year by year, Congress began to water down the operation of national origins. With each change came the denial that any change in the system was contemplated or had been effected; the law had simply been made more "secure." And when changes in the spirit of the system were proposed and pushed—in a small way in 1939 and in a major way in the early 1950's—anti-restrictionists were severely rebuffed, and the system endured. A substantive change in the law which does not alter the *form* of the law will usually succeed, because the compromise is comfortable both to reformers and those whose political necks would be wrung by the electorate for tampering with basic American institutions. When and only when the point is reached at which the final affront is form itself do reformers have a chance to succeed. In the battle for immigration reform, that point was not reached until 1965, thirty-six years after national origins became the law of the land.

THE 1940's

Two contradictory themes emerged from legislation enacted during the 1940's: a toughening of the laws designed to cut down subversion and espionage, and a relaxing of the laws to admit into the country some who were previously barred. The toughening began with the Smith Act, formally known as the Alien Registration Act of 1940. It increased the Government's power to deport undesirable aliens and established a requirement that all aliens except diplomats and those under fourteen be fingerprinted. One year later Congress extended the foreign consul's authority to bar entrance to those suspected of being dangerous to public safety. The Passport Act of 1918 was reenacted, allowing the Government to deny entrance to immigrants on a finding that their presence would be "prejudicial to the best interests of the United States." This law, as we shall later see, could result in the virtual imprisonment, without trial, of an alien who could neither enter nor be deported. Additions to the list of causes for and methods of deportation were made in 1943 and 1944.

Meanwhile, in 1943, Congress for the first time in sixty-one years permitted immigration and naturalization of the Chinese. The ban was lifted because the Chinese were now our allies, and it would be unseemly to deny admission to the nationals of a country with whom we were fighting to rid the world of fascist and racist philosophies. This first breach in the wall we had erected against Asia was modest: The Chinese were allowed only 105 quota numbers a year, fewer than they would be entitled to under a mathematical application of the national origins system. The lifting of the ban, furthermore, did not bring equality in other areas. For instance, under the general immigration laws, the spouses or minor children of American citizens could come to the United States without regard to the quota of their particular country; they were said to be "nonquota immigrants." But the spouse or child, if born in China, of an American citizen, was still required to come within the quota system (no point in mongolizing the nation too quickly). In 1946, Congress relaxed the rule only slightly: Henceforth, the Chinese *wife* of an American citizen would be nonquota. Chinese husbands and children continued to be quota immigrants, and the separation of families continued as national policy.

In 1946 also, the embargo on Asian immigrants was lifted a bit further to permit a limited number of East Indians and Filipinos to emigrate to America. The quota for the entire Indian subcontinent: 100. For the first time, too, since Thind took his case to the Supreme Court, Indians were given the right to be naturalized, benefiting some 4,000 Asian Indians who had lived in the United States since 1923. In spite of the liberalization, and like the Chinese, the Indian spouses and children of American citizens had to come in under the quotas; they were not on a par with the nationals of most other countries.

In December of 1945, President Truman established an executive committee to smooth the flow of refugees into the U.S. within existing quotas. Pressure for the pooling of unused quotas and for other liberalization was evident throughout the next year, and Truman finally called for such legislation in his State of the Union address early in January, 1947. Congress responded one year later with the Displaced Persons Act of 1948, aimed mainly at the million-plus refugees in Europe. In order to maintain the national origins system, the 1948 act required that all refugees admitted under its terms would constitute a burden against one half the future quotas of the countries from which they fled. The mortgaging feature was harsh: For a country like Latvia with 235 quota numbers annually, the 22,157 quota immigrants who came in during the 1940's would mean a delay of nearly a century. By 1952, in fact, one half the Latvian quota was mortgaged until the year 2274.

The Displaced Persons Act provided for a total admission

of 200,000 refugees, limited to those persons who entered Austria, Germany, or Italy before December 22, 1945, a date most observers agreed discriminated against a large number of Jews who fled from Poland in 1946. As usual, Congress cast back to the past to fix a cut-off date, rather than dealing with the present reality. Forty percent of the DP's were required to come from Estonia, Latvia, Lithuania, and Poland; 2,000 (one percent) of the total were authorized for Czechs, and 3,000 for orphans under sixteen. Thirty percent of the total had to be farmers. To top it off, these homeless and destitute people could not enter the United States without a security clearance and a job and housing guarantee. In signing the bill, President Truman said: "This bill is a pattern of discrimination and intolerance wholly inconsistent with the American sense of justice. It mocks the American tradition of fair play and discriminates in callous fashion against persons of the Jewish faith. It also excludes many Catholics who deserve admission."

The Displaced Persons Act was practically unworkable. During 1949, only 2,507 refugees entered the United States under its terms. The Commission on Displaced Persons urged sweeping revisions of the law, and the House passed a moderate reform bill in June of 1949. In the Senate, the chairman of the immigration subcommittee, Nevada Democrat Patrick McCarran, blocked the bill for the year, announcing that upon his return from Europe where he would conduct a fact-finding study, the Senate might reconsider. It did. In 1950, the House and Senate agreed on a compromise that enlarged the total to be admitted: The act specified 415,744 could now enter by June 30, 1951. The 1950 legislation spelled out certain subgroups within the 415,000, such as 54,744 persons expelled from Germany, 18,000 Polish veterans in England, 10,000 Greeks, two categories of orphans, and 300,000 refugees whose admission would be supervised by the United Nation's International Refugee Organization. The act also discarded the 40 and 30 percent provisions of the 1948 statute, but it retained job and housing requirements and failed to remove the provisions for mortgaging quotas.

THE McCARRAN-WALTER ACT

By 1951 the national origins system rested somewhat uneasily as the guardian of the nation's racial mix. The June deadline for European refugees was extended to December to accommodate refugees who had been kept out by the draconic Internal Security Act of 1950, which barred members or former members of "totalitarian" organizations from emigrating to the United States (which in time came to mean members of the Communist party only). Thousands of displaced persons had been nominal members of Fascist and Communist parties in order to survive the holocaust of war and its aftermath. Mussolini had required all schoolchildren to be members of the Fascist Youth Organization; thus most educated Italians were automatically excluded. Charging that the Attorney General and others were out to "sabotage" the Internal Security Act by strict interpretation of its requirements, Congress amended its regulations to cover these people, and they came in. By the time the Displaced Persons Act of 1948 expired, most of its authorized quotas had been used. From 1949 through 1952, more than 660,000 quota immigrants had come to the United States; since of these more than 355,000 were charged against future quotas, it was evident that national origins had been distorted.

To forestall the impending breakdown in American culture, Senator McCarran had been busy since 1947 with hearings and drafting; his aim: the codification of all the scattered immigration and naturalization acts on the federal statute books. McCarran's active partner across the Hill in the House was Representative Francis E. Walter, Democrat of Pennsylvania and chairman of the House Subcommittee responsible for immigration matters.

These two men wielded great power in their respective subcommittees, and in the Congress at large, as fierce defenders of America against infiltration and subversion, earning wide public support in the bitter days of the early 1950's. Both men were elected in Franklin Roosevelt's first landslide in 1932;

neither turned out to be a New Deal liberal. Walter was chairman of the House Un-American Activities Committee, and like McCarran, was constantly attempting to ferret out Communists in the United States. As late as 1960, Walter charged that a large number of churches throughout America were infiltrated with Communists. He was, at the same time, an international liberal of sorts; he had been part of the original House group which urged the adoption of the Marshall Plan following the war.

Perhaps more than any other man, McCarran exemplified the citizen called to Washington to govern. There was nothing fancy about Pat McCarran when he went to the Capitol in the midst of the Depression; he was just a concerned Nevadan, who had waged an intensely personal campaign. He was the people's man because he had been so long a part of them.

Born in Reno in 1876 of Irish immigrants, he studied law while a member of the state legislature in 1930. Having been the district attorney of Nye County from 1906 to 1908, he was elected to the Nevada Supreme Court in 1912 and served as chief judge from 1916 to 1918. Returning to private practice in 1919, McCarran quickly became caught up in a scandal involving the maze of Nevada divorce law. Mary Pickford hired him to obtain a divorce, and McCarran borrowed a "quickie" technique that had been developed by a fellow member of the bar. It seems that through a loophole in the Nevada statute, a person could avoid the six-month residence requirement then prevailing if the defending spouse were served with the legal papers in the same county that the plaintiff spouse happened to be in. The husband conveniently showed up in the right county and was served. Mary Pickford received her divorce that day, and returned to Hollywood to marry Douglas Fairbanks. She gave McCarran her Reno home, the same house she had purchased as evidence of her intent to remain in Nevada for six months. The public was noisily angered: That loophole could ruin the local economy. The father of McCarran's technique was actually indicted by the local authorities; the indictment was dropped when it was pointed out that in

Nevada you cannot commit a crime by following the law. The state legislature amended the same-county rule out of existence, and McCarran settled back to relative obscurity.

He became president of the state bar association in 1920–21 and president of the Truckee River Water Users' Association the following year. From his contacts in that job, he would carry to the Senate for twenty years the fight of local squatters against the Paiute Indians' right to certain land and water. In a number of Senate hearings, described in detail by A. J. Liebling in a *New Yorker* series, McCarran terrorized Indian commissioners and the Interior Department. Of the woman Indian Superintendent appointed in 1933 by President Roosevelt, he said, "I'm not saying she had Leftist tendencies or anything, but these Paiutes turned up at hearings in Washington using the expression 'minority group.'"

No one would ever accuse him of deserting his supporters in Nevada; he was often called the "silver-haired and silver-minded Senator," for he tenaciously looked after Nevada silver interests. He even watched out for Nevada's need for skilled immigrants; in complete disregard of the national origins system, McCarran got through Congress in 1950 a law to allow 250 Basque sheepherders to emigrate to Nevada and other states to aid native wool producers. No quotas were mortgaged that time; McCarran's "private DP bill" admitted the sheepherders above the Spanish quota. This was the man who would recodify American immigration law.

First introduced in 1950, the Immigration and Nationality Act of 1952 underwent joint Congressional hearings in the spring of 1951. These hearings lasted twelve days, during the period from March 6 to April 9 (with usually only one or two committee members in attendance at any one time). No further action was taken that year. By January 29, however, the Senate Judiciary Committee finished its work and reported the bill to the Senate floor; its proposed legislation had grown from McCarran's original 248 pages to 302. On February 14, the House Judiciary Committee reported out its version of the bill; the dissimilarities were not marked. The House took only parts of three days to debate and amend the bill before passing it 206 to 68 on April 25.

Meanwhile, Senators Hubert H. Humphrey of Minnesota and Herbert H. Lehman of New York introduced a new bill in March, co-sponsored by eleven other Senators. The Humphrey-Lehman Bill would have changed the quota system's base year from 1920 to 1950, authorized the redistribution of unused quotas for certain groups of immigrants, and removed both the "mortgages" on quotas that had resulted from the Displaced Persons Act and also racial and sex discriminations. It got nowhere. Despite Senator Lehman's pointed observations that hearings on the McCarran bill had never really been held (because the Judiciary Committee in January had simply reported out what in most respects was the House bill) and that his bill should be given a chance in hearing, McCarran prevailed. He maintained the offensive and refused to be pushed into a defensive position; eight times during the third week in May he categorically refused to answer questions that Senator Lehman wished to put to him. Instead, he prodded with the kind of argument that made it difficult for rational debate to flourish. Opponents, he said, "would wittingly or unwittingly lend themselves to efforts which would poison the bloodstream of the country." In a slight exaggeration of the time span, he added that his bill's provisions "have been the basic provisions of our immigration law for generations and are designed to screen out subversives, the criminals, and the undesirables."

Further, "the times, Mr. President, are too perilous for us to tinker blindly with our basic institutions." And, McCarran added: "If we scrap the national origins formula we will, in the course of a generation or so, change the ethnic and cultural composition of this nation." Raising the specter of communism, McCarran linked all opposition to his bill to the Communist Party in America.

On May 22, the Humphrey-Lehman forces were roundly defeated and McCarran's bill easily passed by voice vote. Minor conflicts between the House and Senate versions were resolved by June 9, when the conference bill was reported out. The

House adopted it 203–53 the next day, and the Senate followed by voice vote the day following that.

As far as national origins is concerned, the McCarran-Walter Act had two principal features. The first was the decision to retain the 1920 census as the basis for the system. In opting for the continuation of outdated statistics, Congress moved a step back from its putative motives. Form was clearly being exalted above substance. Since the entire basis of national origins was to relate present immigration to the "historic population blend," as one defender was later to put it, rejection of the present blend was a denial of the only reason advanced in favor of it.

The second feature of the act was the decision finally to drop racial bars to entry and citizenship. The only groups still in blanket disfavor were the Japanese, Koreans, and Southeast Asians. The McCarran-Walter Act now proposed to admit these groups as immigrants once again; people of all races would be eligible for immigration and naturalization. It was this provision to which McCarran, Walter, and other supporters pointed to prove that they were not guilty of racial prejudice or blindness. Their argument was flawed.

The act replaced the ban on Asians with a new device, the Asia-Pacific triangle. This large geographic area—bounded by parallel 25° south latitude, 165° west longitude, and meridian 60° east—embraced China, Japan, Southeast Asia, India, and most Pacific Islands. Within the Triangle, each independent nation was given a quota of 100, except for China, which retained its 1943 quota of 105 and Japan, which was assigned a quota of 185. The act specified that for the purposes of the minimum quotas, the total within the Triangle could be no more than 2,000—should more than twenty nations be created within the area, they would get a minimum quota at the expense of the nations already included; at the time the act was passed, there were already nineteen countries in existence. Not included in this limitation were the Japanese and Chinese quotas, which could not be reduced, and a special Triangle quota of 100 for people living in areas not otherwise covered. Thus, the maximum allowed under the Asia-Pacific Triangle provision was 2,190 (China, Japan, the other seventeen countries, a new one should it be created, and the Triangle itself).

If many of these quotas were lower than national origins should properly grant them in theory, the act contained an even more discriminatory feature. Anyone whose ancestry was at least half-Asian—meaning by that, a person whose father or mother was born within the Triangle—would himself be chargeable to the Triangle-area quota, regardless of where he was born. Thus, a man born in Britain to a man born in India would not be eligible to come to the United States under the British quota, but would have to take his turn on the Indian waiting list. The rationalization was based on the claim that large numbers of Asians were emigrating to South America; since the Western Hemisphere continued in its nonquota status, Congress must ensure that these Asians do not take advantage of our laws.

The labyrinthian Triangle provisions worked this way:

A native of Canada whose parents were native Canadians could come freely to the United States. His next-door neighbor, also a native Canadian but whose mother was born in Japan, would be chargeable to the quota for Japan, even though his mother emigrated to Canada a half-century before when she was one day old. A native German whose father was Malayan was chargeable to the "Asia-Pacific quota," since Malaya did not have a separate quota. When both parents were born in the Triangle, but in different countries, the descendant was chargeable to the "Asia-Pacific quota," also, rather than to either of the parents' countries. To round out the picture, a person born in Great Britain to a German mother and an Irish father was chargeable to Great Britain. The parents counted only when they were born within the Triangle.

Other features of the act:

It did away with discrimination based on sex, so that Chinese husbands, and Asian spouses generally, were entitled to emigrate as nonquota, assuming their spouses in America were citizens. This ended the arbitrary division between Chinese husbands and wives, and Indian and Filipino spouses.

The act also established new preferences within the general

quota system. The first half of all quotas were to be devoted to those with "high education, technical training, specialized experiences, or exceptional ability" and to their spouses and children. The next 30 percent was reserved for parents of adult U.S. citizens. The remaining 20 percent was for the immediate family of aliens who were already admitted to the U.S. as permanent residents. Should any quotas remain unused after all applicants in the first three categories had been taken care of, then and only then would the mass of common folk, without immediate relatives here, be allowed to make the journey. Even then, adult children and brothers and sisters of U.S. citizens were allotted a maximum of only 25 percent of those remaining numbers. Any latecomer who put his name on the list would stand a better chance of admission if he were a stranger than if he had a brother in this country.

Colonial territories were given a maximum quota of 100; for the first time they were taken out of the general quota category of their parent country. Thus, the natives of Jamaica—against whom this provision was aimed—could no longer be admitted to the United States under Great Britain's quota of 65,000; instead the Jamaican Negro had to compete with his fellow colonials for the 100 annual spots, even though Jamaica was within the Western Hemisphere. Opponents charged that this was but another example of the act's continued racial bias.

The McCarran-Walter Act also included a long list of provisions concerning grounds for deportation and exclusion. It laid down a host of rules and procedures by which a person could be denied the right of naturalization. In most respects, it was considerably tougher than the laws it was supposed to be codifying. The influence of loyalty-phobia and Joseph McCarthy (whose admirer and defender McCarran was) was evident.

Senators Humphrey and Lehman had warned that the act might be vetoed by the President if it were passed in its undiluted form. On June 25, 1952, their predictions proved correct. Noting that it made some improvements in the law—especially the ban on racial exclusion, President Truman went on to denounce the act:

"But now this most desirable provision comes before me embedded in a mass of legislation which would perpetuate injustices of long standing against many other nations of the world, hamper the efforts we are making to rally the men of East and West alike to the cause of freedom, and intensify the repressive and inhumane aspects of our immigration procedures. The price is too high, and in good conscience I cannot agree to pay it."

He continued: "The country by country limitations create a pattern that is insulting to large numbers of our finest citizens, irritating to our allies abroad, and foreign to our purposes and ideals. . . . The basis of this quota system was false and unworthy in 1924. It is even worse now. At the present time, this quota system keeps out the very people we want to bring in. It is incredible to me that, in this year of 1952, we should again be enacting into law such a slur on the patriotism, the capacity, and the decency of a large part of our citizenry. . . . Today, we have entered into an alliance, the North Atlantic Treaty, with Italy, Greece, and Turkey against one of the most terrible threats mankind has ever faced. We are asking them to join with us in protecting the peace of the world. We are helping them to build their defenses, and train their men, in the common cause. But, through this bill we say to their people: You are less worthy to come to this country than Englishmen or Irishmen; you Italians, who need to find homes abroad in the hundreds of thousands—you shall have a quota of 5,645; you Greeks, struggling to assist the helpless victims of a Communist civil war—you shall have a quota of 308; and you Turks, you are brave defenders of the Eastern flank, but you shall have a quota of only 225! . . . In no other realm of our national life are we so hampered and stultified by the dead hand of the past as we are in this field of immigration. We do not limit our cities to their 1920 boundaries—we do not hold our corporations to their 1920 capitalizations—we welcome progress and change to meet changing conditions in every sphere of life except in the field of immigration."

The next day the House overrode the President's veto,

by a resounding 278 to 113 vote. Representative Walter branded the veto message "fictional and amateurish." Two days after the veto, on June 26, the Senate responded to McCarran's plea to override "in God's name, in the name of the American people, in the name of America's future." By a vote of 57–26, the Immigration and Nationality Act of 1952 became law. Had Richard M. Nixon and Lyndon B. Johnson voted the other way, the act would have failed. Yet not since 1917 had an immigration bill excited a Presidential veto; since that time Presidents and Congress had agreed on restrictions and repeal of restrictions. For the moment, the consensus on national origins held.

BEYOND McCARRAN-WALTER

It has been charged that among the reasons for passage in 1952 was Congressional inability to read "highly technical and unduly lengthy bills and reports." Representative Hand moaned that the committee report on the basic House bill was as long as *Gone with the Wind* and that he for one had not had the opportunity to read it. It has been estimated that of the 2,000 pages of reports, no more than 5 percent of those who voted for the act read them. Had the bill been straightforward, this might be an objection, since a Congressman cannot possibly read all the reports about all legislation on which he must vote. But there was nothing simple about H.R. 5678. Complained Senator Blair Moody of Michigan: "Why is this legislation labeled as a codification and, therefore, a simplification, when the test of whether admitting an alien is in the public interest appears as subclause (b) of clause (ii) of [sub-subparagraph I of] subparagraph 28 of subsection (a) of section 212 of Chapter I of Title II of Chapter 6 of Title VIII of the United States Code dealing with immigration matters? What is clear or simple about that?" So unclear, in fact, that Senator Moody didn't even get it right when reading from his prepared speech; he omitted the bracketed reference above to sub-subparagraph I.

The maze of unreadable portions in the statute's text soon compelled changes in its substance. The first to come was the Refugee Relief Act of 1953. The new President and Vice-President were on record in early 1953 to rid McCarran-Walter of its discriminations, or some of them, at any rate. In late January, Representative Celler sponsored a bill which would admit 328,000 European refugees on a nonquota basis within three years. President Eisenhower, citing the situation as an "emergency" four months later, requested nonquota status for 240,000 refugees within the next two years. With Representative Walter squawking that the Relief Act would "destroy the national origins system," the House Judiciary Committee reported the bill and after amendments from the floor, the House in July passed a bill by a 221–185 vote authorizing 217,000 immigrants over the next two-year period. The Senate followed suit a few days later by a 63–30 vote, lowering the total to 209,000. By August, Congress had agreed to the conference committee bill, allowing 209,000 refugees and others from Germany, Austria, Greece, Italy, Holland, Asia, Arabia and certain other classes of people, such as Italians, Greeks, and Dutch with immediate relatives in the United States, and orphans. The act was to expire at the end of 1956.

Because it imposed the same screening controls as the DP Act of 1948 (including a new provision that no person could be admitted unless "complete information" about him was available for "at least two years" prior to his visa request), the administration of the act fell heir to the same debate. At the end of 1954, only 399 orphans and 821 others had been admitted. One of the problems stemmed from the fact that far fewer Italian, Dutch, and Greek refugees were applying for visas (45,000, 15,000, and 15,000 of the total had been allotted to them respectively) than were those nationals with close relatives (who came under separate subtotals within the act). Congress amended the act in August, 1954, to permit the State Department to issue visas without regard to the 1953 division between refugees and those with close relatives. Still, McCarran insisted that the immigrant with a close relative in the United States be required to show that he had obtained housing and a job before he came, otherwise the State Department could not issue him a visa. It was his last victory; he died in Nevada on September 28, 1954.

The Refugee Relief Act was heavily criticized; a welter of debate from within the Administration rose to the public's attention when Edward J. Corsi, the State Department's special adviser on refugees, was fired by the boss of the Refugee Act, Scott McLeod, head of the Bureau of Security and Consular Affairs. Corsi charged that administration of the act was being blocked by an "active minority" of Congressmen and State Department officials. The charges were denied, but President Eisenhower a few weeks later asked Congress to make major changes in the administration of the act, including the complete redistribution of unused quotas. Congress failed to act on the President's requests.

In 1955, with an election impending, President Eisenhower made a massive attack on national origins, in almost every way but name. He called for the substitution of the 1950 census; he wanted to raise the total yearly authorized immigration from 154,000 to 220,000, he wanted to redistribute unused quotas, and he wanted the quotas of countries heavily mortgaged by the Displaced Persons Act to be freed. Senator James O. Eastland, Democrat of Mississippi, who had stepped into McCarran's seat as chairman of the subcommittee, would have none of it.

Not easily discouraged, Majority Leader Lyndon B. Johnson and Senator Everett McKinley Dirksen of Illinois, soon to become the Minority Leader, along with a number of Senators from both parties, introduced a compromise by offering their bill as an amendment to another immigration bill then pending. Senator Eastland complained that it did not have the benefit of committee hearings; Dirksen rejoindered, "I have drawn freely, however, on staff members of the Senate Judiciary Committee." On the last day of the session, the only day the Senate considered the bill, Senator Eastland spoke against the provision to redistribute unused quotas. The 18,500 vacant quotas, if used by low-quota nations, would "change the cultural pattern of our immigration system from northern and western Europeans to southern and eastern Europeans. . . . Ours is a constitutional republic, built upon concepts stemming from cultures which reflect themselves in the historic composition of our population. If we transfer the pattern of our immigration to countries and peoples who have historically maintained a totalitarian concept of government, it will only be a matter of time until our Republic will veer from its traditions of freedom and democracy." This was the standard argument—an influx of less than one third of one percent of the population (assuming that 600,000 mortgaged quotas would be freed and unused quotas redistributed) would result at some undisclosed later time in a radical change in American traditions through an undisclosed method. What changes would occur were kept a secret. No one answered these points directly. Apparently they did not need to, for in spite of the fact that the Johnson-Dirksen compromise amendments were issued to Senators only a short time before in mimeographed form and had not undergone committee scrutiny, the Senate passed them. For the first time in thirty-two years, a serious dent in the substantive basis of national origins had been made in the Senate. But this was the last day of the Second Session of the 84th Congress and it was too late to secure House approval, despite an attempt by New York Republican Kenneth B. Keating.

The battle was far from its end. Though Congress seemed disposed toward reform, it still had to contend with such opinions as those of Robert C. Alexander, the Assistant Administrator for Refugee Relief Program, Bureau of Security and Consular Affairs, who in 1956 wrote in a prestigious law journal:

"In a recent article, Mr. J. B. Matthews, a recognized authority on Communist subversive activity, refers to the questioning of a witness by the Senate Subcommittee on Internal Security, on June 23, 1954, regarding the Communist origin of the now-exposed National Committee to Repeal the McCarran Acts. He states that the witness, who invoked the 5th Amendment of our Constitution in refusing to answer questions concerning the Communist origin of the NCRMA, was the Communist party's top commissar in the field of immigration. This does not mean, of course, that all who criticize the McCarran-Walter Act are Communists, or even Communist sympathizers, but it should cause patriotic Americans who have no political ax to grind to ponder before they join any movement to attack the law."

The late autumn revolution in Hungary numbed opposition by sparking a wave of public sympathy for the refugees. President Eisenhower moved under the McCarran-Walter Act to reserve 5,000 quotas for the Hungarian freedom fighters who had escaped to Austria, and announced that he would "parole" 15,000 additional Hungarians into the United States under section 212(d)(5): "The Attorney General may in his discretion parole into the United States temporarily under such conditions as he may prescribe for emergency reasons or for reasons deemed strictly in the public interest any alien applying for admission to the United States, but such parole of such alien shall not be regarded as an admission of the alien and when the purposes of such parole shall, in the opinion of the Attorney General, have been served the alien shall forthwith return or be returned to the custody from which he was paroled and thereafter his case shall continue to be dealt with in the same manner as that of any other applicant for admission to the United States." This parole clause, sorely lacking in 1939, had rarely been used and little noticed. Most of the President's proposals in 1957 fell on unmoving hands in Congress, but another last-minute attempt, incorporating some important provisions, this time succeeded.

Senator John F. Kennedy, who had sponsored a number of immigration bills in the past few years, introduced a major bill in June that would have patched up many of the holes in the various refugee acts, including the reuniting of separated families, the settling of refugees still unsettled, and the regularization of paroled immigrants' status. "The number of aliens which this bill would admit," Senator Kennedy said on the Senate floor, "is relatively small—less than 90,000 over a two-year period—but the advantages to the United States and the people affected are tremendous. More importantly, however, this bill has great moral significance, having as its basic purpose the preservation of families and the extension of assistance to the homeless. . . . This bill is no panacea nor is it a final answer to the immigration problem. As I have repeatedly stated, I believe that Congress must seriously and thoughtfully reexamine our entire immigration policy. However, the problems of the human beings to which the legislation is primarily addressed cannot await a thorough legislative review."

Representative Walter introduced a narrower bill which was reported by the House Judiciary in mid-August. After conducting an informal poll in Congress, Kennedy realized that the only chance for change that year was the Walter bill. Accordingly, he introduced a similar version in the Senate the day after the House bill was reported. The House passed the bill 295-58 and the Senate by a voice vote on the last day of the session. Senator Kennedy hailed the passage as a "major step forward in our attempts to enact more liberal immigration legislation." The bill erased the mortgages which had lain on eastern and southern European countries since the DP Act of 1948. It extended visas to more than 60,000 persons escaping persecution; many of these visas had been earlier authorized by the Refugee Act and never used. It also gave nonquota status until 1959 to orphans who were being adopted by U.S. citizens.

The next three years were rather slack, but not completely quiescent. In 1958, Congress smoothed out the status of Hungarian parolees, authorizing them to become permanent residents and thus allowing them to apply for citizenship. In 1959, the United States continued its participation in international refugee programs, this time in the United Nations-sponsored World Refugee Year. Congress contributed ten million dollars to U.N. programs conducted under World Refugee Year auspices. Congress also extended the nonquota orphan provision another year. In 1960, Congress passed the Fair Share Law, increasing the parole power of the Attorney General, by which the U.S. would take up to 25 percent of the number of refugees settled elsewhere by the U.N. High Commissioner for Refugees, and extended the orphan provision still another year.

Running for the Presidency in 1960, Senator Kennedy was pledged to end the national origins system. During 1961 and 1962, he was moderate in his proposals to Congress, apparently afraid to risk an all-out fight for repeal. In each of these years, however, the national origins system was further whittled away.

In 1961, Congress made permanent the nonquota orphan provision, and repealed the Asia-Pacific triangle ceiling of 2,000, authorizing instead a 100 quota minimum for each new country. In 1962, Congress approved in the Migration and Refugee Assistance Act the extension of a number of refugee programs, some strictly American, some operated in connection with the United Nations. The principal concern in that year was the wave of more than 100,000 Cuban refugees who entered easily enough under nonquota Western Hemisphere provisions. The escape of Chinese across the mainland to Hong Kong offered another problem, though; after some discussion, President Kennedy decided to parole some 19,000 Chinese into the United States just as 24,000 Hungarians had eventually been admitted under the parole clause.

By now the preliminary work was done. Between 1952 and 1962 the national origins provisions had been so diluted that it was difficult to see what remained of them other than their honorific name. Year after year, modest proposals had snowballed; the accumulative effect is readily observable from just a few statistics:

Between 1953 and 1964, the total number of immigrants admitted to the United States was 3,197,857. Of these, only 1,140,479 came in under the national origins system, just a shade more than one third. The remaining immigrants were either nonquota immigrants allowed under the McCarran-Walter Act (1,681,285) or were admitted under the special legislation just reviewed (376,093).

The disparity between what national origins promised and what it accomplished is observable on a country-by-country basis also. Italy, for instance, with an annual quota of 5,666, or 56,000 over a ten-year period, actually sent 185,491 of its residents during the decade between 1951 and 1960. In 1962 it sent 20,000. And Greece, with an annual quota of 308, sent 47,608 during the years 1951 to 1960, and in 1962 sent 4,408. China, with a quota of 105, managed to get 9,657 in during the decade, and 1,356 in 1962. Japan's meager 185 annual quota provided 46,250 in ten years, and 4,054 in 1962.

National origins had become a shell. It had been vigorously

defended in the past and would continue to be defended, even beyond the day of its defeat. But the battle between substance and form had largely been resolved on the side of substance. Congress had enacted significant exceptions to McCarran-Walter each year since 1957 to accommodate groups throughout the world who could not enter the U.S. under its terms. It was a wearying task—plainly, a longer-range solution than yearly ad hoc legislation was called for. With all its surplusage stripped away, national origins had only its observed-in-the-breach quota system as a rallying point, and reformers now went after its very heart.

6 / *Policy Round 3: Abolition*

As much as the victory of national origins was a product of hysteria and distemper, its abolition was achieved in an atmosphere of relative calm. Not that there was not vehemence, nor even sometimes anger and impatience, but on the whole the battle was fought with the good grace that an advocate, confident of his coming victory, could afford.

Battle lines for the third round of policymaking were drawn as early as 1960, though the victory would wait five years. The Democratic party platform of 1960 urged the abolition: "The national origins quota system of limiting immigration contradicts the founding principles of this nation. It is inconsistent with our beliefs in the rights of man. This system was instituted after World War I as a policy of deliberate discrimination by a Republican Administration and Congress." The 1960 Republican party platform hedged its bet: It advocated replacing the 1920 census with the 1960 census, but otherwise it saw no reason to disturb the admission scheme.

With the election of John Fitzgerald Kennedy as President came something new to the politics of immigration. For the first time a Chief Executive had been elected from an immigrant group that had once been sorely abused during a large span of our history; for the first time, an Irish Catholic had won the right to occupy the oval office in the White House. More significant from the standpoint of immigration reform, however, was the fact that President Kennedy was personally conscious of his immigrant origins and throughout his years in the Senate had been a consistent champion of liberalizing the immigration laws. "I know of no cause," wrote his brother Robert F. Kennedy in 1964, "which President Kennedy championed more warmly than the improvement of our immigration policies." Certainly he was the only President to have written a book (*A Nation of Immigrants*—in 1958 while a Senator) specifically on the subject and specifically for the purpose of promoting reform.

The President and his brothers had been instilled with an appreciation of their family origins. They were highly aware that the family had risen from immigrant stock; they were equally conscious that that stock had been discriminated against in Massachusetts at the time their great-grandparents arrived from Ireland in mid-century. Kennedy's maternal grandfather, John F. Fitzgerald, was a vigorous supporter of liberal immigration policies during his six years in Congress between 1895 and 1900 (and during his later tenure as mayor of Boston). He introduced bills to aid refugees throughout the world. His defense against the detractors of the Irish, detractors who still haunted Congress even in those days, led him to a firm commitment to the rights of all peoples to share in the American civilization. Senator Edward M. Kennedy of Massachusetts recalls childhood chats with his grandfather about this nation of immigrants. Favoring immigrants in Massachusetts is good politics, of course; forty percent of the people in the state today are either foreign-born or children of foreign-born. Mayor Fitzgerald knew it; so did all three Senators Kennedy, but the commitment was deeper than mere politics. Calvin Coolidge and Henry Cabot Lodge, after all, had been on the other side.

The first direct move toward abolition came with President Kennedy's message to Congress of July 23, 1963. It was first in the sense that the legislators and President in 1965 when the battle was won would refer to John Kennedy's call as their start. In a larger sense it was a beginning only because it represented the first vigorous Presidential demand for abolition in many years.

It is probably safe to guess that President Kennedy's sentimental journey to Ireland one month before had had an effect on his July proposal. In June he remarked to a large gathering of Irish citizens, "When my great-grandfather left here to become a cooper in East Boston, he carried nothing with him except a strong religious faith and a strong desire for liberty. If he hadn't left, I would be working at the Albatross Company across the road." In July he wrote: "The use of a national origins system is without basis in either logic or reason. It neither satisfies a national need nor accomplishes an international purpose. In an age of interdependence among nations, such a system is an anachronism, for it discriminates among applicants for admission into the United States on the accident of birth."

The President requested reduction of the worldwide quota system by one fifth for five years; the quotas so released would be placed in a reserve pool from which immigrants would be admitted on a first-come, first-served basis. A number of other provisions would limit the number of immigrants from any given country to 10 percent of the total (about 16,500) and would reallocate the preferences within the quotas to allow 50 percent to go to exceptionally skilled immigrants and the remaining 50 percent to various relatives (adult children, spouses and children of resident aliens) who were ineligible for nonquota status. The President also requested authority to allocate up to 50 percent of the reserve pool during the five years to Britain, Germany, and Ireland if they were disadvantaged by the reduction in their quotas (for these would be the only countries to have quotas reduced). At the end of five years, quotas would be abolished altogether, and the entire world would compete on a first-come, first-served basis for the 164,500 places, subject to the 10 percent limit per country and to the skill and relative preferences within the pool.

The chances for passage looked better than they had in some years. Representative Walter had died on May 31, and although

the new chairman of Subcommittee No. 1 of the House
Judiciary Committee, Michael A. Feighan of Ohio, was known
to share many of Walter's opinions, the fact that fifty-five Congressmen introduced bills identical to Representative Emanuel
Celler's Administration bill and twenty-seven Senators cospon-
sored Senator Philip A. Hart's Administration bill indicated that
there was sympathy for change. Some legislators anxiously
yearned for abolition, not only because they believed in its
principle, but because private immigration bills (2,677 in 1961–
1962) had become too great a burden.

A constant argument put forth by national origins proponents from the very beginning was the necessity for a clear,
definite, and unalterable policy. Again and again, from 1924
to 1965, national origins was justified by the observation that
mathematics would save the country from serious problems. A
concise statement of the philosophy was written in 1956 by the
same Robert Alexander who warned against Communist opposition to the McCarran-Walter Act:

"It seems fairly certain that unless every foreign country's
quota is computed upon the basis of a public, definite, and
identical mathematical formula, so that all countries may know
in advance what their quotas, as well as the quotas of other
countries, will be from year to year, the Government of the
United States may be deluged with both foreign and domestic
complaints and charges of graft, corruption, undue influence,
national bias or prejudice, special favoritism, and perhaps even
national animosity. The flood of diplomatic protests alone could
seriously interfere with the normal conduct of our foreign relations. Moreover, the internal strife which could be created by
some justifiably dissatisfied foreign national origins groups in
the United States could well disrupt our national unity."

Exactly how well the mathematics of immigration worked
was a matter of no little doubt. The quotas did not stop Congress
from enacting an accumulating load of legislative changes nor,
as we shall see, did the mathematical formulas stop Congress and
the Executive branch from administering the laws in a gran-
diosely discriminatory fashion. In fact, every one of the arguments Alexander advanced for the retention of mathematical

formulas had been justifiably advanced in favor of their dissolution.

Nowhere, however, did Congress more reject its own mathematics than in one of its most peculiar institutions: the private bill. Normally, Congress is a governmental body that creates legislation of general applicability to the whole society. The private bill is analogous to petitions presented to the King of England centuries ago by citizens requesting relief from the hardships which certain laws created. Congress reserves this same power to itself, but exercises it in only two general cases: applications for monetary claims against the Government (or for release from claims by the Government against the individual) and requests for relief from the hardships imposed by immigration laws.

Regardless of its outcome, a private bill pending in Congress has an important consequence: It usually delays action by the Departments of State and Justice in a pending immigration case. Thus, if a Congressman agrees to submit a private bill on your behalf to secure relief from threatened deportation, you will probably be safe for a year at least. The Immigration and Naturalization Service normally will not act while a bill is pending in Congress (though this is a "custom" of the Service, not a law that binds them). The delay technique worked best in the case of an immigrant who was to be deported solely because his quota number had not come up, although otherwise qualified to remain in the country. A private bill to allow the immigrant to remain in the country could be reintroduced in each new session of Congress until the quota number came up; even though there is no chance for passage, I.N.S. normally held off.

Private bills are rather cavalierly dealt with in Congress. They can be killed usually if a single member objects, although as a matter of course bills that are cleared by the respective immigration subcommittees generally receive positive action. The classes of hardship cases are as large as the number of roadblocks to immigration thrown up by the McCarran-Walter Act, although the most frequent call for private immigration bills is for those cases dealing with adjustment of status of family members. The cumulative effect of the private calendar in Congress meant (and still means) hours of time spent in the consideration of relatively minor cases that could be handled far better by enacting a more workable general statute. During the 1960's Congress was considering more than 1,000 private bills annually in the immigration area. The private bill points out that the blind faith in "mathematical formulas" was unwarranted; in spite of the McCarran-Walter Act, political pressures were sufficient to destroy its pristine elegance.

Yet despite the wearying load of immigration bills, the time was not propitious for general reform in 1963. Other matters were more pressing—civil rights, tax reform, and the beginning war against poverty. The July message was President Kennedy's last major public act on behalf of immigration reform; four months later he was dead. When the Second Session of the 88th Congress convened in January, 1964, it was met by a southerner who promised to continue his predecessor's policies. On January 13, the President met with Congressional committee members and urged on them swift passage of President Kennedy's July proposal.

It was not to be. Not until June did the House subcommittee begin hearings on national origins (for the first time in twelve years). The six-month delay resulted from a feud which erupted between the subcommittee chairman, Feighan, and Chairman Celler of the parent Judiciary Committee. The accession of a new man to the subcommittee's chair meant, Celler thought, that some degree of control could be imposed on the previously recalcitrant group. Celler refused Feighan's request to hire a new staff and blocked other plans of the new chairman. Feighan, never an ardent sympathizer with immigration reformers, began a series of incredible accusations: Russian spies were inside the C.I.A., inspectors and administrators within the Immigration Service had accepted large bribes to fix cases; Feighan even railed that an Englishman, Richard Burton, should be denied a visa because his alleged misconduct with Elizabeth Taylor, an American citizen, made him unfit to enter.

Feighan struck back with more than words. He activated the twelve-year-old Joint Committee on Immigration and Nationality Policy and was elected chairman. This was accomplished by sending a resolution to committee members which stated that Feighan *was* chairman; a majority signed the resolution without really thinking about the matter, and it was a *fait accompli*. The Joint Committee had met a total of eight minutes in twelve years because Representative Walter saw no need for a rival. Feighan found a use for the committee, and he quickly appointed one of his Congressional assistants staff director and requested $160,000 in operating funds from the House Appropriations committee. House liberals feared Feighan would begin a round of investigations which, though ostensibly aimed at corruption, might in the end be another hunt for Communists in government. The Appropriations Committee rejected Feighan's request for a budget increase from the usual $20,000 annually. He took the fight to the floor of the House in April and lost by a 69-69 tie vote. Feighan had been defeated and with him the immigration bill for that year.

In Feighan's subcommittee, as in the Senate subcommittee, the matter died to await rebirth in President Johnson's State of the Union message January 4, 1965. In the interval Lyndon Johnson won election to the Presidency by the greatest popular margin in the nation's history. With Senator Barry Goldwater in defeat went dozens of Congressmen, giving the President better than a 2 to 1 majority in both houses of Congress.

On January 4, the President said: "Let a just nation throw open . . . the city of promise . . . to those in other lands seeking the promise of America, through an immigration law based on the work a man can do and not where he was born or how he spells his name." On January 13, he presented a message to Congress on immigration reform; its proposals were nearly identical to President Kennedy's of a year and a half before. "The principal reform called for," he wrote, "is the elimination of the national origins quota system. . . . The fundamental, long-time American attitude has been to ask not where a person comes from, but what are his personal qualities. On this basis men and women migrated from every quarter of the globe. . . . Violation of this tradition by the national origins quota system does incalculable harm. The procedures imply that men and women from some countries are, just because of where they come from, more desirable citizens than others. We have no right to disparage the ancestors of millions of our fellow Americans in this way. Relationships with a number of countries, and hence the success of our foreign policy is needlessly impeded by this proposition. . . . No move could more effectively reaffirm our fundamental belief that a man is to be judged—and judged exclusively— on his worth as a human being."

President Johnson's bill was for the most part a tightly drawn piece of legislation. It had benefited from the hearings in 1964, and some changes had been made—for instance, the President's authority to reserve quotas from the reserve pool had been reduced from 50 to 30 percent. In major matters, it was the same bill, with the same philosophy. Since its greatest departure from the past forty years was its explicit abolition of the national origins system and the Asia-Pacific Triangle, the Administration was careful to emphasize that everything else remained unaltered. Aside from a few relatively minor liberalizations, the bill would not "open the floodgates," it would not flood the labor market and depress the wage, it would not throw American workers out of jobs. Indeed, the primary emphasis in this, the new "new" immigration, was the highly skilled, professional man. Skilled personnel were to receive the first preference, even above relatives, a situation which Congress would ultimately reverse. But the Administration was correctly aware that the major charge hurled against the bill would be induced by the old fear of being swamped. Time and again the bill's supporters were to point out that it authorized no more than some 7,000 additional immigrants per year under the quota system. (To which opponents would reply that total annual quota immigrants actually were less than the total allowed by McCarran-Walter. Since British-Irish-German quotas were not fully utilized the actual increase would be greater. The implication—that McCarran-Walter authorized more immigrants than could be safely absorbed—defeated the argument.) Time and again witnesses would answer that in their opinions the pending bill would have nothing but beneficial effects on the American economy. And significantly, no opposition testimony could be produced to show any adverse effects. Rabid opponents *asserted* the harm; they could not prove it. In all but its repeal of national origins, the bill was a conservative measure.

IN THE SENATE

On February 10 the Immigration and Naturalization Subcommittee of the Senate Judiciary Committee began its hearings. The Congressional hearing is a ritual that exposes to anyone who cares to enter the marbled hearing rooms both the majesty of a sovereign people deliberating on its national policy and the pettiness of individuals who though perhaps sincerely motivated talk only to confuse and rarely listen. Most Congressional hearings can be broken into three distinct parts: testimony of high government officials who are intimately involved in the subject matter under discussion, either supporting or opposing; testimony of interested Congressmen, Senators, and other government officials, state and local; and the testimony of private persons of every description, from the representatives of the great multimillion member labor unions to the single little lady from across the river who is plainly scared at what her representatives in Washington are about to do.

The parliamentary situation in the Senate subcommittee was somewhat unusual. Generally a subcommittee chairman, appointed by the full committee chairman, will control the hearings —in duration, in numbers and names of witnesses, even in the direction the questioning may go. Some subcommittee chairmen are more generous than others; rarely are they so generous as Senator James O. Eastland of Mississippi, chairman of both the parent committee and the subcommittee. A longstanding foe of immigration reform, he simply chose not to attend at all; except for one brief appearance he abdicated his privilege of presiding. Next in line for the role of chairman were John L. McClellan of Arkansas and Sam J. Ervin, Jr., of North Carolina. Both were initial opponents of the legislation; besides, McClellan had his own important Government Operations Committee to attend to, and Ervin relished the position of devil's advocate, a role in which he would have been hampered had he also the responsibilities of acting chairman.

Neither was reluctant to let that part go to Edward M. Kennedy of Massachusetts. (Philip A. Hart of Michigan was Kennedy's junior on the committee and did not object; nor did the three Republican members, Everett McKinley Dirksen, Hiram L. Fong of Hawaii, and Jacob K. Javits of New York.) It was not mere happenstance on Senator Kennedy's part that led to his presiding over the abolition of national origins. The immigration issue is deeply personal with him, and he has an active desire to be involved. He is highly conscious of carrying on his brother's mission, and he saw in 1965 that the overthrow of the old immigration order was part of President Kennedy's unfinished business. Furthermore, he had played the role of freshman Senator well during the two previous years. Anxious to avoid any possible reproach that he was taking advantage of his relationship with the President, he stayed quiet from 1962 to 1964, watching and learning from his elders. He began to fit into the inner club of the Senate, a place which most observers say had eluded his brother the President. He persisted in showing to Eastland his interest in the committee assignment, an interest buttressed by the fact that as his maiden parliamentary effort in the Senate, he would be the bill's floor manager, the active leader of Administration forces. Finally, he just returned to the Senate following a severe injury in an airplane crash, which had necessitated his sitting out his campaign for reelection; the natural sympathy for one who had narrowly avoided death worked in his favor.

He thus became the acting chairman, though this was not a formal title, for the chairman was alive and well. It was the informal relationship with Senator Eastland that pointed to Senator Kennedy's increasing posture in the upper house. The desire to be the Senate's chief immigration spokesman was prompted also by the realization that it was an excellent way in which a young Senator could develop a special competence in foreign relations. During the three years following the 1965 hearings, Edward Kennedy attended international meetings concerned with immigration and refugee issues (including trips to Vietnam to learn firsthand of the awful plight of refugees there); these trips and tours have put him in contact with scores of cabinet ministers and foreign officials throughout the world.

It is the function of a Congressional subcommittee to investigate proposed legislation referred to it and to recommend its
adoption (after making such amendments as it deems proper)
or to let it lie. From the subcommittee, the bill must go to the
full committee, which has the power to repeat the entire procedure, though it will almost never hold separate hearings. Where
consensus exists, the full committee will rubber-stamp the subcommittee's bill. Where there is complete lack of agreement, the
parent committee can shelve the bill altogether.

The Subcommittee on Immigration and Naturalization began
its hearings in a national atmosphere of tolerance and consensus.
The then great master of the consensus had issued the call for a
Great Society and this was one of its necessary measures. The
subcommittee also began with the understanding that there was
a possible 4 to 4 split in the thinking of its members. Senators
Kennedy, Hart, Javits, and Fong would certainly vote to abolish
national origins; Senators Eastland, McClellan, and Ervin would
certainly vote to retain (it was then thought). Senator Dirksen
might be prevailed upon to go either way—he was later to prove
that he was less interested in the entire matter than he was in
his pet amendment to the Constitution permitting states to apportion their legislatures on a nonpopulation basis. His possible
refusal to support the Administration bill would be used to
extort the Judiciary Committee's acquiescence in reporting out
his amendment. The only certain thing in the committee was that
Eastland would not actively block the Administration bill, because he knew that in the final count it would have overwhelming
Senate support. Early on, the President let it be known that he
was for a bill repealing national origins in any form; he gave
instructions that if a bill were reported at all, the Chief Executive
would back it. This knowledge made it easier to come to compromise; it also made it easier to water down his original
proposals.

But the subcommittee began on an optimistic note; its first
series of hearings in February and March scheduled key executive and legislative figures, including the Secretaries of State,
Labor, and Health, Education, and Welfare, the Attorney General, an Assistant Attorney General, the Surgeon General, and a

former Attorney General, Robert F. Kennedy, who occupied that office when the original bill had been drafted. Supporters of the bill had a number of themes they had to promote to dampen opposition: that national origins damaged our relations with other countries, that the new bill would not open the floodgates and inundate America with illiterate foreigners, that the new-comers would not take jobs away from hungry Americans, that national origins was morally wrong.

Foreign Affairs

The principal proponent of the argument that national origins had seriously damaged United States foreign relations was Secretary of State Dean Rusk. He was accompanied by James J. Hines of the Office of the Legal Adviser, State Department, and Abba P. Schwartz, Administrator of the Bureau of Security and Consular Affairs; these two men were the chief formulators of the State Department's position on the bill.

Ever since Congress had voted to exclude the Japanese, the State Department had been plagued by the foreign repercussions of national origins. Japanese exclusion was such a blow to the nationals of that country that it became a contributing cause of Japan's attack on the United States in 1941. From the mid-1920's, convinced that the United States considered the Japanese an inferior and worthless people, Japan reciprocated the feeling, becoming more and more anti-American during the following decade.

In 1965 the nationals of no country were absolutely refused admission, so the problem of defining the difficulty was more subtle, but no less acute. "We continue to be judged abroad by a basic provision of law which suggests that prospective immigrants are selected on the basis of their national origins," said the Secretary. "I know this to be a fact because I have been approached on a number of occasions by foreign ministers who expressed their belief that this principle discriminates against their countries where, although frequently ignored or overlooked or paid little attention in this country, it proves to be a point of high sensitivity among the other countries who are directly concerned. They were not complaining about numbers but about the principle which they considered discriminatory."

Asked to elaborate, Rusk responded: "We have had formal and most urgent representations by the Governments of Jamaica and Trinidad and Tobago in notes to the United States, and in conversations between their high officials and myself and our high officials in our own government, pointing out the discrimination which they have, perhaps accidentally, fallen into [though they had become independent Western Hemisphere nations, they were still chargeable to the colonial subquotas of their former Eastern Hemisphere governors], and that it is a matter of high sensitivity in their countries. We have also had foreign ministers of other countries who are in a low-quota status—highly restrictive quota status, where there are long backlogs of unfilled immigration applications—tell us that this has become a matter of high sensitivity to them. . . . I would like to emphasize this, however, that in every case they are not saying, 'We are interested in numbers.' They are not saying, 'We are concerned about how many people from outside of the United States you feel it is wise for you to admit. What we are concerned about is the sense that we are different than others, that you look upon us as second- or third-class possibilities, or that you consider your own citizens, who are formerly of our country, as, somehow, second-class citizens.'"

This was the basis of the foreign relations argument. It was never denied by Administration opponents; it was simply talked around. Chief among the sidetrackers was Sam J. Ervin, one of the Senate's most skilled lawyers and dialecticians, a man who argues cases before the Supreme Court while actively pursuing legislative ends in Congress. (The senatorial tradition of advocacy before the bar of the Supreme Court is an old but wavering one, going back at least to the days of Daniel Webster.)

Ervin is noted as a scholar and a gentleman, and though a firm supporter of much of the South's segregationist ways, he is a liberal on other issues of civil rights and individual freedoms. He has demonstrated his sensitivity by his stand on the mounting threat to individual privacy, on military justice, and on many other subjects over which he has jurisdiction as chairman of the subcommittee on constitutional rights.

As the South's representative on the immigration subcommittee, Ervin was prosecutor for his cause. As supporters would later concede, his contribution to the bill was major, and his personal switch was one of the most dramatic in recent history. If most legislative hearings do not change minds but rather reinforce the positions which participants had before they began, here was a major instance of the cumulative weight of testimony bringing one man to question his own beliefs. Throughout, Ervin was a sharp questioner, and he began his probe of national origins by questioning the foreign policy motives of the United States:

> SENATOR ERVIN. Now, aren't we chasing ourselves around in a circle, when we send the Peace Corps abroad in order to lift those people up, and we are spending money for helping undeveloped countries, and then we admit to this country their most skilled people, aren't we leaving them in the fix from which we are trying to extricate them? . . . I am reminded of Aesop's fable where a man was blowing on his hands out in the cold weather and when he was asked what he was blowing on his hands for, he said to warm them. Then when he went into the house, and when they brought his porridge for breakfast, he started blowing on the porridge, and when asked what he was blowing on his porridge for he said to cool it—in effect blowing both hot and cold. And so it is with this Peace Corps, we send the Peace Corps abroad to help and then are encouraging these people to leave those countries and come over here.

The obvious response is that it was very sensible indeed for the man to warm his hands and cool his porridge; different circumstances require different responses. Yet Secretary Rusk was not entirely responsive to Ervin's point. Rusk argued for a "free exchange of talented people" and noted that Ervin's objection "doesn't work an offsetting basis. An increase in trained people all over the world is going on at a very rapid rate." Ervin's point was made again and again by Administration opponents, as well as by Ervin himself, but the cuteness of the metaphor outdid the argument, as the answer was further refined, until Assistant Attorney General Norbert A. Schlei finally made it moot. Schlei, a principal drafter of the Administration bill, forced Ervin during one colloquy in March to an abrupt change of subject:

> SENATOR ERVIN. Do you not see any contradiction in a country like the United States inviting highly skilled people to come here and having a policy which sends out Americans to try to teach skills to people of underdeveloped countries?

> MR. SCHLEI. I think that freedom of movement is a great thing, Senator. People come here only if they want to come and if their government wants to let them, and all we are saying is that if they want to come and their government will let them, they are welcome to come here. There is no way of holding people prisoner around the world if they want to go live somewhere else. I think you have to let them, and I do not see any inconsistency in our immigration policy and our Peace Corps, for example.

> SENATOR ERVIN. . . . I think it is blowing a little bit hot from one side of the mouth and a little bit cold out of the other side of the mouth, though all the blowing is done with the same breath.

> MR. SCHLEI. Senator, whoever enacted the McCarran-Walter Act thought it made sense to have that first preference [for skilled immigrants], at least within national quotas.

> SENATOR ERVIN. I agree.

> MR. SCHLEI. We are simply making it worldwide rather than limited as it is within the national origins system.

> SENATOR ERVIN. I certainly agree that we should have that first preference, but I also say that the first preference in this bill—which is virtually identical with the first preference in the McCarran-Walter Act—does not give us any assurance that we are going to increase to any substantial degree the skilled people coming in under the first preference.

Within one minute, Senator Ervin went from worrying that immigrants would be too skilled for their former countries' own good to worrying that they would not be skilled enough. That the United States was blowing hot and cold was forgotten.

On a broader scale, Senator Robert Kennedy responded during the body of his testimony: "The decisions whether to remain in one's country of birth must always be a matter of individual conscience and decision. The East Germans attempted to justify the Berlin Wall on the grounds that the emigration of highly skilled people was depriving them of a needed national resource. We rightly answered that no such need could justify denying the right of emigration. Second, skills are no longer only a national resource; they belong to, and help, the world. When Einstein, Fermi, Teller, Bethe, Bohr, and their many colleagues came here, they 'deprived' their countries of talent. But the weapons they developed here protect their native lands, protect us, and protect free people everywhere."

A friendly questioner is an invaluable aid in Congressional hearings, for the proper answer can be elicited smoothly and painlessly. With Senators Kennedy, Fong, and Javits, Secretary Rusk was able to present a lucid summary of the debate with the most telling argument to be made throughout the year: that, after all, this new legislation was not really very radical, that its impact would be far more important in correcting an ugly impression of America in the minds of foreigners than it would in encouraging mass migrations as in days gone by:

SENATOR FONG. It is not the numbers, it is the principle?

SECRETARY RUSK. That is correct.

SENATOR FONG. If we say we can only allow five people to come into the United States, but we do not put it on a race basis, they will be satisfied?

SECRETARY RUSK. They may not be entirely happy, but at least they wouldn't be unhappy over the point of discrimination.

SENATOR FONG. They realize, after all, immigration is a matter for us to be concerned about.

SECRETARY RUSK. That is correct, no question about it.

SENATOR FONG. But they feel that if we are going to have a law, let's have a law that is based on equality and justice and fairness.

SECRETARY RUSK. That is correct, sir.

SENATOR FONG. And isn't it a fact that throughout the

history of the United States we have gone forward, we started in 1882 with the first law, it was extended for ten years, it culminated in the 1924 act, in which we barred all Asiatic immigration, and subsequently we allowed the Chinese to be naturalized, and then we had a quota for the Chinese and then we allowed the Indians and Burmese to be naturalized, and isn't it a fact that we have come a long way in our immigration laws?

SECRETARY RUSK. Yes indeed.

SENATOR FONG. Isn't this the last mile that we are trying to travel now, to eliminate all vestiges of discrimination in our land?

SECRETARY RUSK. That is correct, Senator. Let me, if I may, take just a moment, in addition to the point that you have made very well. Our actual practice, in this postwar period, has been much better, from the point of view of our attitude toward the rest of the world than has been the underlying theory of our law. You see, only 34 percent of the permanent immigrants who came to the United States in the last decade have come under the quota system. The Congress itself has performed an immigration service far beyond that which would be called for by the narrow application of the principles of the basic law. So that one of the things that we would like to do is to get this underlying principle of the law brought into conformity to the way we have acted during this postwar period.

SENATOR FONG. So we are actually not doing anything radically different from what we have done; is that correct?

SECRETARY RUSK. That is correct, sir.

Labor and Employment Problems

The great bugaboo of the twenties, aside from a dislike of subversive and inferior races, was the dread that America could not absorb massive migrations of immigrants. More immigrants meant more competition for jobs, lower wages, and a general depression of the national economy. From the earliest essays against the Chinese, this had been a prime theme in the restrictionist movement. Its temper may have softened, especially since the American Federation of Labor in 1946 had reversed its position and welcomed skilled immigrants to the land of labor shortage, but supporters of the bill felt that the argument had retained its vigor, and it was therefore crucial to rebut the assertion, constantly made, that immigration reform would loose the floodtides once again.

Secretary of Labor W. Willard Wirtz led off. "Of the 1959–62 annual average of 97,600 quota immigrants, an average of approximately 48,600 were added to our labor force each year. The rest of the number have been housewives, children, and others with no indicated occupation. Under S. 500 [the Administration's Senate bill] when it is fully operative in its fifth year, it is estimated that nearly 60 percent of increased admissions due to full use of the 165,800 quota will likewise be nonworkers. This means that an additional yearly number of about 23,900 quota immigrants would be expected to enter the labor force. In a total force that is estimated to reach 86 million by 1970, the yearly addition of 23,900 would have no appreciable impact. Qualitatively, the increased immigration of persons of high education, specialized experience, exceptional ability or capable of filling labor shortages could be beneficial."

If they would not have an appreciable quantitative economic impact generally, still less would they take individual jobs away from American workers: "Nobody is more acutely aware than we are, all of us here, of the impact of the fact that there are between 3.5 and 4 million people unemployed in this country. We have been a little the victims of our generalization about that. Despite the fact that there are 3.5 to 4 million people unemployed in this country, there are very real needs in the work force today, and, to a considerable extent, those would-be immigrants under this bill would fit into that need area. We are short in a number of categories. . . . I point to the fact that under the present law approximately 8,800 quota immigrants entering the labor force annually are professional and technical workers. We need professional and technical workers. Another 8,600 are craftsmen, foremen, and kindred workers. We need people of that kind. . . . What this proposal would do . . . would be to increase the opportunities for workers with needed abilities to come in under the quota." In a word, the unemployed citizens and the skilled immigrants are not interchangeable; an unemployed general construction worker does not become a doctor, and doctors are in short supply.

Secretary Wirtz emphasized the change that the proposed bill would bring. Under McCarran-Walter, the first-preference, skilled immigrants had to prove that they had a *specific* job awaiting them, a difficult requirement to meet since the employer in most cases had to agree to hire the immigrant sight unseen. In fact, the requirement was a dodge, simply another way to restrict the flow of immigrants. The proposed bill would admit a skilled immigrant, without a specific job prospect, as long as his skills conformed to a list prepared by the Department of Labor, which would ensure that his abilities were "especially advantageous to" the United States.

Senator Ervin expressed the fears of the restrictionists; does not the change in fact remove the "pretty good guarantee they will not come over here and take a job from somebody?" Not at all, responded Wirtz, for a chemist does not compete in the market for steelworkers. It was not much remarked on by either side that a doctor who by state law is ineligible to practice medicine while awaiting citizenship may well compete in the labor market of lesser skills.

Senator Fong brought out the positive aspect of skilled immigration. "I once read," he remarked to Secretary Wirtz, "that a doctor of philosophy is backstopped by 10 engineers, and the 10 engineers employ 50 to 150 skilled workers." To which Wirtz added: "The other side of the same point is equally important. We have Ph.D.'s today who are doing a lot of work for which they ought to have assistance. . . . We have a very real shortage at the sub-Ph.D. level and we are today wasting a good many of the talents and the time of our most skilled people because we have a shortage at the second level."

Still another point raised by the Senator from Hawaii was that in getting a foreign doctor, America was attracting a resource for which it did not have to pay training costs. "A doctor," said the Secretary of Labor, "costs, and I will get a better answer for the record, but it is about $35,000. I guess we would both agree that the value of the resource is much greater than that. That is the cost of it, but the resource is all that that doctor would do for hundreds of people during his service. I agree with your point."

One week later, Hugh Scott, the Republican Senator from Pennsylvania, underscored the issues raised by Fong and Wirtz. Ervin asked whether he thought it wise to admit immigrants in view of the fact that the President of the United States had officially declared a belt of poverty running from Scott's state through Ervin's. "Well, sir," Scott replied, "I came from a state which had quite substantial unemployment, greater than the national average, and whose unemployment is now less than the national average, and I know of many instances where recent immigrants have come over here say twenty years ago, twenty-five years ago, established plants and businesses, quite a lot of them around Wilkes-Barre and Scranton, for example, in the clothing business. There are others all through Pennsylvania whose arrival in this country twenty years later meant the employment of a great many native white Americans, and I would say that immigration as far as Pennsylvania is concerned has provided a source of employment rather than a contribution to unemployment." As often happened, Ervin's perhaps crafty, perhaps unthinking, confusion of general limitation with national origins backfired. Senator Scott was willing to admit that there should be a general limitation, but showed that even McCarran-Walter allowed skilled immigrants, that these immigrants had not damaged the economy, that the new bill would not bring in enough more to upset the economy, and that in any case none of this had anything to do with national origins. As Secretary Wirtz had earlier testified, the employability of a skilled individual does not depend on his country of birth.

The final argument against skilled immigrants was self-defeating. Senator Ervin worried that "a man could be brought in to do work because of a shortage, and the very day he gets here if he finds the wages a little better, the working conditions a little improved in some other occupation which he is capable of performing, then he can enter competition for employment in that occupation no matter how many Americans are available."

That must be a remote possibility, however. The more skilled a person, the less likely he will be able to secure work in another specialty. A tailor will not be an adept laboratory technician; and he will be unlikely to compete for such a job the next day. Any job for which he can compete, if it entails lesser skills, is highly unlikely to pay more. So he is likely to remain in the field in which he was trained. And if at the margin there is some job competition, as long as he is not working more cheaply than native Americans, it is an exceedingly anticapitalistic position to deny him the job.

Discrimination

It was on the question of discrimination and the related issue of the immigrant contribution to America that Senator Ervin had the most trouble. He hammered at the point that any classification is discriminatory in some sense; but he never let on that he understood some discriminations to be more offensive than others. Yet the barrage of evidence from witnesses that the national origins system was discriminatory was enough eventually to convert even Ervin. Because of his great desire to be consistent above all, he helped forge the compromise that let the bill through.

The evidence of discrimination was strong; as Senator Robert Kennedy said: "Last year I noted that a maid or an unskilled laborer from a northern European country can enter this country within a matter of weeks, while scientists or doctors or other highly skilled persons from less favored countries wait for months and years.

"Since I spoke then, about 3,000 more housemaids and unskilled laborers from northern Europe have come here. And the doctors and chemists and biologists are still waiting.

"And others are waiting as well—American citizens, waiting for their parents and brothers and children. An American citizen whose mother is Greek must wait more than five years before she can get a visa. An American citizen whose brother, or sister, or married son or daughter is Italian or Australian, Spanish or Portuguese, Japanese or Korean, Indian or Filipino, cannot expect a visa for them until Congress passes a special bill. The last such bill, passed in 1962, admitted all such relatives who had first applied more than eight years earlier.

"A system which allows an American citizen to bring to this country a maid or a gardener overnight—but forces him to wait eight years for his sister—makes no sense at all."

Other testimony indicated that some immigrants from Japan and Turkey faced waiting periods in 1965 of up to 322 years. The only reason for their wait: their national origin.

Furthermore, the rigidity in the system made the discrimination exceedingly cruel. One case of many cited shows the point. A naturalized citizen living in Providence, Rhode Island, wished to send for his daughter from Italy, following the death of her husband there. The daughter was eligible for a second-preference visa but her three minor children were not; were the mother to come she would endure at least a four-year separation from them. The system forced a choice between reunion in America with her father who would support her, or remaining behind with her children.

Ervin tried his best:

> SENATOR ERVIN. This bill would say to the people in the British Isles, for example, no more is your maximum quota possible. Under this bill it shall be identical with the maximum possible quota of Indonesia, would it not?

> MR. SCHLEI. Yes; fundamentally, that is true.

> SENATOR ERVIN. Now an Englishman might well say, "Well, it is discrimination against me to say that the privilege of an Englishman to go to America should be identical with that of an Indonesian." Could he not say that just as well as you say there is discrimination now?

Of course, so might it be argued that letting the black man vote discriminates against the white man, because now the white vote will be worth proportionately less than it was before. But that would be a curious definition of discrimination. As curious as the statement which the racist philosopher H. S. Chamberlain made in the last century that the Italian Dante was obviously "Teutonic" because Martin Luther had a "powerful head which in every particular is the very opposite of Dante's and by this very fact betrays the intimate relationship."

Ervin plugged away: "You read in the paper about the demonstration at the American Embassy in Moscow yesterday, did you not?"

Mr. Schlei. Yes, I did, sir.

Senator Ervin. Do you not rejoice in the fact that Americans do not resort to demonstrations of that kind against the embassies of other countries?

Mr. Schlei. Generally speaking, sir, I do.

Senator Ervin. And do you not agree that the people of England and Ireland and Germany do not participate in exhibitions of that kind at embassies of other countries?

Mr. Schlei. Yes, sir.

Senator Ervin. Would that not indicate that perhaps the people of Ireland, England, and Germany have got a higher respect for law than some of other nations?

Mr. Schlei. I think things that happen in the Soviet Union have a very low evidentiary value. I think that sometimes things happen over there because the government directs that they happen.

Senator Ervin. Yes, and as a matter of fact this bill would say to the people of that country that the same quota would be applied to them as the people of England, Germany, or Ireland.

Secretary Celebrezze. I think Christ would be excluded under the present law, Senator.

Senator Ervin. He would be excluded under this bill even if He came from a country whose quota was not exhausted because of His poverty.

Secretary Celebrezze. No, not necessarily. You forget that He was a pretty good carpenter.

Senator Ervin. Yes; but He would have been excluded under this bill because of His poverty. He couldn't pay the head tax.

Senator Ervin. Now everybody says this bill provides for equality. It would put the same limit on the number of immigrants from the Chinese Republic as it puts on Greece, which means that a Greek would have an eighty-three times better chance to come to America than a person residing in the Republic of China. Don't you think the people of China could very well say that is a discrimination against them? That shows that the United States would prefer a person of Greek origin eighty-three times above a person of Chinese origin.

MR. [NICHOLAS S.] LIMPERIS. If that is the effect of the calculation, prima facie, yes. I don't know as to the figures.

SENATOR ERVIN. That is the reason I can't go along with the idea that this bill eliminates the discrimination.

Another tack the Senator from North Carolina took was the observation that a mathematical formula cannot be discriminatory; at the least, it is less discriminatory than the new system which would substitute the judgment of the foreign consul whether the immigrant was really qualified (although Ervin neglected to note that, as we shall see, the consul would have to make this determination under either law).

SENATOR ERVIN. Anyway, under the McCarran-Walter Act, the quota of each nation is determined by a mathematical formula, is it not?

MR. [JAMES B.] CAREY. It is a discriminatory formula.

SENATOR ERVIN. But it is a mathematical formula.

MR. CAREY. It is based on the superiority of the Anglo-Saxon group of which I am a member and it is unfair; it is undemocratic and it is an insult to people throughout the rest of the world.

SENATOR ERVIN. Yes. I understand that, Mr. Carey, but still it is a mathematical formula, is that not so, whether it is the most outrageous one in the world or not?

MR. CAREY. There are a lot of things that can be done, Senator, in the name of mathematics.

The mathematics of the system so pleased the Senator that he came up with what must pass as the most ingenious justification for national origins ever propounded. "If the United States admitted each year on the basis of the immigration law the total number of immigrants it was going to admit, Congress would be very reluctant to pass any special legislation to admit people in case of emergency. That is one of the greatest arguments I know for having our basic immigration law restrict immigration: it enables Congress in the cases of emergencies to pass special legislation to deal with them." As if 154,000 immigrants annually were a magic number, on which the President's Council of Economic Advisers swore; as if national origins is the only way to arrive at restricted immigration. Still, he persisted:

SENATOR ERVIN. Well, even under the national origins quota system, people are admitted to the United States on exactly the same basis; namely, on the basis of one-sixth of one percent to their contribution to the population of America.

MR. [JUDGE JUVENAL] MARCHISIO. However, no one is so naive as to believe that that formula was predicated only for the purpose of limiting it, but to keep out people who are not of Anglo-Saxon origin, and even the proponents of it in 1924 in urging its passage said that such formula would preserve—which it has not—the percentage of superiority in this country of Nordic races—the same thing that Hitler in 1937, in addressing the German Reichstag, in a speech to them, quoted our 1924 National Origins Act as proof that the people of America believed in his theory of racial supremacy.

There were two points Senator Ervin did not come to grips with. First, the question of validity of the mathematics that went into the formula. As Senator Paul Douglas of Illinois reminded the committee: "In 1924 it was decided to apportion the quotas according to the composition of our population in 1920. Well, how did they determine the composition of population in 1920? They went over the census schedules and those who had what they regarded as English, Irish, or Scottish names were listed as English, Irish, and Scottish. And similarly with the Germans. Now, of course, what had been going on during this time had been that those with polysyllabic names from eastern Europe and from Greece had, in very large numbers, changed and shortened their names, and had adopted anglicized names. As a result, we had enormous numbers, no one can quite tell how many, of eastern Europeans, southern Europeans, and southeastern Europeans listed as Englishmen, Irishmen, Scots, and the rest. So the very basis of that apportionment of nationality quotas was biased and wrong."

Second, no matter how much obfuscation was indulged in, it was impossible to deny the discrimination inherent in McCarran-Walter's treatment of Asians and Negroes. In 1920, the population of the United States was 105,710,620. Yet the basis of national origins was 94,800,000. In the following colloquy, Senator Ervin seemed loathe to interrupt:

SENATOR FONG. Senator Douglas, I do not believe that the statement by Senator McCarran, that the bill is not anti-Semitic nor antireligious, went far enough. He certainly had a discriminatory feature in the bill when he said that, for example, an East Indian, whose family migrated to England for five generations, would be attributable to the Indian rather than to the English quota.

SENATOR DOUGLAS. It was definitely anti-Oriental. . . .

SENATOR FONG. In fact, that a person of Asian or Pacific ancestry who is found in the Western Hemisphere, for example, and whose family had been there for generations, or in any part of Europe, is not attributable to the country in which he is born, is certainly discriminatory.

SENATOR DOUGLAS. That is correct. And of course there are large numbers of Orientals in the islands of the Caribbean.

SENATOR FONG. So the Walter-McCarran Act is a very discriminatory act as far as it relates to the Asia-Pacific Triangle.

SENATOR DOUGLAS. I do not want to say anything against Senator McCarran, but I was in the Senate when he introduced the bill and I heard his opening speech, and I think you will find this in the *Record*, unless he took it out of the *Record* before publication. He said he wanted to prevent, "polluting the bloodstream of the United States." I do not regard Greeks or Italians or Poles or Japanese or

Chinese, if selected on the basis of keeping out criminals, keeping out subversives, and the rest—I do not regard them as polluting the bloodstream of this country.

SENATOR ERVIN. If the Senator will yield.

SENATOR FONG. I yield.

SENATOR ERVIN. I believe I read some of Senator Mc-Carran's speeches in the last few days, and I believe when Senator McCarran was talking about that, he was talking simply about the provisions of the act which excluded certain persons who had criminal records and subversives and not about people generally. I believe the Senator will find that. I read the speech.

SENATOR DOUGLAS. You can make any defense you wish, but I heard that remark, and I noticed the gleam in his eye as he said it, because I was sitting just two feet from him.

Contribution and Assimilation

Closely allied to the question of discrimination is its intended justification. Discriminations which are reasonable, after all, can legitimately serve as the basis for legislation. If Senator Ervin could not dissuade others from the belief that national origins was discriminatory, perhaps he could at least justify it.

The first half of the justification was an attempt to prove that the national origins system was based on the "contribution" that peoples of various nationalities made to the United States. It was not always clear how Ervin determined this, but most of the time it was apparent that the greatness of the contribution was to be measured purely by the number of people who came from each country; the greater the number, obviously the greater the contribution.

SENATOR ERVIN. Mr. Secretary, as a matter of fact, do you know of any people in the world that have contributed more to making America than those particular ethnic groups that I mentioned and that are singled out for preference in the McCarran-Walter Act?

SECRETARY RUSK. I think, sir, the very fact that we are, perhaps 60 million of us, directly traceable to British origin means that to that extent those 60 million have contributed to the country, that is true.

SENATOR ERVIN. In other words, you take the English-speaking people, they gave us our language, they gave us our common law, they gave a large part of our political philosophy. . . .

SECRETARY RUSK. We have been enriched by contributions in science, the arts, letters, culture, from all over the world. Now, these are important contributions, but the Greeks themselves made a very decisive contribution in the very early stages that is not reflected.

SENATOR ERVIN. The reason I say this bill is discriminatory against those people is because it puts them on exactly the same plane as the people of Ethiopia are put, where the people of Ethiopia have the same right to come to the United States under this bill as the people from England, the people of France, the people of Germany, the people of Holland, and I don't think—with all due respect to Ethiopia —I don't know of any contributions that Ethiopia has made to the making of America.

SENATOR RUSK. Senator, the issue is not, as I see it, whether they come from Ethiopia, but who is the man, what is he like, what is his character, what are his capabilities, will he make a good citizen—not whether he came from Britain or Ethiopia, but what can he contribute here, and whether he would make a good citizen. We cannot, by any stretch of the imagination say that the twenty million Negroes here in this country have not made an enormous contribution to all aspects of American life.

SENATOR ERVIN. The point I am making is, we discriminate every day in every phase of life, we make discriminations in law, we make them in our personal actions, we discriminate in our opinions, on what kind of folks we are, we discriminate by the girls we marry, choose one and object to the choice of another, or they object to us. Now, it seems to me, this so-called discrimination—in some aspects, a smear word—this discrimination that you speak of, we all have it, a man of great intellect is able to distinguish between different things. Now, what is wrong with that, what harm is there in discriminating if it is discriminating in favor of people that have made a great contribution to America, that have developed America, in preference to people that have done nothing for America?

Secretary Rusk. Well, we are not challenging the importance of distinguishing in our immigration policy to give first preference to those who have special talents and skills and may make a special contribution to the country. . . . We still will maintain the distinguishing features so that we can select among classes and groups to give preference in terms of individuals in this country, but not on the basis of race or national origin.

Senator Ervin. The bill starts out with discrimination, because it gives first claim to those who are gifted, and it discriminates in their favor against those who are not gifted. So there is a discrimination. Personally, I don't see any harm in giving a preference to people who belong to ethnic groups which make America.

Senator Ervin. Would you say that these people [from middle and southern Europe] have made as great a contribution to the United States as people from the British Isles?

Senator Kennedy of New York. I am not in any position to tell. I think we can make a study of it together, but I am not in any position to tell.

Senator Ervin. The people of the British Isles gave us our language, did they not, the language spoken in the United States, the language in which our laws are written?

Senator Kennedy of New York. I suppose if you take that from the British Isles, you can say it was the people from Norway, Sweden, Normandy, and Germany.

Senator Ervin. Did the British not give us much of

our legal system which you were extolling so eloquently a while ago, habeas corpus rule and so on?

SENATOR KENNEDY of New York. Are you talking about England, about the Magna Carta, or are you talking about what has been done here by the immigrants? Are you talking about the establishment of Jamestown? The work that was done in Jamestown? It was done mainly by six people from Poland.

SENATOR ERVIN. I have not said, Mr. Secretary, that those people did not make contributions.

SECRETARY CELEBREZZE. The difference is, Senator, that I have seen the struggle these people have had. I have seen these people. They were brought here, if you please, because there was a shortage in unskilled labor. I have seen these people break their backs for twelve hours a day and to say to them as a nationality that this group has contributed more to America than they have is wrong, because you do not contribute to America, to the good of this country, by numbers alone. One person of Polish origin can contribute much more in certain instances than 100 people of English origin and I say on the other hand one person of English ancestry sometimes contributes more than 100 people of Polish or Italian ancestry. The basic philosophy, the basis from which you start, Senator, is wrong and you build greater wrongs on top of it.

ATTORNEY GENERAL KATZENBACH. Do you think, Senator, that a maid from Ireland will contribute more to the United States than a trained doctor from an Asian country?

SENATOR ERVIN. I think Ireland has made an excellent contribution to our country, including Governors and Senators, two of whom are present.

SENATOR KENNEDY. Thank you.

SENATOR ERVIN. Frankly, if it comes down to the choice of people from the Congo and those from Ireland, I am going to discriminate in favor of the people from Ireland because they have made the greater contribution.

SENATOR ERVIN. You certainly do not gainsay the fact that these people made the greatest contribution to our population?

MR. [DAVID] CARLINER. Now, here again, you mean in terms of the numbers of people, they made the greatest contribution?

SENATOR ERVIN. Yes; that is what the McCarran-Walter Act put it on, the numbers of people they contributed.

MR. CARLINER. Well, they made the greatest contribution in terms of numbers. That is what we are complaining about.

SENATOR ERVIN. Since they made the greatest contribution in terms of numbers, they made the greatest contribution necessarily to the settlement of the country, did they not?

MR. CARLINER. In terms of numbers.

SENATOR ERVIN. Well, yes; that is the way it is counted?

MR. CARLINER. Yes.

This approach was obviously not conducive to sharp distinctions. If you can state a position on which people of philosophically opposite positions can agree, you have probably not stated a very great profundity. It remains to try to justify discriminations against aliens on the basis of their relative assimilabilities. Senator Ervin threw out the bait, but few were willing to bite:

SENATOR ERVIN. History teaches me that a person of Hellenic descent is very readily assimilated into American life.

MR. LIMPERIS. That is correct.

SENATOR ERVIN. And that the people of Greek descent are dispersed throughout this nation, and they do not live in communities to themselves like the people of so many other nations who have come. And also it teaches me that they can be readily assimilated. Now, do you think that a person who has had no experience in self-government and no particular desire for self-government is as readily assimilated into the American way of life as a person of Hellenic descent who does have those capacities?

MR. LIMPERIS. No, sir; but I believe that he can be assimilated into the system. This is the attraction of my country.

SENATOR ERVIN. This thing would give Russia the same maximum quota that we would give Italy or any other country.

MR. [JOSEPH A. L.] ERRIGO. Why not? What is wrong with the Russian people? We fight the Russian Government, not the Russian people. Our relationship with the Russian—

SENATOR ERVIN. I really believe that a people that have been living under a totalitarian government like Russia are less experienced in government than the people in the United States and for that reason I would be in favor of giving a favored quota somewhere else rather than enlarging the Russian quota.

MR. ERRIGO. I would say, Senator, if you check your history, you will find out that the most downtrodden people of the world have been the Irish people, and you won't find any nation more democratic than the Irish.

SENATOR ERVIN. I have always heard that the Irish ruled all the countries on earth except Ireland.

Other examples of the assimilability of the world's peoples were discussed, too numerous to mention here. Perhaps it is not entirely a quirk of America but a pattern of life everywhere that we have a penchant for one-word or simple-minded explanations, without which we remain unsatisfied. Senator Ervin required such one-word answers. Thus he asked whether Indonesians will assimilate more quickly than Irishmen, and expected an answer. The very question was absurd given the answer that was required, for the Indonesian chemist who speaks English may assimilate far more rapidly than the Irish mill-hand who moves to New York City. The answer Senator Ervin sought is not to be found in the question, as he supposed. To the kind of contribution immigrants would make in the

future the Senator did not address himself, concerned as he
was with the contributions made in the past.

Western Hemisphere Immigration

On one issue Senator Ervin seemed to hold the upper
hand, at least from a debater's point of view. That was the
question whether to impose a numerical limitation on Western
Hemisphere immigration, which had been exempted from
quotas even during the height of the racist fervor. It was
Ervin's contention that if he were to accept the argument
that national origins was discriminatory because it said some
people were better than others, the new system would have
to be applied to the Western Hemisphere, because the old
system said they were the best peoples of all.

> SENATOR ERVIN. I am just wondering if your observa-
> tion about the fact that there is room for expansion in the
> Western Hemisphere, whereas there is less room for expan-
> sion in the other areas of the earth, does not make the
> discrimination in favor of the Western Hemisphere as
> against these other areas even a worse discrimination
> since you are basing this matter on the cause of justice.
> In other words, you are going to discriminate against
> people where they are overpopulated, but you are going
> to give special preference to those where there is no over-
> population and room for air.

> ATTORNEY GENERAL KATZENBACH. I would not and
> have not characterized it as discrimination. I think of it
> this way, Senator; I think that the United States at this
> stage in our development is justified in having an immi-
> gration policy which limits the number of immigrants that
> come into this country. This is true to protect the employ-
> ment status and it is true to protect our national objec-
> tives. . . . I think if you are restricting immigration, you
> are doing it because of a national policy that says you
> cannot absorb hundreds and thousands and millions of
> immigrants without doing damage to your own national
> economy. That is not a problem as far as the Western
> Hemisphere is concerned because the bulk of that immi-

gration comes from Mexico and from Canada. . . . If there were great numbers who were coming to the United States from the Western Hemisphere, then it would seem to me that the matter would have sufficient seriousness to attempt to restrict immigration from those countries. In the interim, it seems to me it is not a practical matter. Other countries have not objected to this or characterized it as a discrimination. It is part of a good neighbor policy and part of our interest in Latin America to promote this kind of freedom. I think that it helps our foreign policy objectives to do that.

SENATOR ERVIN. Do you not think it is a discrimination against all the people in the Eastern Hemisphere to say to them that they have to come in under a very small quota system, but that everybody in the Western Hemisphere can move into the United States provided they have good health and are not subversive?

SECRETARY WIRTZ. I would use a different word than "discrimination." There is surely a difference in the treatment, and on the broad universal logic I suppose you would have trouble drawing that line. I still have enough of the impulse which you suggest to want to see our relationships with Canada and some of the others treated differently. I do not think anybody's mind is free of all cant or prejudice.

SENATOR ERVIN. What can you call it, Mr. Secretary?

SECRETARY WIRTZ. I would call it difference, Senator.

This kind of admission would have had small effect had it not been highlighted by the fact that proponents of abolition sought a change in the status of two countries—Jamaica and Trinidad-Tobago—which had recently achieved independent status. These islands were excluded from an existing law which provided nonquota status for Western Hemisphere countries which became independent. In asking that the two members of the British Commonwealth be granted nonquota status, the sponsors of S. 500 raised anew the entire question of the Western Hemisphere's general exemption. Although Secretary Rusk and others assured the subcommittee that Eastern Hemisphere countries did not feel aggrieved at the Western Hemisphere's special right in this connection, the point was open to doubt, and it provided a wedge for compromise.

The Opposition

In view of the vehemence of past opposition, it was surprising in a sense how little the present opposition counted. Two factors accounted for its lessening importance. First, almost all "respectable" groups representing large numbers of Americans sided with proponents of repeal. Most professional economists, businessmen, and labor groups saw no danger in the Administration's proposals. The AFL-CIO's chief representative, James L. Carey, so stated. Every immigrant group rallied behind the Administration. There were no dissenting government officials.

Only the relatively few professional restrictionist groups remained. Many of these groups, such as the American Legion and the Daughters of the American Revolution, though widely respected for their work in other areas, had long held such uniformly negative views on changing immigration policy that their automatic response to this legislation did not seem to affect many politicians. The other groups, such as the New Jersey Coalition, the Maryland Coalition of Patriotic Societies, and the League of Christian Women, simply did not command enough support.

In the second place, much of their opposition had been neutralized by the solicitous attention Senator Edward Kennedy paid their leaders. He invited them to his office and to lunch to seek their views. It was not the flattery implicit in such meetings alone that conditioned these groups. Senator Kennedy made a patient and strong pitch for their understanding. Most left his office unconvinced, but enough aware of the problems to admit, "Yes, it doesn't work, does it; we need a new system, don't we?" Although many of these groups testified in their usual bellicose tones, they did almost nothing to stir up feeling across the land. John Trevor, Jr., who has taken his father's place as head of the American Coalition of Patriotic

Societies, faced a different climate of opinion entirely. Still, the opinions presented at the hearings were almost as colorful as they had been in their heyday:

IRRELEVANCE: "Liberty Lobby does not believe that the function of a diplomat is to run around apologizing for the imaginary faults of this country. If our immigration law, with all its loopholes and exceptions, is to be referred to by our own Attorney General as "cruel" and "outrageous," what term then is left to describe the Berlin Wall, the genocide of Tibet, or the prisons of Castro Cuba?"

DISTORTION: "Can [our diplomats] not answer that the law, in fact, does not choose, at all, but is based on a completely objective, statistical census? And that the census on which it was based was not just arbitrarily or carefully selected, but was the latest census available at the time the law was passed?" (Liberty Lobby)

COMMUNISM: "Are those right who say that the U.S. State Department is more important in protecting and promoting the interests of communism than the Communists? When in the world's history has a nation so widely opened its gates to a Trojan horse and welcomed the enemies within?" (National Economic Council, Inc.)

INGRATITUDE: "We should remember that people accustomed to such marginal existence in their own land will tend to live fully here, to hoard our bounteous minimum wages and our humanitarian welfare handouts, and then either send their savings abroad or go back with them to live like princes in their native land." (New Jersey Coalition)

GUILT BY ASSOCIATION: "Not to be ignored is the further fact that the breakdown of the Immigration and Nationality Act of 1952 has been one of the major objectives of the Communists since this legislation was passed. . . . There may well be some embarrassment to proponents of weakening amendments when it is recalled that, according to the House Committee on Un-American Activities, the Communist party has created, and now controls in fifteen key states, 180 'front' organizations dedicated exclusively to the purpose of creating 'grassroots' support in Congress to destroy the act—which is what most of the proposed amendments would do." (Daughters of the American Revolution)

SCARE: You who wish to use immigrants in the United States do not love your country for which it stands. You love power. You force integration with the excuse of serving humanity—all must be 50–50. The average white citizen is losing his right to your phony cause. Those of you who serve the 'humanitarian' cause by using Freudian propaganda, create a huge guilt complex among our Americans. You are condoning the most inhumane practice by trying to destroy a nation's beautiful culture and personality, to replace it with ignorance, crime, disease, and greed. Any philosophy we read or follow—be it Hebrew, communism, Christianity, law of survival, cannibalism, 'King Lutherism,' atheism or—perhaps simply, the straight history of all nations; we know that one culture is destined to change under the infiltration of foreign culture, be it high or low." (Baltimore Anti-Communist League in Affiliation with the Catholic Anti-Communist Committee of Baltimore)

IGNORANCE: "Virtually every argument that I have seen in behalf of the Hart-Celler bill, which seeks to abolish the national origins quota and admit immigrants to America in the ratio to their proportion to the world's population, is an inapplicable slogan." (Federation of Republican Women, Atlanta)

RABID FEAR: "In the beginning this country happens to have been settled chiefly by Nordic types. . . . Must we deliver these legacies to the hordes of Red Chinese, Indians, Congolese cannibals just to disclaim having any pride in our identity as a nation?" (Federation of Republican Women)

Through eleven days of such testimony, the subcommittee was unfailingly polite. In part the subcommittee's consideration was due to the fact that rarely were more than two members present; usually only one Senator attended, solely for the purpose of allowing others to have their say. Senator Eastland had declared that these were to be "open" hearings—anyone who desired could file an intention to testify with the subcommittee and would be permitted to present his case.

Sometimes the case was very brief, a single statement of the group's resolution. One lady on behalf of the Sons and Daughters of Liberty, after reading the short resolution, said, "That is the view of the order and it is purely personal in a way—not my own—I am with the folks, of course, but I do think—I am very green on most of these subjects and I don't know why they picked me to come here, but thank you." To which Senator Kennedy responded: "We are delighted to have you here. Could you tell me what your membership is?" "Well," she replied, "our membership in the District at this time is around, I think it is ninety-six."

Sometimes the witness was not at all sure what the subject of the hearings was and cared little; he or she had a pet peeve on which to expound. One such lady, on her own behalf, began: "I am opposed to any change in the McCarran-Walter immigration law which will allow more people to enter this country. Indeed after hearing my paper on the serious condition of our water situation, you may agree with me that we should have emigration for a while instead of immigration." Then she launched into a dissertation about the United States water pollution crisis. Senator Kennedy seemed nonplussed:

> SENATOR KENNEDY. I share your concern about that. But I don't feel that adjusting our immigration policy to provide a greater equity in its administration and in its disposition is directly related to the problem, as significant and as serious as it is, of the pollution of our streams and air.
>
> MRS. WILLIAMS. Well, I don't know of a better reason for keeping people out of the country than that. Water is as important to us as food.
>
> SENATOR KENNEDY. I certainly share that.
>
> MRS. WILLIAMS. And polluted water can cause disease and everything. Dreadful.

The remainder of her statement was printed in the record, but not received as testimony. With some difficulty, Senator Kennedy persuaded her to leave the hearing room.

From such testimony as the foregoing, it is evident that the opposition mounted a puerile attack at best. At worst, it conceded defeat. The American Coalition of Patriotic Societies, for instance, introduced a formal resolution calling for strict maintenance of national origins and at the same time its representative testified that the American Coalition supported the House bill being pushed by Representative Feighan, a bill which did away with national origins. Admitted the American Coalition's representative, "It becomes more apparent that the quota system has been reduced to a deceptive myth." In the afterglow of the 1964 elections, at a time when the 89th Congress was in the midst of enacting Great Society legislation, the spirit of the 1920's had collapsed.

IN THE HOUSE

Subcommittee No. 1 of the House Judiciary Committee held hearings simultaneously with the Senate. Although many of the witnesses were the same, a somewhat different parliamentary situation prevailed within the committee. Five new members were added and one old member was dropped, giving a 5 to 4 margin in favor of the Hart-Celler bill. It was thought Subcommittee Chairman Feighan was somewhat chastened by a primary battle for his seat; his failure to support a change in the national origins system the year before had cost him support back home. Now he began hearings determined to make some changes. During the spring while the House hearings continued, Feighan had several talks with the President. These conferences led to Feighan's own bill, submitted on June 1.

The Feighan bill differed substantially from the Administration proposal. It did not include a Western Hemisphere quota, but it eliminated the five-year transition period and imposed a total numerical limitation on each country of 20,000, rather than the 10 percent proposed by the Hart-Celler bill. Feighan reversed the order of preference, placing relatives ahead of highly skilled and professional people. His bill included many labor unions' requests, the most important of which was that an immigrant who came under one of the labor preferences would first have to be granted a certificate by the Secretary of Labor attesting to the fact that the immigrant would not be taking away a job from citizen workers. This was perhaps more restrictive than the old law which required merely that an immigrant could not enter if he did not have a job. Still, the Feighan proposal would mean a lessening of the burden on the immigrant in most cases.

The subcommittee on July 22 reported a blend of the original Celler bill and the newer Feighan bill to the full committee. A week later in the full committee, a dissident member of the subcommittee, Clark MacGregor, a Republican of Minnesota, proposed a Western Hemisphere limitation of 115,000. He was beaten 22 to 11 and the next week the Judiciary Committee reported out its immigration bill, H.R. 2580, 27 to 4. The bill abolished the Asia-Pacific Triangle immediately. It reduced the five-year transition period for the abolition of national origins to three years, authorized the redistribution of unused quotas to oversubscribed countries during the three-year period, and provided a 20,000 limit on immigrants annually from any one country. In addition to numerous other provisions, it established an eight-tier preference system within the Eastern Hemisphere total of 170,000 per year, to which the Senate later concurred:

(1) 20 percent for adult, unmarried children of U.S. citizens;

(2) 20 percent for spouses and unmarried children of resident aliens, plus any unused amounts of the first preference;

(3) 10 percent for "qualified immigrants who are members of the professions, or who because of their exceptional ability in the sciences or the arts will substantially benefit prospectively the national economy, cultural interests, or welfare of the United States." This preference is *not* entitled to unused portions of the first two preferences.

(4) 10 percent for married children of citizens, plus unused portions of the first through third preferences;

(5) 24 percent for brothers or sisters of citizens, plus unused portions of first through fourth preferences;

(6) 10 percent for "qualified immigrants who are capable of performing specified skilled or unskilled labor, not of a temporary or seasonal nature, for which a shortage of employable and willing persons exists in the United States;"

(7) 6 percent for refugees from communism, countries in the Middle East [or from "catastrophic natural calamities"; a provision later added by the Senate and concurred in by the House]; half this number may be used to adjust the status of refugees already in the United States for two years;

(8) any of the 170,000 places still left are to go to applicants otherwise qualified (*e.g.*, not subversive) under the terms of the existing Immigration and Naturalization Act.

On August 25 the House of Representatives passed the bill by a lopsided margin of 318 to 95, rejecting after initially accepting a MacGregor amendment to provide a Western Hemisphere limitation. Representative Emanuel Celler, in calling for the historic vote, said that he had "inveighed against this national origins theory away back in 1924. I made a speech then against this theory. I am glad I am living today and have lived to see that my theories have been vindicated, that we are now to obliterate and nullify and cancel out this abomination called the national theory of immigration."

During the weeks just gone by, Celler had been engaged in a continuation of his feud with Feighan, and some observers thought the dispute might jeopardize the entire bill. Feighan had requested and received in the House legislative appropriations bill $120,000 to reactivate the Joint Committee on Immigration and Naturalization Policy, which had been inactive now for fourteen years. Afraid that Feighan would engage in "witch-hunts," Celler asked the Senate Appropriations Committee to delete the operating funds; the Senate obliged, reducing Feighan's funds to $24,100. Stung by Celler's unusual request to the other body, Feighan blasted his chairman when the appropriations conference report was accepted by both houses. Celler replied that none of this would have happened had Feighan not attempted to go over his boss's head. Said Celler, "I am going to tell you that nobody is going to ride in front of me when I ride the horse of the Judiciary Committee."

The House had finished its relatively brief hearings on June 1. The Senate subcommittee's hearings lingered on until August 3, at which time the subcommittee began deliberations on the final bill. In a meeting with the Attorney General on the same day the House passed H.R. 2580, August 25, Senators Ervin and Dirksen obtained a pledge that the Admin.istration would not fight an annual limitation on Western Hem.sphere immigration of 120,000. In addition, a Dirksen proposal was accepted under which a Select Commission on Western Hemisphere Immigration would make an intensive study and report back to the Congress in three years; if new legislation did not modify the plan, the 120,000 limit would go into effect July 1, 1968. The next day the subcommittee accepted the Ervin-Dirksen proposal by a 5 to 3 vote (Kennedy, Hart, and Javits against), thus substantiating the Administration worries that without an agreement not to fight, that bloc might have killed the bill altogether.

For two more weeks the bill remained stalled in the Senate Judiciary Committee, while Dirksen employed a number of tactics to force consideration of his unrelated reapportionment amendment. Dirksen had been angered over the Supreme Court's 1964 ruling that under the federal Constitution both houses of state legislatures must be apportioned on a "one man, one vote" basis. Earlier in the summer he had sought to push a constitutional amendment through the Senate. Failing to get the bill reported out by the Judiciary Committee, he forced the issue on the floor by making piecemeal amendments to a pending resolution which would have proclaimed a National Baseball Week. Like the Tin Woodsman in the Kingdom of Oz, the bill's body was cut off and replaced with the text of Dirksen's amendment. Then the head—the "enacting clause"—was lopped off and replaced with Dirksen's title. Behold, an entirely new bill already on the floor of the Senate, free of the unnecessary time wasted in going through committee. But a constitutional amendment requires two-thirds vote, and under the active leadership of Senator Douglas, aided by Senators William Proxmire of Wisconsin and Joseph Tydings of Maryland, thirty-nine members rallied and Dirksen's amendment was killed.

Dirksen did not give up, and now he forced a changed version through the Judiciary Committee by his threat to hold up the immigration bill. Under Judiciary Committee rules, the objection by a single member is enough to stop the committee's consideration of any bill altogether. When the committee bowed and released the reapportionment amendment, Dirksen withdrew his objection to the immigration bill and by a 14 to 2 vote (Eastland and McClellan against), the Judiciary Committee reported the finished bill to the Senate floor for debate and a final vote.

Debate was relatively gentle. Old themes were echoed by Senators Eastland, McClellan, Strom Thurmond of South Carolina, and Allen J. Ellender of Louisiana. In one of the only references during the entire year to the national origins impact on Negroes, Senator Robert Kennedy forced the Senator from Florida, Spessard L. Holland, to a startling disclosure. The Florida Democrat had been arguing the usual argument and was asked to justify the 1924 and 1952 acts' exclusion of Negroes from the national origins system. Said Holland: "The Senator from Florida, after having talked with a great many people of that origin, has not been able to find many of them who have the slightest idea as to what tribe or nation or area or geographic region their people came from." The flabbiest excuse for the internal inconsistencies of national origins having been given, there was nothing new to offer. On September 22, the Senate passed its version of H.R. 2580 by a vote of 76 to 18. All but two opposed were southerners.

The conference committee reconciled the different versions of the bill in the Senate's favor: The limitation on Western Hemisphere immigration would be kept. Other changes, incidental to this story, were made and the bill was sent back to each house. The Senate passed the bill on September 30 by voice vote; that same day the House agreed to the measure 320 to 69.

Three days later, the abolition of national origins was signed into law. President Johnson, at a special ceremony in New York, affixed his signature to Public Law 89–236 on October 3, 1965. On the same day that Sukarno was being ousted from control of Indonesia, that Cuban refugees were offered U.S. asylum, that the Pope prepared to come to the United Nations, and that the Dodgers beat the Braves for the National League

Pennant, the President spoke at the base of the American flag seventy-five yards from the Statue of Liberty.

"This bill is not a revolutionary bill," he said. "It does not affect the lives of millions. It will not reshape the structure of our daily lives, or add importantly to our wealth and power.

"Yet it is still one of the most important acts of this Congress and this Administration.

"For it repairs a deep and painful flaw in the fabric of American justice, it corrects a cruel and enduring wrong in the conduct of the American nation. It will make us truer to ourselves as a country and as a people. It will strengthen us in a hundred unseen ways.

"Now, under the monument which has welcomed so many, the American nation returns to the finest of its traditions.

"The days of unlimited immigration are past. But those who come will come because of what they are—not because of the land from which they sprung."

In the final analysis, the new law succeeded primarily because the old law had failed. By 1964 only one third of the total immigration fell under the quota provisions of the 1952 legislation. As Representative Celler asked rhetorically: "Are we really suddenly and dramatically departing from that which we presumably had held sacred for forty years? Obviously no. Instead of clean surgery we have indulged in operations of occasional blood infusion into a moribund system."

The struggle of substance over form is first necessarily piecemeal—this is the lesson of the years between 1952 and 1965. Beyond a certain point, a point different for each piece of legislation, no doubt, the terms of the battle shift; no longer is the form exalted over the substance, and even the opponents of change begin to admit that they value the form above the substance. Once the opposition can be forced to such an admission, they cannot long stave off defeat. Such an admission had finally been made by 1965.

The American people supported the change; so we suspect, anyway, from the whims of public sentiment recorded on a random day by the poll takers. In this case the matter is not entirely free from doubt, for each side put forth its own poll to show that the public was for and against the impending legislation. On May 31 the Harris poll was headlined in the *Washington Post*: "U.S. Public Is Strongly Opposed to Easing of Immigration Laws." This poll, claimed the private groups which lobbied to preserve the system, showed that the American public would resist change by a 2 to 1 margin. Supporters of change, on the other hand, cited the Gallup poll, which was headlined on July 25 in the same newspaper as follows: "Gallup Poll Shows Widespread Public Support for the Elimination of the National Origins Quota System."

A close inspection of what the polls actually asked resolves the apparent contradiction. The Harris poll emphasized the President's proposal "to allow more people into the United States as immigrants." People were against opening the doors, 2 to 1. That this question and its consequent play in the syndicated column is not entirely fair was not pointed out; the Harris column simply told the people's response to the Harris questions. It did not justify its choice of questions. Buried farther in the Harris poll itself was the question of skills vs. national origins; even in this poll, 36 percent thought it would be better to base the law on skills, and 29 percent thought it would be better to foster national origins, while 15 percent saw no differences, and 20 percent weren't sure.

The Gallup poll, on the other hand, pinpointed far more accurately the essence of the pending bill: National origins was rejected in favor of occupational skills by the Gallup sample, 51 percent to 32 percent (with 17 percent of no mind at all). The only possible contradiction, in fact, was over Harris's initial point: According to Gallup, 47 percent of the American public favored maintaining immigration at its present level or increasing it, while 33 percent wanted it decreased (and 20 percent just didn't know).

If polls are one measure, so are the votes of Congress, at least when the votes are overwhelming. In the Senate, all but two of the eighteen members who voted against the Senate's original bill on September 22 were southerners. The two non-southerners were Carl Hayden of Arizona, a Democrat, and

Norris Cotton of New Hampshire, a Republican. Alabama, Georgia, Mississippi, South Carolina, and Virginia contributed two Nays each. Arkansas, Florida, Kentucky, Louisiana, North Carolina (Ervin voted Yea), and West Virginia contributed one Nay each. The West, the Midwest, the Southwest, and the North almost unanimously supported the bill.

In the House, the story is much the same, although the greater number of members increased the chance that parochialism in all regions would lead to Nays. Of the 95 negative votes recorded on August 25 for the original House bill (without a Western Hemisphere limitation), 78 were from southern states (Alabama, Arkansas, Florida, Georgia, Kentucky, Louisiana, Mississippi, Missouri, North Carolina, South Carolina, Tennessee, Texas, and Virginia); not all were solidly against. The remaining 17 Nays were scattered among California (3), Idaho (1), Indiana (4), Iowa (1), Nevada (1), New Mexico (2), Ohio (2), Oklahoma (2), and Wisconsin (1), and all but five of these votes were cast by Republicans. The West-South alliance was dissolved; the West's former racial fears apparently disintegrated. The North, which had once tipped the scales in favor of restriction, came out one short of unanimous for repeal.

Despite its resounding victory, the new law continues misunderstood by some. Despite its resounding renunciation, the national origins system continues to be exalted by those who expected too much of it, feared too much of immigrants, and doubted too much of America. Marion T. Bennett, a former member of Congress from Missouri (1943–1949) and a consultant to the drafters of the McCarran-Walter Act, expressed this viewpoint in an article in *The Annals of the American Academy of Political and Social Science*. Said he:

"By 1965 the political atmosphere would change completely, and in an era of expanding civil rights for minorities, our pluralistic and egalitarian-bent society would reject, through Congress by public law, the concept that white, Anglo-Saxon western European culture need remain the cornerstone of a truly viable democratic society or was worthy of preservation, though none denied it the nation's debt and honor."

That this is a gross misreading of the legislation and of American history need hardly be underscored. Congress did not reject any such notion at all. What it did deny was that American culture, whatever it is, would be wrecked by abolishing the national origins system. Sadly, for some, national origins is like an old love who, though unfaithful, continues to enflame.

7 / Administration,
The Raw Nerve of Policy

Cherished deep in the American tradition is the vibrant thought that ours is a "government of laws and not of men." Of course, this can never be more than an ideal, and the persistence of the notion that the ideal exists as actuality may keep us from seeking the acts of men. The ideal to be sought must be a "government of men who obey the laws"; to deny this is to give human qualities to "the law," to expect the law to work mechanically and automatically without human intervention.

If man was made by God, it did not seem unsuitable for President Kennedy to note in his Inaugural (a quadrennial address in which it is mandatory to "invoke His blessings") that "here on earth God's work must truly be our own." How much more true must this be of law, an invention of man.

Alas that this simple, sobering fact causes anguish even in the most pure-minded of public servants. If ours is a government of men who must obey the law, what is the law and how is it to be obeyed? An examination of almost any "law" will show that it consists of directions in a fractured version of the English language. Language is an imperfect means of communication in law because the attempt to make directions concise inevitably leads to exceptions, while the attempt to make the language broad enough to encompass all exceptions inevitably makes it ambiguous.

Thus the public servant as well as the common man is faced with an extraordinary dilemma, for an even-handed administration of the laws, as well as an honest attempt to follow the law, may be an impossibility. "A government of men who obey the law" or "a government of men who administer the law even-handedly" is supposed to mean a system of law in which a man's passions and emotions and predispositions—those irrelevancies of life—do not intrude. Is that not why lawyers are thought of as precise-thinking men for whom logic has displaced passion? But men do not think in a vacuum; a Republican Attorney General may well enforce the same law differently than a Democratic Attorney General and both may be perfectly honest and fair. Men do make a difference.

Something other than the mere statement of the law is obviously required if our government is to approach the humane ideal. That something else is this: adherence to the underlying *purpose* of the law we sometimes call *policy.* Though purpose has eluded the capture of science, it remains the bedrock of law and human existence. The remark that it would be better to live under Soviet law and American legal procedures than under American law and Soviet legal procedures calls to the mind's center stage the paramount importance of purpose in life and in law. A paradox it is, then, that laws so rarely include their purposes. But this is partly the trouble with self-defining definitions, partly caused by the fact that the shortness of time leads us to write laws before we fully consider our purposes, and partly due to the sometimes astonishing reality that what is a purpose for one occasion may be but a limited aspect of an unseen larger purpose.

Perhaps in no other area of our public law have purposes been so widely ignored, so largely confused, and so ill-considered as in the actual administration of our immigration laws. Public officials who have dealt in immigration affairs have consistently claimed, and acquired, more power throughout our history to deny procedural safeguards than any save those who have been obliged to keep Negroes and Indians in their proper places. The guarantees of "due process," of trial by jury, and of the right to confront accusing witnesses, absolutely guaranteed to citizens, have often been lost on the human beings we call aliens. The explanations of administrative behavior, designed to prove that the administrators are only following the law, at times have seemed to come straight from the matinee of Alice's Teaparty.

A detailed history of the administration of American immigration laws is beyond the scope of the present essay. Beginning with the statutes and judicial interpretations that sprang up in the 1880's, administrative law in this field, as in all fields, has grown increasingly complex. Legal doctrine for the most part has been unclear; the Supreme Court has equivocated on so many occasions that even the present state of the law, in this advanced age, is messy. But no discussion of the national origins system can fail to take at least a peek at the glacial tips of our domestic policy regarding foreigners.

EXCLUSION AND DEPORTATION

Immigration officials have usually asked for, and often obtained, unfettered discretion in the exclusion and deportation of aliens. Because aliens are not part of the "body politic," the sovereign power of the United States, vested in Congress and the President, can deal as it sees fit with them, without restraints. So it has been argued and so it has been held.

Unquestionably, the greatest discretion lies in the hands of those empowered to *exclude* foreigners from entering the United States. American consular officers abroad have the final authority to deny immigrant visas. Section 221(g) states that "no visa or other documentation shall be issued to an alien if . . . it appears to the consular officer, from statements in the application, or in the papers submitted therewith, that such alien is ineligible to receive a visa or other documentation." There is no right of appeal to any higher authority; not the officer's boss, not the ambassador, not the Attorney General, not American courts, not the President.

Under this provision, two Chinese-born sons of an American citizen were denied admission from Hong Kong on the grounds that they could not prove their kinship with their father. The stories of the two boys—aged twenty-two and eighteen—were identical with each other and with their father's except in one particular: the location of a *movable* washstand in their Chinese living room. One son, who had not been back to China in five years, remembered the washstand on the north side. The son, newly arrived in Hong Kong, remembered it on the south side. Their application for admission was rejected because of this discrepancy. The Hong Kong consular officer denied visas in another case to fifteen-year-old and thirteen-year-old brothers, anxious to join their father, an American citizen, because "applicant Yee Suey Keung testified that the village toilet accommodated two people at one time, his applicant brother stated that the village toilet accommodated only one person."

Sometimes the consular officer may make a mistake and allow the dangerous alien to enter America. Ellen Knauff was one such case. Born in Germany, a citizen of Czechoslovakia, she served as a WAAF in the British Royal Air Force during World War II and married a naturalized American soldier in Germany, where she had returned to help the U.S. Occupation Forces. She had been cleared to come to the U.S. under the War Brides Act, enacted by Congress to expedite admissions for the wives of persons who had served honorably in the armed forces. In Ellen Knauff's case, it proved a colossal irony.

When she landed, she was incarcerated at Ellis Island, branded a security risk: Her entrance, said Attorney General Tom C. Clark, would be "prejudicial to the interests of the United States." Mrs. Knauff was refused a hearing and never informed as to the nature of the charges against her. She was ordered deported and the decision of the Attorney General was upheld by the District Court for the Southern District of New York, the Court of Appeals for the Second Circuit, and the United States Supreme Court. Participating in the 5 to 4 vote which ruled that the power to exclude was plenary and due process need not be observed, was the now-elevated former Attorney General who had started all the fuss. Said Justice Minton for the majority: "Whatever the procedure authorized by Congress is, it is due process as far as an alien denied entry is concerned."

Her lawyers fought on. To his credit, Representative Walter introduced a bill in Congress to permit Mrs. Knauff to remain in the country and the bill was unanimously passed by the House (though later tabled in the Senate). Another round of hearings was begun in the lower courts.

When the Second Circuit denied her appeal for habeas corpus to free her from Ellis Island, where she had been virtually imprisoned for months, the Immigration Service immediately announced that it would deport her, despite the fact that the Court of Appeals had suggested that her lawyers could apply to the Supreme Court for a stay of deportation and her lawyers had announced they would do so. The denial of her stay of deportation was issued at four o'clock in the afternoon; the Immigration Service wanted her on an eleven o'clock flight out of the country the next morning.

Her lawyers went to Justice Robert H. Jackson in Washington, who as circuit justice for the Second Circuit had the power to enjoin an administrative official temporarily in such a case. "As the case comes to me," he said in a rare move ordering the Immigration Service to change its plans, "I am informed that preparations are complete at the airport to deport her in a matter of minutes." So dangerous was Ellen Knauff that a case which had dragged on from August 28, 1948, to May 17, 1950, could not wait a day longer. Justice Jackson noted that unless he issued the stay the Supreme Court's jurisdiction would be defeated and the pending legislation in Congress would be mooted.

Said Justice Jackson in his stay decision: "If the Department had at any time shown even probable grounds to believe that the presence of this woman a few days more in this country might jeopardize national security, even infinitesimally, I should refuse the stay. But the Department of Justice has not only had opportunity, it has been importuned to show the courts or Congress any reason for its exclusion order.

"Not only is the petitioner unable to learn what the specific charges against her are, neither can the courts which are asked to play at least a consenting part in her exclusion, nor the Congress, which is in the midst of an effort to stop it. It overtaxes credulity to believe that it would jeopardize the security of the United States to impart to coordinate branches of the Government some inkling of the charges against this woman." For more than seven months, Mrs. Knauff was held at Ellis Island, while Congress debated in the dark, for the Department of Justice was still not talking.

When her husband arrived in January of 1951, released from active duty, the dangerous security risk he had married was released into his custody. Two months later she was given her first opportunity to be heard by the Immigration Service, more than two years after her original incarceration. At the hearing, Mrs. Knauff's lawyers were virtually barred from cross-examining a witness who claimed that her papers were not in order. The only testimony introduced was "hearsay": the witnesses themselves had not seen or heard anything to indicate that Mrs. Knauff was disloyal or a spy, but "other people" had told them so. One of the witnesses, whose charges two and a half years before had been used to justify exclusion, in fact had not been approached by the Government until three weeks before the hearing. The hearing was so blatantly lacking in due process that had it concerned an American citizen any court would have tossed out its findings automatically. But this was the hearing of an alien, excluded at the gate, and the Service concluded that she was an alien who "it was reasonable to suspect would work contrary to the laws of the nation against espionage, sabotage, public disorder and subversive activities." This decision was upheld by the commissioner of the Service in May, and she was returned to Ellis Island.

The hearing proved the department's undoing, however. Enough statements were made to allow Mrs. Knauff's lawyers, friends, and newspaper reporters (for her fate had now become a national cause célèbre) to show that misstatements, distortions, and actual perjury had been committed. The commissioner's decision allowed the case to be appealed to the Board of Immigration Appeals. Three months later, and more than three years after she was first detained, the independently-minded appeals board upset the detention order and on concurrence of the Attorney General, Ellen Knauff was admitted to the United States. Said the board in a 4 to 1 decision, there simply was not the requisite "substantial evidence" required by law (which, translated from legal parlance, means there was not a shred of evidence) to bar her entrance.

Why had Ellen Knauff terrorized the United States Department of Justice? No one is entirely sure, but it is suspected that a girl whom Mr. Knauff had previously been seeing was annoyed when he left her for Ellen, and began to spread malicious rumors about Ellen's being a paid informant of the enemy. The department was determined not to admit to its mistakes, and so a woman was denied three years of her life to preserve (unsuccessfully) the integrity of a department of the United States.

An alien falls under the rules regarding "exclusion" whenever he is seeking entrance to the United States; except in rare situations (such as an unintentional or forced departure), "seeking entrance" is broadly construed. Thus, a Hungarian national who had lived in upstate New York as a permanent resident alien for a quarter-century was barred when he sought reentry after an unsuccessful trip to see his ailing mother in Romania. Again, no hearing was granted, no reasons offered, except that his admission would be against the best interests of the United States. The Service refused to state its reasons, even privately to a federal judge. The excluded alien then applied for admission to twenty-five other countries, all of which turned him down. The Supreme Court in 1953 upheld his virtual imprisonment on Ellis Island; Congress, after all, had placed the final decision in the hands of the Attorney General. (After three years' detention, when the department could safely assume the public had forgotten him, this Hungarian capable of shaking the foundations of America was afforded a hearing and allowed to return to his wife and family.)

Deportation has presented a slightly more difficult problem for the arrogance of Congress and I.N.S. to contend with. The first difficulty stems from the fact that the 5th Amendment to the Constitution, adopted in 1791, provides that "no *person* shall be denied life, liberty, or property without due process of law." The phrase is repeated as a command to the states in the 14th Amendment, ratified following the Civil War. In the first great test of the constitutional meaning of "person," the Supreme Court held it to include even an alien.

Under the San Francisco municipal code in the 1880's, laundry operators were required to obtain a permit from the city board of supervisors. The city fathers explained that the permit was necessary in order to insure against fire hazards and unsanitary establishments. Of the 320 laundrymen in the city, 240 were Chinese, and 310 of the laundries were in wooden buildings. When the time came for the issuance of the licenses, 150 Chinese launderers were denied permits on the grounds that their wooden buildings were firetraps. Curiously enough, 80 non-Chinese launderers were granted licenses, though they conducted their businesses in substantially similar wooden buildings. The laundrymen who continued operation without licenses were convicted of the crime and sent to prison. Two fought back: In a case that eventually went to the United States Supreme Court, Yick Wo and Wo Lee argued that city officials who acted in a manner so obviously discriminatory were guilty of violating the 14th Amendment to the Constitution, which declares that "no state . . . shall deny to any person within its jurisdiction the equal protection of the laws." The city administrators responded that the equal protection clause was aimed at the state, by its own words, that they were city officials, merely local administrators. Furthermore, these Chinese were not even citizens; they were merely resident aliens who unfortunately had been allowed to come to America at a time when no restrictions barred the way.

In a case which has become a major part of the foundation of American public law, the Supreme Court ordered the California jailer to release his prisoners and the board of supervisors to issue licenses. Said the Court: "Though the law itself be fair on its face and impartial in appearance, yet, if it is applied and administered by public authority with an evil eye and an unequal hand, so as practically to make unjust and illegal discriminations between persons in similar circumstances, material to their rights, the denial of equal justice is still within the prohibition of the Constitution." The alien won this round because the city officials were not sophisticated enough; in time they would think up more subtle means of circumventing the clear policy of the case.

Ten years later the Constitution was held to protect aliens who were *unlawfully* in the country. A United States commissioner, at a hearing held before him, ascertained that certain Chinese nationals were illegally within the United States; he sentenced them to sixty days at hard labor and then to deportation, under the 1892 exclusion act providing "that any such Chinese person or person of Chinese descent convicted and adjudged to be not lawfully entitled to be and remain in the United States, shall be imprisoned at hard labor for a period of not exceeding one year, and thereafter removed from the United States." The Government argued in support of the section's constitutionality that Congress had created a "political offense," a crime whose commission need not be determined under constitutional ground rules.

In *Wong Wing v. United States*, the Supreme Court demurred. Noting that it was settled that aliens might be deported upon a finding of executive officials, the Court said: "But when Congress sees fit to further promote such a policy by subjecting the persons of such aliens to infamous punishment at hard labor, or by confiscating their property, we think such legislation, to be valid, must provide for a judicial trial to establish the guilt of the accused. . . . It is not consistent with the theory of our government that the legislature should, after having defined an offense as an infamous crime, find the fact of guilt and adjudge the punishment by one of its own agents."

The Service persisted. It insisted that an alien within the United States could be deported without even a hearing. Kaoru Yamataya landed in Seattle in 1901; immigration inspectors decided she was a pauper and a person likely to become a public charge, excludable under the law. The Supreme Court held, citing a variety of precedents, that it was legitimate for Congress to place the enforcement of its policy in the hands of executive officials (a power denied with some vehemence, though on other grounds, to California state inspectors in 1875).

The lady claimed, however, that she should be given the

right to defend herself against the charges at a hearing. The immigration inspector contended that an alien "may be deported without previous notice of any purpose to deport him, and without any opportunity on his part to show by competent evidence before the executive officers charged with the execution of the Acts of Congress, that he is not here in violation of the law." Presumably, it was cheaper to forego the hearing, and economy is always the desideratum in government proceedings. The Court didn't mind the expense. Administrative officials cannot disregard requirements of due process of law—even an alien, once in the country, is entitled to "all opportunity to be heard upon the questions involving his right to be and remain in the United States."

Just how much that right meant, however, is apparent from the disposition of the *Japanese Immigrant Case*. Miss Yamataya was given only "informal" notice of the proceedings against her; she spoke no English and did not understand the nature or import of the questions propounded. Nevertheless, said a majority of the justices, she *was* heard (if sounds are words). It is not for the judiciary to review the *adequacy* of the hearing—she should have complained to the Secretary of the Treasury, who had the final administrative authority; but she had not complained. Thus a great constitutional principle enunciated forcefully was denied life in the next breath: "If the appellant's want of knowledge of the English language put her at some disadvantage in the investigation conducted by that officer, that was her misfortune." The dissent of 1888 in Jung Ah Lung's case came of age.

In 1922 the Court was faced with the bald assertion that no judicial trial was necessary for a person who claimed to be a *citizen*. The Service insisted that an administrative hearing was enough, and finding that no citizenship existed, was ready to deport. The Court reversed.

Consistently, the Immigration and Naturalization Service has sought to avoid the Constitution, to avoid sound practices, to be higher than the law. Perhaps the most arrogant claim ever made by the Service was that repudiated in *Wong Yang Sung v. Mc-Grath*. In 1946 Congress enacted the Administrative Procedure

Act (sponsored by McCarran in the Senate), by which it hoped
to remedy many grave defects in the practice of administrative
law by federal agencies, which had grown enormously in scope
of jurisdiction and impact since their birth in the New Deal.
One of the fundamental purposes of the A.P.A. was "to curtail
and change the practice of embodying in one person or agency
the duties of prosecutor and judge." The act provided that the
administrative agencies' judicial sections, which hear cases, must
be separate from the rule-making sections of the agencies. The
man who investigates should not be the man who hears the
case, just as the prosecutor should not be judge. Separate classes
of hearing and investigating inspectors were created. By its
terms, the Administrative Procedure Act was to govern all agencies which were required by statute to hold hearings, unless the
other statute specified a different arrangement.

Wong Yang Sung, born in China, was a merchant seaman
charged with overstaying his shore leave in the United States. At
a hearing an immigrant inspector recommended deportation, and
his decision was affirmed by the acting commissioner and the
Board of Immigration Appeals. Wong appealed solely on the
grounds that the Service had not followed the procedural requirements of the A.P.A.

I.N.S. first argued that it was not bound by the act because
no statute required the Service to hold hearings in deportation
cases. This was an incredible claim, not because it was inaccurate
but because of what it assumed. The *Japanese Immigrant Case*
had held forty-seven years before that aliens are constitutionally
entitled to a hearing in deportation cases. Since a hearing is a
constitutional necessity, there is patently no need for a statute
creating the right. Accordingly, the Supreme Court found the
I.N.S. argument too much to swallow: "The difficulty with any
argument premised on the proposition that the deportation
statute does not require a hearing is that, without such a hearing,
there would be no constitutional authority for deportation." Even
though the statute governing deportation procedures does not
mention the necessity for a hearing, the Supreme Court had read
such necessity into the statute to save it from invalidity. "We
would hardly attribute to Congress a purpose to be less scru-

pulous about the fairness of a hearing necessitated by the Constitution than one granted by it as a matter of expediency," said the Court. Other contentions of the Service were brushed aside and Wong was ordered released for a proper hearing.

The A.P.A. was not constitutionally necessary, however. Soon after the Court decided *Wong Yang Sung,* Congress removed from the Service the necessity of complying with the Court's ruling. Stuck on the end of an unrelated appropriation bill, Congress explicitly exempted the Service from the obligation of keeping the prosecutory and judicial functions separate. Two years later the McCarran-Walter Act repealed the rider, but did not restore the status quo ante. Instead, special procedures were established: A "special inquiry officer" conducts the hearing even though he may act as a lawyer for the Government. Although the individual special inquiry officer cannot hear a case which he helped investigate, he may nevertheless "present and receive evidence, and interrogate, examine, and cross-examine the alien or witness." He is subject to the control of district directors of the Immigration Service. Complained Justices Hugo L. Black and Felix Frankfurter in a 1955 case, it is "hard to defend the fairness of a practice that subjects judges to the power and control of prosecutors."

So weak is the alien's case, however, that if the procedural niceties are observed, he can be deported almost without question. In one of the most classic deportation cases, a number of resident aliens were banished for acts that were not illegal when committed. A Greek, an Italian, and a Russian all belonged to the Communist party at various times during the 1920's and 1930's. All were sympathetic toward its philosophy, but each disavowed any belief in the necessity of violent overthrow of the Government. Their memberships were terminated before the Smith Act of 1940 went into effect. Under the terms of that act, an alien could be deported for membership in an organization which advocated overthrow of the Government by force and violence, even though the membership existed entirely before the law was enacted. The Supreme Court upheld the act's constitutionality. After reaffirming the paramount power of Congress to deal with aliens as it sees fit, the Court, speaking through Mr.

described by General George Marshall as the most decorate
military unit in America, considering its size and span of servic
Masaoka's four brothers were also members of the 442d, an
among them the five garnered thirty separate combat decora
tions. One of his brothers was killed, one totally disabled
Insurance benefits paid Masaoka's mother enough to purchas
land for a home in Pasadena; but California "escheated"—too
—the land. She was racially ineligible to have an interest in rea
property in the state.

It was not her first indignity. After the Japanese attack o
Pearl Harbor, Mrs. Masaoka was imprisoned along with 110,00
other persons of Japanese ancestry—citizens and aliens alike. I
was as if the 1870's were being replayed. Distinguished citizen
and utter racists were of one voice: Japanese-Americans *migh*
be loyal to the fatherland (which they had never seen). Wh
can say? In a time of grave danger, they must be evacuated t
"war relocation centers." Leading the call for evacuation wa
Earl Warren, then state attorney general. The constitutionalit
of the executive evacuation order was upheld by the Suprem
Court; abandoning previous tests concerning the reasonablenes
of the evidence which prompted the Executive to act, the Cou
declared that it was not for it to say that in a dangerous hou
the commanding general in the Pacific might be in error. Indus
trious and hard-working *citizens* and resident aliens were de
prived of their liberty and fleeced of their property (and est
mates of later reparations put the reimbursement at ten cents o
the dollar).

In 1944 the military authorities made a colossal mistake
They admitted that Mitsuye Endo, an American citizen, wa
loyal to the United States, but claimed the power to detain he
anyway. The Supreme Court unanimously disagreed. Said Justic
William O. Douglas: "Loyalty is a matter of the heart and min
not of race, creed, or color. . . . He who is loyal is by definitio
not a spy or a saboteur. When the power to detain is deriv
from the power to protect the war effort against espionage an
sabotage, detention which has no relationship to that objective
unauthorized." The Court repented (without conceding its ea

Justice Jackson, denied that the "ex post facto" section of the
Constitution applied. That provision, he said, protects an accused
from "criminal" punishment only. But everyone knows that deportation is merely a "remedy" for a "civil" offense. He quoted
Justice Holmes, who was in a decidedly nineteenth century frame
of mind when he said, "The determination by facts that might
constitute a crime under local law is not a conviction of crime,
nor is the deportation a punishment; it is simply a refusal by
the Government to harbor persons whom it does not want. The
coincidence of the local penal law with the policy of Congress
is an accident." Justice Jackson noted that since the Communist
party had expelled aliens as a matter of strategy, "Congress may
have believed that the party tactics threw upon the Government
an almost impossible burden if it attempted to separate those
who sincerely renounced Communist principles of force and
violence from those who left the party the better to serve it.
Congress, exercising the wide discretion that it alone has in
these matters, declined to accept that as the Government's
burden."

The administrative procedures for exclusion and deportation today are essentially those enacted in McCarran-Walter. The
claimed liberalizations were merely of form, not substance. The
Immigration and Naturalization Service, though it has become
somewhat tempered in its conduct, is still outside the "framework and the pattern of the Administrative Procedure Act," the
drafters of McCarran-Walter to the contrary notwithstanding.

Today's reasons for which the I.N.S. can order deportation
or exclusion run to six pages; the McCarran-Walter Act is posi-
tively draconic in its grounds. Statutes of limitation, common in
all criminal law, both state and federal, were abolished in many
types of deportation cases. Yet in most states a person can rob,
rape, or murder and, if not caught within a specified period
(almost always less than ten years), cannot be prosecuted.

The power to deport has often been used for the most trivial
offenses. Failure to report an address during the month of January, as required by law, will permit an order of deportation,
even decades later. A resident alien who takes a spur-of-the-
moment, half-day sightseeing trip to Mexico and returns to his

Texas home has entered the country illegally upon his return. His continued residence is a violation of current law and he could be summarily deported (whereas a trip to Oklahoma would have been perfectly safe).

I.N.S. has actually initiated proceedings on grounds as slight as these. The Service has succeeded in deporting an alien resident for the following reason. A sixty-nine-year-old Portuguese man had lived for twenty-six years (from 1929 to 1955) with a woman not his wife. Unfortunately, he had been separated from his lawful wife since 1921, but she refused to divorce him. In 1955 deportation proceedings were begun when it was discovered that during the course of living with the woman who was not his wife, he "had intermittent sexual relations with her." Adultery is an act of "moral turpitude" within the meaning of section 101(f)(2), for which an alien is deportable. He applied for suspension of deportation under a provision in the law permitting relaxation of the rules for "exceptional and extremely unusual hardship": the woman was now fifty-nine years old and sick; she was supported entirely by his weekly salary of twenty-nine dollars. His request for suspension was denied and he was deported.

An immigrant can even be deported for divorcing his American spouse within two years after entry; the burden of proving that the marriage was not intended to evade the immigration law is on the immigrant. The act says that the immigrant must "satisfy" the Attorney General that he did not intend to evade.

On and on goes the list; cases that have resulted from the deportation provisions number in the thousands. Pleasant as it may be to contemplate the folly of the deportation and exclusion sections, there are other aspects of administration that must equally command our attention.

ALIEN LAND LAWS

During the second and third decades of the twentieth century, the Pacific states—California, Oregon, Washington—enacted a series of so-called alien land laws. In effect, these laws forbade the sale and renting to and ownership and leasing

of land by aliens "ineligible to naturalization." The laws were harsh and were upheld by the Supreme Court in a number of cases in 1923. The reasons by now should be all too familiar The Court ruled that since Congress created two classes of persons within the United States—those eligible and those in eligible for citizenship—a state could constitutionally make differences turn on the distinction. The Court agreed with a low federal judge in Washington State who considered the matter "It is obvious that one who is not a citizen and cannot become one lacks an interest in, and the power to effectually work for the welfare of, the state, and, so lacking, the state may rightfully de him the right to own and lease real estate within its boundari If one incapable of citizenship may lease or own real estate is within the realm of possibility that every foot of land with the state might pass to the ownership or possession of n citizens." This decision was rendered despite the plain langu of an 1870 Congressional statute explicitly directed toward regulation of naturalization: "All persons within the jurisdic of the United States shall have the same right in every S and Territory to make and enforce contracts, to sue, be pai give evidence, and to the full and equal benefit of all laws proceedings for the security of persons and property as is enj by white citizens, and shall be subject to like punishment, penalties, taxes, licenses, and exactions of every kind, and other." The act was held, in a different context, to apply to as well as citizens, and then ignored.

The state land laws were strictly enforced. In the late a large number of "escheat" cases came to the public's atte and helped provide the indignation necessary to endin racial bars to citizenship. One of the most compelling inc was the story of Mike M. Masaoka, Washington represe of the Japanese American Citizens League, and a tireless le during 1952 for the passage of the McCarran-Walter Act b it dropped the ban on Japanese immigration and natural Masaoka was a member of the 442d Regimental Combat formed entirely of Japanese-American volunteers during War II to show that these people were as loyal to Am any who fought for her during the war. The regime

lier error), and in early January, 1945, most of the detained Japanese-Americans were freed.

The release of these prisoners did not end their troubles. Mrs. Masaoka's land was confiscated. So was the farm of Mrs. Roy K. Hirata, an American citizen, because her husband, an alien, helped her cultivate crops and lived with her on the farm. A California statute made it illegal for an alien to "enjoy, use, occupy, be, or remain on the land or have a beneficial interest in the land, its crops, or its proceeds."

Perhaps worse was the treatment of American-born Akira Iwamura, an original evacuee who volunteered and was accepted for Army combat duty in the South Pacific. When he returned home, California demanded he forfeit his land because his alien parents had purchased the land in his name when he was still a minor, eight years before. Iwamura's father had operated the farm following his release from a war relocation center. The California Supreme Court had already declared the alien land laws constitutional, so Iwamura's only hope was to repurchase his land in order to "quiet title." California said, in effect, that although it was illegal for Iwamura to retain the land, he could possess it despite the law, if he paid in cash a sum equal to half the land's assessed valuation. This kind of extortion was widely repeated throughout the state and always upheld.

The Supreme Court moved circumspectly against this state which had spawned *Yick Wo v. Hopkins*. In 1943, California passed a law which when later amended forbade the issuance of commercial fishing licenses to "aliens ineligible to citizenship." Torao Takahashi, a resident alien from Japan, had been issued such a license annually since 1915. Upon his release from a wartime center in 1945, he was denied a license and he sued. The state claimed that it was protecting the "community interest" in the commercial fish within the three-mile limit of domestic waters; since there were only so many fish, the first to be denied the right to catch them should be aliens who have a lesser interest in the community's welfare. Furthermore, California added, since fish outside the three-mile limit were indistinguishable from fish inside the limit, the aliens could constitutionally be barred from fishing anywhere. The Court denied the power. Its decision stated that the distinction which Congress made between aliens eligible and ineligible for citizenship could not be carried over by the states to deny some people the right to earn a living, because it was an unconstitutional denial of the equal protection of the laws. Because the case did not involve the land laws, the Court could make no ruling concerning them.

Of the seventy-nine escheat actions filed under the California law, seventy-three were against the Japanese, and fifty-nine of these were begun after the outbreak of World War II. The results were so harsh that one case eventually made its way to the Supreme Court. Fred Oyama's father, a Japanese alien resident, purchased six acres of farm land in 1934, placing title in the name of his six-year-old son, born in California. The father was appointed guardian of the land by a California county court. In 1942 the entire family was evacuated, and two years later while the Oyamas were still in camps, the state filed its escheat petition. Under California law, a presumption exists that land purchased in a minor child's name is a *gift* to the child. The trial court, upheld by the state supreme court, presumed that when an alien ineligible to citizenship makes such a purchase, not a gift but a *trust* results in which the son holds the land for the benefit of the father, a violation of the alien land law. Thus, one class of citizens—those with Japanese alien fathers—had the burden of proving there was no trust intended; all other citizens had no such burden. The Court never reached the underlying question whether the land law itself was constitutional. Even assuming it was, the Court said, "it does not follow that there is no constitutional limit to the means which may be used to enforce it."

The Supreme Court never took the final easy step. The state supreme court had early said the purpose of the law was to "discourage the coming of the Japanese into this state." Since Congress had authorized the Japanese to come and to remain in the state, the conflict with federal law must surely have rendered the state law unconstitutional. Nevertheless, the *Oyama* case discouraged further attempts at escheating. In 1950 Congress authorized naturalization for alien Japanese who were permanent residents at that time, a halfway measure. The alien land laws were finally mooted, of course, by the ending of ineligibility in 1952.

EXPATRIATION

In spite of the general rule, enunciated with certain exceptions during the past century by the Supreme Court, that Congress is supreme in immigration and naturalization matters, in one narrow aspect the Court has recently found a higher law. Congress provided in a series of enactments a number of ways by which an American citizen—whether naturalized or native-born—could lose his citizenship. These ways included living abroad more than three years at a time if naturalized, desertion from the armed forces, and voting in a foreign election. In 1958, the case of a soldier convicted by general court-martial of war-time desertion and sentenced to forfeiture of citizenship came to the Supreme Court. Denying Congress the power to declare such forfeitures, the Court found the penalty "more primitive than torture," since it makes the person "stateless" and leads to "the total destruction of the individual's status in organized society."

The Court next disposed of the contention that the Constitution allowed a naturalized citizen to be shorn of his citizenship simply because he lived abroad for three years in the country where he had formerly been a national. The same regulation did not apply to native-born citizens, of course. Since the Constitution makes no distinction between citizens of any type, the Congressionally-mandated penalty for remaining away was an attempt to create a forbidden second-class citizenship, and was struck down in 1964.

Three years later a host of Congressionally-sanctioned reasons for expatriation cascaded out of the statute books as the result of one vote in an Israeli general election. A naturalized U.S. citizen left for Israel in 1950 where he subsequently cast a ballot in an election for the Knesset. When he applied for a passport renewal in 1960, the Department of State turned him down. His vote had cost him his citizenship, the department ruled, citing a section of the naturalization law it had no choice but to follow. With this conclusion the Supreme Court disagreed in 1967, sweeping away the law itself. "In our country," wrote Justice Black for the majority, "the people are sovereign and the Government cannot sever its relationship to the people. Our Constitution governs us and we must never forget that our Constitution limits the Government to those powers specifically granted or those that are necessary and proper to carry out the specifically granted ones." He perceived a grave danger in the power of a group of people temporarily organized in a majority in Congress to deny citizenship to a group whom they disliked. "Our holding," the Court said, "does no more than to give to this citizen that which is his own, the constitutional right to remain a citizen in a free country unless he voluntarily relinquishes that citizenship."

REFORM TO COME

Notable as the abolition of national origins was, it is only a beginning step in the long-range reform of American immigration policy. The Immigration Act of 1965, despite the achievement of its primary purpose, was imperfect legislation, even for what it attempted. The doors were suddenly thrown open, but they do not all open on the same room; the preference system within the first come, first-served policy has skewed the nature of immigrant admission.

Immigrants from southern Europe, especially Italy, Greece, and Portugal, tend to emigrate in family units: A man with an already-established family will go to America, later to send for his wife, children, brothers, and sisters. These latter, in turn, bid their relatives. Since the immigrant breadwinner is not yet a citizen, his family must enter under the second preference provision which gives 20 percent of the 170,000 available places, or 34,000 visas (plus any unused portion of the 34,000 first preference visas). The northern European immigrant, by contrast, traditionally founds a family in America. Thus he must enter under the third or sixth preferences, which impose an absolute limitation of 17,000 visas each. And although one of the basic purposes of the new act was to allow pooling of unused "quotas," the still-existing rigidities in the preference system cause many visas to remain untaken while backlogs grow. For instance, only 2,000 first-preference visas out of 34,000 allotted are desired by "unmarried sons or daughters of U.S. citizens." But the third preference generated a backlog of 50,000 people by June 30, 1968, when this sort of thing was supposed to end. The backlog is there because the statute forbids the reallocation of first preference visas to the professional people in the third preference. Given that situation, the immigrant who must enter the sixth preference, for persons of lesser skills capable of filling labor shortages, has an even more reduced chance of entering when he wishes.

Most hopeless of all are the "eighth preference" hopefuls; these people who do not actually come under any preference at all can take only the leftovers. In this position are, ironically enough, the former prime candidates for admission to the United States: Irish, German, Dutch, and other northern European citizens, people with fewer relatives and less education. The Irish laborer, cook, or bartender, for instance, who used to find it easy to come, now finds it next to impossible.

In an outrage over a situation which they claim will reduce their compatriots' immigration from 5,000 to 500 annually, the American-Irish Immigration Committee protested vigorously in New York ceremonies down Fifth Avenue on St. Patrick's Day, 1968. The chairman of the group, founded in 1967, protested, somewhat hypocritically, that "the Irish can never stand satisfied until the disgraceful blot of the present United States immigration policy is erased."

Perhaps "you can't win them all," but the sponsors of the 1965 act are seriously concerned about the undesirable effects of the preference system. Edward Kennedy and twenty cosponsors introduced an omnibus reform bill in the Senate, and a similar bill was introduced by Emanuel Celler in the House during the 1967 and 1968 sessions of Congress. Suggestions to clean up backlogs accumulated under national origins and to make more smooth the operation of the labor certification system have been incorporated.

There has not been, however, any solid plan for dealing with the new complaints of the northern European. President Kennedy's bill, and the original draft of President Johnson's bill, had provided for an immigration board, with the power to reserve and reallocate a percentage of the worldwide visas to countries disadvantaged by the legislative change, at least during the initial phase-out of national origins. Even this modest plan was defeated; its opponents, notably Representative Michael Feighan, objected to the granting away of Congress's legislative powers to a quasi-executive agency which could alter the preference system, within limits, at will. Although on the surface it was a ludicrous objection, since constitutionally the Congress could not give its power away even if it wanted to, it was not at heart merely an idle objection. Feighan was simply observing the great political truism that it is far easier in America to preserve the legislative status quo than to change it. Thus it took so long for immigration laws to be rewritten, and thus it would take so long for any drastic changes to be made in the new law, once enacted. The meaty question, never argued on its precise merits, was to what extent Congress should create a scheme to be administered by an executive agency which would prove impregnable to change. In other words, could Congress write a law which it would be politically capable of revising as changing world circumstances warrant? The question will have to be answered. That there is an answer to Feighan's objection seems obvious, since every other part of the immigration law is administered at the present time by executive agencies. How else indeed could the policy be carried out?

A second major problem involves Western Hemisphere immigration. The Select Commission, established by the 1965 act, was unable to make a final recommendation in its last report of January, 1968. "While the Commission majority favors some type of immigration limitation in the New World as in the Old, implementation of the labor certification provisions of our new legislation is as yet insufficiently advanced to permit a meaningful judgment on the role of this device in the general limitation of immigration. With this situation in mind, the Commission recommends that the effective date for the imposition of the 120,000 ceiling on Western Hemisphere Immigration be extended from July 1, 1968, to July 1, 1969."

The proposal to delay was not without precedent. During the year's wait, the Commission hoped to take advantage of an interesting coincidence that developed between the implementation of the Labor Department's certification program and the actual reduction in Western Hemisphere immigration. The 1965 act requires the Secretary of Labor to certify that applicants for immigrant visas will not take jobs from Americans and that their skills are important to the United States. Doctors, mathematicians, chemists, have no difficulty, since these professions are so understaffed that the Labor Department requires neither a job offer nor departmental review of any individual case. The number of professional immigrants from the Western Hemisphere is not as high as the number of semiprofessional and skilled workers, such as welders, machinists, psychiatric aides, and stenographers; these people may come in without a specific job offer, but the department does review each case to insure that the stenographer does not head for an area in which a surplus of stenographers already exists. Finally, the department maintains a third list, of low-skill occupations, which bars their applicants from entering. Obviously depending upon economic conditions in the United States, the Labor Department could adjust its lists to control the flow of immigrants from Canada, Central American, and South American countries.

Apparently, this is precisely what has happened. In 1965, 174,237 immigrants were admitted from the Western Hemisphere. In 1966, the new labor certification provisions cut Western Hemisphere immigration to 121,877, including relatives not coming under the proposed ceiling. Since the new figure is so close to the proposed 120,000 limitation, the Commission evidently felt that the ceiling itself may be unnecessary. In any event, it wanted a year to find out.

Events during the spring of 1968 completely overshadowed any possibility of legislation, however. On March 17, Senator Robert F. Kennedy announced his candidacy for the Presidency, and his brother devoted his full attention to the campaign. With the legislative leader away, the contemplated delaying statute was shelved. And when tragedy struck the Kennedy family anew on June 5, following the California primary, all hope for legislation in 1968 vanished. Edward Kennedy withdrew from Senate battles during June, and the July 1 deadline passed unnoted. National origins was dead, but the Western Hemisphere limitations came to life as called for by the 1965 act. The 120,000 ceiling applied to the entire hemisphere; there are no preferences and no maximums placed on immigrants from any particular country. It would be possible, therefore, though unlikely, for the entire 120,000 visas to go to one nation. But in view of that possibility and a growing dissatisfaction with the operation of the Eastern Hemisphere preference system, reformers look forward to continuing the debate in Congress in January, 1969, after the campaign hiatus.

No less important than the refinement of the system which limits the quantity of immigration is the reformation of the system which regulates the quality. In proposing a board of visa appeals, Senator Edward Kennedy said on the Senate floor: "There are many cases on record in which the denial of a visa [to "relatives of a U.S. citizen or a permanent resident alien"] by an American consul abroad has raised justifiable skepticism. Some of these denial cases have been finally settled through the enactment of private immigration bills. It is true that an informal appeal process currently operates within the Department of State, but regardless of the department's findings, the final decision rests with the consul abroad. I believe an independent board of visa appeals—under law—will help assure a more equitable treatment of denial cases." Opponents of any restriction on the absolute power of minor bureaucrats to deny visa applications can be expected to resist strenuously, as they have since 1952, when the limited right of appeal was done away with by the McCarran-Walter Act. How such opponents reconcile their trust in consular officials and distrust in a Presidentially- and Congressionally-appointed Immigration Appeals Board is unknown.

Necessary also is a statute of limitations in deportation cases. Except in some capital crimes, statutes prescribe time limitations on the Government's power to prosecute all crimes.

Deportation, of course, is a civil penalty for the non-crime of (usually technical) violations of the immigration laws. "The alien may have resided in this country since childhood," said Senator Kennedy, "or for twenty or thirty years or more. He may have been the product of our society—but he is denied its justice and its equity under the law. The absence of a statute of limitations from the basic immigration law is a tragic shortcoming—a glaring injustice which has caused undue personal hardship and anxiety in the lives of many."

Above all, the fundamental requirements of due process must be imposed on the Immigration and Naturalization Service. Hasty hearings, without adequate concern for the need of counsel, greatly impede the ability of the average immigrant to defend himself against unwarranted charges. The lack of a solid basis for judicial review, with all the safeguards of the federal Constitution, means that only the most patently biased and illegal administrative proceedings will be stopped. As long as the notion persists that in America aliens, simply because they are aliens, are entitled to a lesser class of rights than citizens, so long will indignities and indecencies be committed in the name of the United States. Indeed, as long as aliens are denied due process, even citizens are unsafe.

One of the grossest examples of harassment by the I.N.S. against an American citizen concerned the case of an unlucky person born in Canada while his American parents were on vacation. Since his parents were native-Americans, by law the son was a citizen also. But the father had no birth certificate, and this presented a ticklish problem when the now forty-four-year-old son vacationed in Canada and attempted to return. He was held by the immigration authorities on a charge of failure to prove his American citizenship. The Service refused to accept marriage and death certificates of the father, listing an American birthplace. The Service refused to accept official birth certificates of the man's two sisters, stating the father to be a native-born American. The Service refused to accept sworn statements from the sisters, attesting to the birthplace of their father.

Instead, I.N.S. arrested the disputed "citizen" in his home without a warrant, clearly an unconstitutional act if the arrested person is a citizen and an unconstitutional act even if an alien for all crimes but that of being born elsewhere. For four months he was held in jail, denied a hearing, and denied the right to contact his United States Senators. Finally he obtained a lawyer and following a short hearing the hearing officer concluded the man *was* a citizen of the United States. Was the man freed? He would have been had this been a trial for any other offense, but this was an immigration hearing and the constitutional prohibition against double jeopardy does not apply. He was released from jail on "conditional parole"; to avoid rejailing he would have to report to an immigration office monthly, pending review. Six months later the hearing was "reopened." A forty-minute hearing affirmed his citizenship. The case was reviewed anew. Finally, after an expensive review by the Board of Immigration Appeals, he won his case. Yet with even more impunity, the Service has held incoming immigrants for more than a year at a time, without a hearing, without preferring charges, without an explanation. These practices were affirmed in the McCarran-Walter Act and are still possible today.

Still another large-scale problem remains to be solved: the unconstitutional restriction by every state of the immigrants' right to practice their professions. It is the policy of the Federal Government, in both the McCarran-Walter Act and the 1965 amendments, to encourage the immigration of professional and other highly skilled foreigners. The preference systems in both acts make this policy explicit and undeniably clear. Yet it is a startling fact that the laws of every state deny to aliens the right to practice many professions. In one or more states, you must be a citizen of the United States to be an accountant, architect, attorney, dentist, nurse, optometrist, osteopath, physician, surveyor and professional engineer, veterinarian, and many more.

The ostensible justification for the prohibition is the "police power of the state" to protect its citizens from conditions which may be detrimental to their health, safety, or welfare. It is difficult to see how the mere fact of alienage alone can be detrimental, however. In light of the *Takahashi* and other Supreme Court decisions it may well be an unconstitutional assertion of the police power, on the grounds that the denial violates the equal protection guarantee of the 14th Amendment.

In any event, the existing state bans are clearly unconstitutional on another ground, suggested above: Under the supremacy clause of the Constitution, any state law conflicting with federal law is invalid. To admit a doctor to the United States because of a severe shortage of physicians, only to turn around and deny him the right to practice medicine for at least the five years it takes to gain citizenship is an obvious conflict, and an unwise one, too. To support himself, the physician is forced to take a job involving lesser skills, one which might have been filled by an American citizen, but one which in any case involves a tremendous economic waste.

It is well within the power of Congress to void the alienage provisions of state licensing statutes, while establishing qualification tests to ensure that the resident alien is up to American standards in the profession. Without such legislation, American immigration policy can hardly be implemented, and the Congressional motives once again must surely be considered suspect.

Compared to the devilish complexities of the main body of administrative procedure, the national origins system may seem dull and relatively unimportant. In many ways, that appearance was true, since the morass of administrative bottlenecks and procedural unfairnesses have persisted with vigor following the demise of national origins. Yet it was precisely because national origins was so simple and so obviously biased that it could be disposed of so much more easily once the grand assault was made. The continuing power of the Immigration and Naturalization Service and the Department of Justice, in conjunction with the Departments of State and Labor, to exercise wide power with virtually no "due process" restraints in matters of deportation and exclusion, can be more easily justified because the law's wording is so often vague. The American people have had honest differences of opinions, say the departments sworn to uphold the law; they have not always had the time to resolve these differences. So Congress has passed laws which not only blend opposing principles (what we call "compromise") but which also blur language (what we call "ambiguity"). If you have at least a little of what you wanted you won't overturn the whole; if you can't tell exactly what you got, how do you know you didn't get what you sought? In the gaps among the law which administrators rush to fill, our government, at least insofar as immigration is concerned, continues to be of men, not law.

maintaining freedom. It is important to realize that the Bill of Rights was a historical response to the fact that America was, even at that time, a nation of immigrants. Perhaps there might have been a Bill of Rights anyway; for some of these rights were guaranteed in the earlier law of the land and even found expression in ancient documents in England. But there can be no doubt that the clamor for amendments to the new Constitution, and the purpose behind them, was motivated in no small part by the diversity of life in America.

To protect a group of men from domination by a state-financed religion, there must be a "wall of separation" between church and state, wrote Thomas Jefferson. So the 1st Amendment provides that "Congress shall make no law respecting an establishment of religion or prohibiting the free exercise thereof," a bar which has been extended to state legislatures as well. And if people are to protect this right, they must be given the equally important freedoms of speech and press and petition. These essential doctrines of our constitutional firmament were not mere abstractions created in the ordered minds of eighteenth-century lawyers. They were the response of a nation of many peoples to the requirement that they each be free.

Our history has repeated this truth many times. Against the encroachments of an "American" majority, immigrant minorities tested their basic freedoms in countless court cases. Many of the most important Supreme Court cases spelling out the reach of fundamental rights bear the names of aliens, immigrants, and their descendants: Yick Wo, Endo, Takahashi, Oyama, and Afroyim.

Rights are not protected only by courts, of course. Informal adjustments are made at all levels of society before it becomes necessary to repair to the formality of judicial declarations. But whether through discourse in a courtroom or the stark power of the ballot, the fact that there has been the widest possible diversity among ethnic and religious groups has, in spite of the tensions created, been a primary factor in the preservation of the democratic ideal.

It was repeatedly noted during the 1965 debates that many eminent men would have failed to obtain admission to the

8 / *Afterlude:*
The Immigrant Contribution

How common it still is in America to find someone named Palucchi or Cadwicirz. "Hey Palucchi, are you Italian? Cadwicirz, are you Polish?" Poor Palucchi, poor Cadwicirz—they and their parents were born in America—neither speaks Italian or Polish; Palucchi's mother's maiden name was Smith and Cadwicirz's O'Leary, and they have been neither to Germany (where Smith was originally Schmidt) nor to Ireland. "No, we are Americans." And poor little Randi Greenstein, asked by her fellow fourth-graders whether her family would have turkey on Thanksgiving. Informed that they always did, her classmates looked incredulous: "Is Thanksgiving a Jewish holiday also?"

If the "immigrants *were* American history," as Oscar Handlin has put it, it is not enough to tell simply the individual doings of a few outstanding men, or to note that even our language is a mosaic built from the words of many tongues. Or that our diet consists of contributions from many kitchens. Or to note the foreign influence in our art, music, literature, and science. To be sure, it is interesting to know that the most widely sold Christmas song of all times was written by a Jewish immigrant from Russia with a German name, Irving Berlin ("White Christmas"). It is interesting to know that many of the scientists in America who were involved in the World War II race for atomic power were immigrants not all of whom were Nordic. But the impact of immigrants on our national life is far greater than the sum of its parts.

If two words could summarize America, they would be "activity" and "freedom." More than to anything else, Americans point with pride to their land of ceaseless creating and building, carried on by a free and spirited people. Without the central fact of immigration, it would be difficult to conceive that either of these conditions could have been fulfilled in the New World.

Despair may have driven some from their ancient roots to America, but despair alone will not account even for these journeys. Driving most emigrants from Europe, South America, and Asia (though sadly not from Africa) were the hope of a new start and the belief that growth and development were possible. As a group, immigrants newly arrived in America have an abundance of one quality without which creation and construction are impossible: an accommodation for change. Here "natural selection" was at work—the conscious selection of a new land and a new life. Those who were most traditional, most reluctant to change, stayed home. In countless ways the desire for change manifested itself among the immigrant groups: the acceptance of a new language, new political systems, new modes of expression, new foods, new methods of agriculture and industry, new tools and technologies.

American "know-how" is not some mysterious hereditary quirk of peoples indigenous to the Western Hemisphere; it is a by-product of a pragmatic people who have a job to do and who fervently believe that their children will have a better life than they. This was a contribution of the immigrant and it developed *because* they were immigrants who grasped the enormous potential of the willingness to abide change. It is not at all coincidental that the mounting despair of Negroes in the late 1960's springs from the one group in America which did not

freely emigrate and which has not been allowed to realize its potential.

Emma Lazarus's dream was not a literal rendition of historic truth; it had the ring of truth, the partial truth which makes a poem meaningful, and the license of song, which makes it poetic. The poem inscribed on the Statue of Liberty is less a statement of fact than a ringing challenge. "Give us your tired, your poor, your huddled masses yearning to breathe free, your wretched refuse . . ." And see what we in America will make of them; and see what they will make of themselves in America. The challenge is that given even the worst from the Old World, they cannot fail to better themselves and the New.

Not all immigrants were eager to tolerate change, it must be conceded. Some groups that came to America in order to avoid the conformity into which they were forced in Europe found themselves suddenly free to do what they had detested: force conformity on someone else. The Puritans, for instance, detested the Anglican Church in England but they were powerless to reject it for their own as long as they remained on the eastern banks of the Atlantic. When they gained control of Massachusetts, they expelled many who worshipped a slightly different God. Other groups with not such highly-stylized notions of wrong and right were more willing to tolerate difference, but they did not seek it out; they were content to live their own lives apart from the groups around them.

A country so large and so rich in natural resources as America could not remain forever a haven for people who wished to segregate themselves from the remainder of humanity. Physical proximity and a growing economy, even as early as the late eighteenth century, impressed a community of interest upon the colonists. When they rebelled, it was with the conscious desire that people should be free to fulfill their own destinies.

Because there were so many different people with so many different beliefs, the committee which drafted the Constitution was aware that upon the survival of these different peoples depended the survival of freedom in their newly-won nation.

Furthermore, the differences could be used as a vehicle for

United States—Christopher Columbus because the Italian quota was long oversubscribed; Alexander Hamilton, because he was a British colonial and the colonies had similar quotas still. Few ever noted that men at least as notable as these did fail admission: men from Italy, Russia, Greece, Africa, Asia, Hungary, and everywhere else; men who may have been geniuses, who may have invented that which is even yet not invented, organized companies not yet dreamed of, propounded still unknown theories —these men *were* refused.

It was also noted by opponents of the 1965 legislation that to open the gates to a random cross-section of the world's population is a policy that no other country in the world can claim. Indeed, one of our closest allies—politically and culturally— decided in the early months of 1968 to refuse admission to its own *citizens* who were living out of the country. When Kenya gained its independence from Great Britain a few years earlier, its people were given the right to choose their citizenship. A number of East Indians living in Kenya opted for British citizenship, which under the common law of England carried with it the right to enter or leave the country. When Kenya began forcing the Asian aliens out, the British feared the influx of the few thousand who were leaving. The Government proposed and Parliament passed an act to limit admissions to 1,500 per year; the outcry prompted the Labor Party to agree to accept those citizens who had nowhere else to go.

Senators Eastland and McClellan, dissenting in the Senate Judiciary Committee Report on the 1965 arguments, were obviously in error when they argued: "Other countries exercise this right [to refuse admission] daily and their motives are not questioned. *But not the United States.* Oh! No! [sic] We must get down on bended knees and apologize and please don't be offended because we are exercising this very same sovereign right to say who shall and who shall not enter the United States." For motives *were* questioned; and the fact remains that, as Senators Eastland, McClellan, and others argued repeatedly in 1965, the policies of other countries should not necessarily bear on our own policies. There can be no question that the immigration laws of most countries are highly restrictive: Argentina, Australia,

Canada, Guatemala, Honduras, Nicaragua, South Africa, and Venezuela all have restrictive policies based in part on race. Many more countries severely limit immigration. But the Eastland-McClellan point, that the American immigration policy-to-be was unlike that existing anywhere in the world, was a point against their own position. For *America* is unlike any country in the world with respect to its immigrant contribution, its political structure, and its democratic ideals.

Senator Ervin did raise a point in criticism which we would do well to heed: When we get oratorical and emotional, he said, we say we want the tired and poor and despised, but we really take the brilliant and energetic only. Our preference system is effectively geared to keep out the lone, rude immigrant of our simpler days. Although America is a nation of immigrants, we are becoming increasingly less an immigrant society, and the dangers from becoming too homogeneous should be contemplated. When the nation drew inward on itself, fearing the outside conspiracies that loomed everywhere, and forgetting its transplanted origins, hysterical legislation threatened the premises of American democracy. "Internal security" laws cannot flourish where optimism prevails, and optimism demands a look at the path from which we have come to know the path toward which we are going.

In the end, all the economic, political, and cultural analysis really proves nothing. Obviously some immigrants coming to rat-infested slums, without adequate means of support, unable to speak English, will encounter and even cause problems. Obviously, some immigrants will have contempt for local institutions. Obviously, some immigrants will commit crimes. Obviously, some immigrants will be more talented than some Americans and compete successfully for jobs. And obviously, some immigrants will bring new ideas and cause changes in the American condition. But why not? So will many Americans do these things.

The new immigration act expresses a broad philosophy, as all far-reaching legislation does, unmeasurable by economic indicators, technical reports, administrative science, or city planners. It digs a broad channel, allowing the current to take a new direction. It reaffirms America's traditional faith in itself and in the cleansing and creative effects of an open society. Alone among the great nations, it allows men of all origins, races, creeds, and religions to enter and participate in its unfinished tasks. In this solitary immigration policy is mirrored—now more closely than in decades—America's larger uniqueness. Are Americans extinct? We might have been, but we show signs of reviving.

NOTES AND BIBLIOGRAPHY

CHAPTER 1

Page 3, 4. Both statements quoted in Johan J. Smertenko, "The Emerging Hyphen," *Harper's*, August, 1951, p. 63.

4. See *Life* Magazine, October 15, 1951, p. 55, for the story of the Oriental orphan.

5. The case of the loyal lady was *Ex Parte Endo*, 323 U.S. 283 (1944).

8. The case was *Henderson v. Mayor of City of New York*, 92 U.S. 259 (1876).

9. Quoted in John Higham, *Strangers in the Land, Patterns of American Nativism 1860–1925* (Rutgers University Press, New Brunswick, N.J., 1955), p. 44. Though we may scoff at the belief today that crime is hereditary, recent evidence suggests that it is possible that chromosomal abnormality may account for a tendency to commit antisocial acts. See *The New York Times*, April 14, 1968, p. 1.

9. The Chinese Exclusion Case is *Chae Chan Ping v. United States*, 130 U.S. 581 (1889).

10. For a typical Feighan query, see "Immigration," Hearings before Subcommittee No. 1 of the House Committee on the Judiciary, 88.2, Part I, at pp. 213–214 (1964).

10. The great desegregation decision is *Brown v. Board of Education*, 347 U.S. 483 (1954). The Washington, D.C., case decided the same day is *Bolling v. Sharpe*, 347 U.S. 497 (1954).

CHAPTER 2

Page 13. This chapter is based in large part on the accounts in Higham, *Strangers in the Land, supra,* probably the most thorough and knowledgeable history of the people, events, and passions leading to restriction in the 1920's; in Malwyn Allen Jones, *American Immigration* (The University of Chicago Press, Chicago, 1960), an excellent and more recent but somewhat condensed study of the same theme; and in George M. Stephenson's *A History of American Immigration, 1820–1924* (Russell & Russell, Inc., New York, 1964), first published in 1924, close to the events in question, and therefore far more equivocal than the others (and sometimes, regrettably, palpably in error).

13. This fact is reported by President Kennedy in his book, *A Nation of Immigrants* (Harper & Row, New York, 1964), p. 69.

15. *Chy Lung v. Freeman*, 92 U.S. 275 (1875), was the case that invalidated the early California law.

16. *The Passenger Cases* can be found in the reports at 48 U.S. (7 How.) 283 (1849).

16. The case was *Henderson v. Mayor of City of New York*, 92 U.S. 259 (1876).

16. Quoted in Stephenson, p. 259.

17. For a glimpse of California in the 1870's and for an analysis of the California Constitution enacted under Kearney's influence, see James Bryce, *The American Commonwealth*, vol. 2, chapter 89, and also the Note to Chapter 89 in the Appendix, for a letter from Kearney to Bryce.

17. The case distinguishing among black, yellow, and white was *In re Ah Yup*, 5 Sawy. 155, 1 F. Cas 223 (F. Cas. 104) (Cir. Ct. D. Cal. 1878).

18. *Chew Heong v. United States*, 112 U.S. 536 (1884).

19. *United States v. Jung Ah Lung*, 124 U.S. 621 (1888).

20. The Chinese Exclusion Case is *Chae Chan Ping v. United States*, 130 U.S. 581 (1889).

20. *Fong Yue Ting v. United States*, 149 U.S. 698 (1893).

25. Senate Resolution 68 is quoted in *Congressional Record*, June 22, 1906, p. 8919.

26. Until recently the subject of how turn-of-the-century immigrants lived, felt, fought, won, and lost was left for the pages of sentimental studies of particular nationality groups. It was Oscar Handlin who focused a discerning historian's eye on the reception of immigrants and on their common plight in America. *The Uprooted* (Little, Brown & Co., Boston), a sensitive and artistic history, was first published in 1952.

28. Quoted in Higham, p. 133.

30. See Higham, p. 122, for Spencer's statement.

31. For a detailed study of the New England intellectual response to increased immigration and the growth of restrictionist sentiment in Brahmin Boston, see Barbara M. Solomon, *Ancestors and Immigrants* (Harvard University Press, Cambridge, 1956).

32. Lodge quoted in Higham, p. 142.

32. Walker quoted in Higham, p. 143.

33. Walker quoted in Solomon, p. 76.

33. The description of Chamberlain's book is found in Ashley Montagu, *Man's Most Dangerous Myth: The Fallacy of Race* (World Publishing Co., New York, 1964), 4th edition, p. 58.

34. For a discussion of Galton's theories, and his statement, see Theodosius Dobzhansky, *Heredity and the Nature of Man* (Harcourt Brace & World, New York, 1964), pp. 52ff, and Montagu, p. 224.

37. Grant quoted in Higham, p. 156, and Solomon, p. 201.

38. Grant's summation quoted in David Spitz, *Patterns of Anti-Democratic Thought* (Free Press, New York, 1965, revised edition), pp. 177–178; this book contains a short discussion of Grant's and related political philosophies.

39. Darwin quoted in Arnold M. Rose, ed., *Race Prejudice and Discrimination* (Alfred A. Knopf, New York, 1951), p. 437.

40. The Irish incidents are based on William V. Shannon, *The American Irish* (Macmillan, New York, 1963), pp. 43–45, and Carl Wittke, *We Who Built America* (Prentice-Hall, New York, 1939), pp. 489ff.
41. The Haymarket incident is based on Higham, and Marcus L. Hansen, *The Immigrant in American History* (Harvard University Press, Cambridge, 1940), pp. 87ff. The editorial comments are quoted in Higham, pp. 54f.
43. Blaine is quoted in Stephenson, p. 270.
44. Watson is quoted in Higham, p. 186.
44. For a good summary with citations of the applicable statutes, see Jack Wasserman, "The Immigration and Nationality Act of 1952—Our New Alien and Sedition Law," 27 Temple L.Q. 62 (1953).
46. Foran bill backer quoted in Jones, p. 252.
48. The authority is Jones, pp. 180f.
49. Wilson is quoted in Higham, pp. 192f.
50. For Roosevelt's suggestion, see Higham, p. 209.
51. Justice Holmes's famous lines are from *Schenck v. United States*, 249 U.S. 47 (1919).
51. For a complete study of the Red Scare, see Robert K. Murray, *Red Scare* (McGraw-Hill paperbacks, New York, 1964); see also, Allan L. Damon, "The Great Red Scare," *American Heritage*, February, 1968.
52. Palmer is quoted in Damon, p. 26.
53. *The Times* is quoted in Damon, p. 75.
54. See Preston W. Slosson, *The Great Crusade and After, 1914–1928* (Macmillan, New York, 1930), pp. 293ff, for Europe's reaction to America and vice versa.

CHAPTER 3

Page 55. For good analyses of the climate of the early 1920's as it related to immigration restriction, see Higham, chapter 10, Slosson, chapter 13, and Mark Sullivan, *Our Times,* Part 6, "The Twenties" (Charles Scribner's Sons, New York, 1935), chapter 9.
61. MacLafferty's plea is in *Congressional Record,* May 9, 1924, p. 8237.
61. Miller's comments: *Congressional Record,* April 8, 1924, p. 5885.
62. Gilbert's conclusions, *Congressional Record,* April 12, 1924, p. 6260.
63-64. *Ozawa v. United States,* 260 U.S. 178 (1922). *Yamashita v. Hinkle, Secretary of State of State of Washington,* 260 U.S. 199 (1922).
64. *United States v. Thind,* 261 U.S. 204 (1923).
65. *United States v. Wong Kim Ark,* 169 U.S. 649 (1898). *Elks v. Wilson,* 112 U.S. 94 ((1884).
67. Dickstein's complaint: *Congressional Record,* May 9, 1924, p. 8238.
68. See *The New York Times,* May 27, 1924, page 1, for events of preceding day, and page 20, column 2, for editorial comment.

72. The McCormack-Reed exchange is in "National Origins Provision of Immigration Law," Hearings before the Committee on Immigration, United States Senate, 70.2 (1929), pp. 140–141.

73-80. Shipstead's testimony is taken from the above Senate hearings, pp. 166–171.

80. Hill's concessions are found in the same hearings, pp. 22–23.

82. Hoover's remarks are quoted in Robert A. Divine, *American Immigration Policy, 1924–1952* (Yale University Press, New Haven, 1957), pp. 78–79.

CHAPTER 4

Page 85. *Frothingham v. Mellon,* 262 U.S. 447 (1923).

85. For lucid and eminently readable discussions of the concept of race, its validity, and its effects on dealings of men with each other, see Montagu, *Man's Most Dangerous Myth: The Fallacy of Race;* Dobzhansky, *Heredity and the Nature of Man;* and Clyde Kluckhohn, *Mirror for Man* (McGraw-Hill, New York, 1949). See also Spitz, *Patterns of Anti-Democratic Thought.*

89. The classification is taken from Dobzhansky, pp. 83–84.

91. The Kluckhohn quotation is from *Mirror for Man,* pp. 110–112.

92. For a fuller development of this blatant misconception as to the nature of African cranial sutures and for a collection of other misconceptions, see Montagu, pp. 294ff.

93. Boas quoted in Kluckhohn, p. 108.

94. The Railroad Car Case was *Plessy v. Ferguson,* 163 U.S. 537 (1896).

95. It was overruled in 1954 by *Brown v. Board of Education,* 347 U.S. 483 (1954).

96. The Miscegenation Case is *Loving v. Virginia,* 388 U.S. 1 (1967).

98. The secretary-general's assertion is contained in "National Origins," 1929 Senate Hearings, p. 126.

CHAPTER 5

P. 99-101. The *St. Louis* drama is based on the account in Arthur D. Morse, "Voyage to Doom," *Look* Magazine, November 28, 1967, on p. 58. The FDR letter is quoted therein at p. 69. See also, for more detailed treatment of the U.S. failure to respond with sympathetic immigration policies to Nazi atrocities, Morse, *While Six Million Died* (Random House, New York, 1968).

103. For more detailed discussion of the Smith Act of 1940, see Jack Wasserman, "The Immigration and Nationality Act of 1952—Our New Alien and Sedition Law," 27 Temple L.Q. 62 (1953). See also the summary of events relating to postwar immigration policy in *Congressional Quarterly, Congress and the Nation,* pp. 218–232 (1964).

105. Quoted in *Congress and the Nation,* p. 219.

108. See A. J. Liebling's amusing and highly readable chronicle of a pathetic part of Congress's past, and of the character of

Senator McCarran and the part he played in the Indian land fraud, *The New Yorker,* "The Lake of the Cui-Ui Eaters," a four-part series during January, 1955.

108. McCarran quotation from Liebling, January 22, 1955, *The New Yorker,* p. 52.

109. McCarran's statements from *Congressional Quarterly Almanac,* 1952, p. 158.

113. President Truman's veto message is in Poyntz Tyler, ed., *Immigration and the United States* (The H. W. Wilson Co., New York, 1956), pp. 99ff.

114. On Congressional inability to read the McCarran-Walter Act, see Wasserman, *supra,* p. 79.

115. Walter quotation: *Congressional Quarterly, Congress and the Nation,* p. 228.

116. Eastland's soliloquy is at p. 15004, *Congressional Record,* July 27, 1956.

117. Alexander's remarks from his article, "A Defense of the McCarran-Walter Act," 21 Law and Contemporary Problems 383, 386 (1956).

118. Senator John F. Kennedy's floor statements are at p. 8348, *Congressional Record,* June 5, 1957; and at p. 16719, *Congressional Record,* August 30, 1957.

CHAPTER 6

Page 123. Robert Kennedy's comment is at p. ix. *A Nation of Immigrants.*

123. For an example of Congressman Fitzgerald's speeches, see *Congressional Record Appendix,* January 27, 1897, p. 45.

125. Alexander's mathematics argument is at p. 392 of his article "A Defense of the McCarran-Walter Act."

126. Private immigration bills are discussed in Note, "Private Bills in Congress," 79 Harvard L. Rev. 1684 (1966).

127. See *Congressional Quarterly Almanac,* 1965, pp. 459–482, for summary of the course of debate. See also, on the Celler-Feighan feud, Duke and Meisler, "Immigration: Quotas vs. Quality," *The Reporter,* January 14, 1965, pp. 30f.

133 ff. See the two-volume "Immigration," Hearings before the Subcommittee on Immigration and Naturalization of the Committee on the Judiciary, United States Senate, 89.1 (1965), for the complete record of testimony. All excerpts are taken from these volumes.

133 f. Rusk's testimony: Part I, pp. 46–84.

135. Ervin's "hot and cold" argument: Part II, pp. 733–734.

136. Ervin-Schlei colloquy: Part I, p. 286.

137. Robert F. Kennedy statement: Part I, p. 225.

137. Rusk-Fong colloquy: Part I, p. 72.

139. Wirtz statement: Part I, pp. 84–85, 92.

140. Wirtz-Fong colloquy: Part I, pp. 114f.

141. Scott-Ervin colloquy: Part I, p. 137.

142. On the employability of skilled individuals, see Part I, p. 124.

142. Robert F. Kennedy on discrimination: Part I, p. 216.

143. Chamberlain quoted in Spitz, *Patterns of Anti-Democratic Thought*, p. 182.
144. Ervin-Schlei colloquy: Part I, p. 277.
144. Celebrezze-Ervin colloquy: Part I, p. 342.
145. Ervin-Limperis colloquy: Part II, p. 401.
145. Ervin-Carey colloquy: Part II, p. 477.
146. For Ervin's emergency legislation justification, see Part II, p. 416.
146. Ervin-Marchisio colloquy: Part II, p. 503.
146. Douglas statement: Part I, p. 155.
147. Fong-Douglas colloquy: Part I, p. 165.
150. Ervin-Rusk colloquy: Part I, pp. 62–63.
150. Ervin-Robert Kennedy colloquy: Part I, p. 240.
151. Celebrezze-Ervin colloquy: Part I, pp. 345–346.
151. Ervin-Katzenbach colloquy: Part I, p. 20.
152. Carliner-Ervin colloquy: Part II, p. 460. Mr. Carliner's testimony is worth reading in its entirety (pp. 427–467). It is among the most articulate in the record.
153. Ervin-Limperis colloquy: Part II, p. 384.
153. Ervin-Errigo colloquy: Part II, pp. 423–424.
154. Ervin-Katzenbach colloquy: Part I, pp. 19–20.
155. Ervin-Wirtz colloquy: Part I, p. 107.
157. Liberty Lobby: Part II, p. 666.
157. National Economic Council: Part II, p. 680.
157. New Jersey Coalition: Part II, p. 683.
157. D.A.R. statement: Part II, p. 711.
158. Baltimore Anti-Communist League: Part II, p. 766.
158. Federation of Republican Women: Part II, pp. 835–837.
159. Sons and Daughters of Liberty: Part II, p. 692.
159. Statement on water pollution: Part II, pp. 693–700.
160. For summary of House debate, see *Congressional Quarterly Almanac*, 1965, pp. 468–473.
162. Celler quoted in *Congressional Quarterly Almanac*, 1965, p. 463.
165. President Johnson's message: *The New York Times*, October 4, 1965, p. 1.
165. Celler's statement: "Immigration," Hearings Before House Subcommittee No. 1 of the Committee on the Judiciary, 88.2 (1964), Part I, p. 4.
166. For Harris and Gallup polls, see Senate Hearings, 1965, Part II, pp. 666, 847.
167. Bennett, "The Immigration and Nationality Act of 1952, as Amended to 1965," The Annals of the American Academy of Political and Social Science, *The New Immigration*, September, 1966, p. 134.

CHAPTER 7

For case histories relating to administrative snags and cruelties, the reader is referred to J. Campbell Bruce, *The Golden Door* (Random House, New York, 1954); Edith Lowenstein, *The Alien and the Immigration Law* (Common Council for American Unity, Oceana Publications,

New York, 1958); and Ellen R. Knauff *The Ellen Knauff Story* (W. W. Norton & Company, New York, 1952).

Page 172. Examples are from Bruce, pp. 75–78.

172. The account of Mrs. Knauff's ordeal is based on her book. See also Walter Gellhorn, *American Rights* (Macmillan, New York, 1963).

173. Mrs. Knauff's case was *United States ex rel. Knauff v. Shaughnessy*, 338 U.S. 537 (1950).

175. The Hungarian Exclusion Case is *Shaughnessy v. United States ex rel. Mezei*, 345 U.S. 206 (1953).

176. The Chinese Laundry Case is *Yick Wo v. Hopkins*, 118 U.S. 356 (1886).

177. *Wong Wing v. United States*, 163 U.S. 228 (1896).

178. The Japanese Immigrant Case is *Yamataya v. Fisher*, 189 U.S. 86 (1903).

178. *Ng Fung Ho v. White*, 259 U.S. 276 (1922).

178. *Wong Yang Sung v. McGrath*, 339 U.S. 33 (1950).

179. The quoted parts of the Administrative Procedure Act are Sections 236 and 242.

180. Black and Frankfurter dissent in *Marcello v. Bonds*, 349 U. S. 302, 319 (1955). For a discussion of the A.P.A. as it relates to immigration practice, see Heckman, "Our Immigration Laws, a Continuing Affront to the Administrative Procedure Act," 41 *Georgetown L. J.* 364 (1953).

180. The Deportation Case is *Harisiades v. Shaughnessy*, 342 U.S. 580 (1952).

181. Justice Holmes is quoted in *Bugajewitz v. Adams*, 228 U.S. 585 (1913).

181. "Framework" quotation from H.R. Report No. 2096, 82.2 (1952) at p. 127.

182. See Lowenstein, for hundreds of such cases.

183. The 1923 case is *Terrace v. Thompson*, 263 U.S. 193 (1923), quoting from 274 F. 841 (1923).

183. Act of May 31, 1870, 8 USC 41.

184. See the testimony of Mike M. Masaoka, Senate Hearings, 1965, Part II, pp. 619–631.

184. For indictment of the American war evacuation program, see Allan R. Bosworth, *America's Concentration Camps* (W. W. Norton & Company, New York, 1967), and Eugene V. Rostow, "The Japanese American Cases—A Disaster," 54 Yale L.J. 489 (1945).

184. The case which upheld the evacuation is *Hirabayashi v. United States*, 320 U.S. 81 (1943).

184. The case of the loyal lady is *Ex parte Endo*, 323 U.S. 283 (1944).

185. Concerning the Hirata story, see Blake Clark, "Why Shouldn't They Be Americans?" *The Freeman*, July 16, 1951.

186. The story is recounted in *Takahashi v. Fish & Game Commission* 334, U.S. 410 (1948).

186. The case is *Oyama v. California*, 332 U.S. 633 (1948). For a

good summary of Japanese immigration and treatment and the law of California and Congress, see Justice Murphy's concurring opinion at 650. See also Bradford Smith, *Americans from Japan* (J. B. Lippincott, New York, 1948), and Edward K. Strong, *The Second-Generation Japanese Problem* (Stanford University Press, Stanford, 1934).

187. Expatriation as penalty for desertion: *Trop v. Dulles,* 356 U.S. 86 (1958).

187. Expatriation as penalty for living abroad: *Schneider v. Rusk,* 377 U.S. 163 (1964).

188. Expatriation for voting in foreign elections: *Afroyim v. Rusk,* 387 U.S. 253 (1967).

189. Concerning the Irish, see *The New York Times,* March 16, 1968.

190. Quotation from *Report of the Select Commission on Western Hemisphere Immigration,* January, 1968, p. 11.

192. Senator Edward M. Kennedy's statement appears at pp. 14628–9. *Congressional Record,* October 11, 1967.

193. The account is from Bruce, *The Golden Door,* pp. 18–23.

CHAPTER 8

Page 197. Handlin's comment is from *The Uprooted,* p. 3.

201. Senate Rept. No. 748, 89.1 (1965), at p. 52.

Page 216. Table 1 is from *Statistical Abstract of the United States, 1967,* U.S. Department of Commerce, 1967.

218. Table 2 is from *Congressional Quarterly Almanac,* 1965 (Washington, D.C., Congressional Quarterly, Inc., 1965), p. 460

220. Table 3 is from *Statistical Abstract, 1967.*

NOTES FOR FURTHER READING

In addition to the books and articles referred to in the *Notes,* many of which have extensive reference bibliographies, a few other books and articles of special interest are noted briefly below.

Abbott, Edith, *Historical Aspects of the Immigration Problem* (University of Chicago Press, Chicago, 1926). A collection of documents.

Berkson, Isaac B., *Theories of Americanization* (Columbia University Press, New York, 1920). A case study of the Americanization of Jews in America.

Bernard, William S., ed., *American Immigration Policy—a Reappraisal* (Harper & Row, New York, 1950). A sympathetic study of the need for immigration reform, 1950. Good statistical analyses of immigrants' impact on the economy, on population growth, and on the problems of adjustment. Also, a discussion of other countries' experiences with immigration.

Bowers, David F., ed., *Foreign Influences in American Life* (Princeton University Press, New York, 1944). A series of essays on the immigrant and his role in America; bibliographies to 1944. Essays on social and cultural impact are rather technical. Good essays on the role of foreign thinking in art, literature, and philosophy, especially for the role Darwinian thought has played.

Brown, Francis J., and Roucek, Joseph S., eds., *One America* (Prentice-Hall, New York, 1952, 3d edition). A copious collection of essays on diverse minority groups within the United States and their relationships with themselves and "native" America.

"Developments in the Law—Immigration and Nationality," 66 Harv. L. Rev. 643 (1953). A lengthy, technical discussion of the McCarran-Walter Act.

Fairchild, Henry P., ed., *Immigrant Backgrounds* (John Wiley & Sons, New York, 1927). A series of nationality sketches, circa 1927. Generally sympathetic, but too concise to be authoritative.

Garis, Roy L., *Immigration Restriction: A Study of the Opposition to and Regulation of Immigration into the United States* (Macmillan, New York, 1927). An account of the politics and arguments against the national origins system, by a passionate advocate of the 1890 restriction plan.

Glazer, Nathan, and Moynihan, Daniel P., *Beyond the Melting Pot* (Harvard University and Massachusetts Institute of Technology Presses, Cambridge, 1963). The classic modern study of New York City's Negroes, Puerto Ricans, Jews, Italians, and Irish. The thesis is that the melting pot, in its simplest form, is no longer tenable in New York; ethnic groups have not and will not blend into one great middle gray. What has happened and what remains to be done is the subject of this study.

Hansen, Marcus L., *The Atlantic Migration, 1607–1860* (Harvard University Press, Cambridge, 1940). The classic study of American immigration to 1860. Gives a good insight into the formative years of America up to the point at which post-Civil War industrialization leads into the modern era.

Immigration and Nationality Act, with amendments and notes (Committee Print, House Committee on the Judiciary, 5th edition, revised through December 31, 1965). An up-to-date compendium of the Immigration and Nationality Act, containing a verbatim copy of the act and some annotation.

Jaffe, Louis, "The Philosophy of Our Immigration Laws," 21 Law and Contemporary Problems 358 (1956). This essay, and a number of other essays in the same issue of the journal, comprise a rounded discussion of the state of immigration policy in 1956.

Maisel, Albert Q., *They All Chose America* (Thomas Nelson & Sons, New York, 1957). Sketches of immigrant groups and problems they are currently facing. Well-written and informative.

"The New Immigration," The Annals of the American Academy of Political and Social Science, September, 1966. A symposium on the facts and problems of post-World War II immigration, including articles on the 1965 legislation. A valuable general discussion.

Schermerhorn, R. A., *These Our People* (D. C. Heath & Company, Boston, 1949). A look at various ethnic groups, such as Latin Americans, American Indians, eastern Europeans, Jews, and Negroes, from the point of view of racial myths and cultural differences and problems in assimilation.

Scully, Thomas, "Is the Door Open Again?—A Survey of Our New Immigration Law," 13 U.C.L.A. L. Rev. 227 (1966). Just what it says, and not overly technical.

Senior, Clarence, *Strangers, then Neighbors* (Freedom Books, New York, 1960). A concise case study of the Puerto Rican migration to the mainland and their problems of assimilation.

Udell, Gilman G., *Naturalization Laws*, Government Printing Office, Washington, 1964). A collection of naturalization laws since the turn of the century, now not quite up to date. Lack of index makes this a difficult book to use.

Warner, W. Lloyd, and Srole, Leo, *The Social Systems of American Ethnic Groups* (Yale University Press, New Haven, 1945). Personal histories and discussion of ethnic groups, their languages, associations, churches, and families. An examination of assimilation and the melting pot.

White, Lyman C., *Three Hundred Thousand New Americans* (Harper & Row, New York, 1957). Immigrants were not left simply to their own resources; especially after World War II there were a number of agencies which helped them adjust to a new life. This is the story of one such agency, the United Service for New Americans; and it contains a good glimpse of the problems and promise of the new land in modern day.

APPENDIX

TABLE 1

Annual Immigration Quotas, by Country, under Successive Immigration Laws and Amendments: 1921 to 1965

COUNTRY	1921 Act (3 percent, 1910)	1924 ACT		1952 Immigration and Nationality Act, as amended (1965 quota)
		Effective 1924 (2 percent, 1890)[1]	Effective 1929 (national origin ratio)[2]	
All countries	356,995	164,667	[3]153,714	[4]158,561
Europe	355,406	161,546	150,591	149,697
Austria	7,451	785	1,413	1,405
Belgium	1,563	512	1,304	1,297
Bulgaria	302	100	100	100
Czechoslovakia	14,282	3,073	2,874	2,859
Denmark[5]	5,694	2,789	1,181	1,175
Finland	3,921	471	569	566
France	5,729	3,954	3,086	3,069
Germany	68,059	51,227	25,957	25,814
Great Britain[6]	77,342	34,007	65,721	65,361
Greece	3,294	100	307	308
Hungary	5,638	473	869	865
Iceland	(5)	100	100	100
Ireland[6]	(6)	28,567	17,853	17,756
Italy	42,057	3,845	5,802	5,666
Netherlands	3,607	1,648	3,153	3,136
Norway	12,202	6,453	2,377	2,364
Poland	25,827	5,982	6,524	6,488
Portugal	2,520	503	440	438
Romania	7,419	603	295	289
Spain	912	131	252	250
Sweden	20,042	9,561	3,314	3,295

Switzerland	3,752	2,081	1,707	1,698
Turkey	656	100	226	225
U.S.S.R.	34,284	2,248	2,784	2,697
Yugoslavia	6,426	671	845	942
Other Europe	2,427	1,562	1,538	1,534
Asia	1,043	1,300	1,323	3,690
Africa	122	1,200	1,200	4,274
Australia, New Zealand, and other Oceania	359	221	200	4,700
North America	(6)	(6)	(6)	200
Jamaica	(6)	(6)	(6)	100
Trinidad and Tobago	(6)	(6)	(6)	100
All others	65	400	400	—

— Represent zero.

[1] Presidential Proclamation 1703 of June 30, 1924.

[2] Presidential Proclamation 1872 of March 22, 1929.

[3] Quota was 153,714 in 1930-1931; 153,831 in 1932-1933; 153,774 in 1934-1944; 153,879 in 1945-1946; 153,929 in 1947-1949; 154,206 in 1950: and 154,277 in 1951-1952.

[4] Quota was 154,657 in 1953-1956 (Presidential Proclamation 2980 of June 30, 1952); 154,857 in 1957; 154,957 in 1958; 154,857 in 1959; 154,887 in 1960; 156,487 in 1961; 156,687 in 1962; 156,987 in 1963; and 158,161 in 1964.

[5] Prior to 1924, Iceland included with Denmark.

[6] Prior to 1924, all Ireland included with Great Britain; thereafter, only Northern Ireland. Prior to 1963, Jamaica and Trinidad and Tobago included with Great Britain.

Source: Dept. of Justice, Immigration and Naturalization Service; *Annual Report*.

TABLE 2

Immigrants Admitted to the United States, Fiscal 1953–64

CLASS	1953–64	1953[1]	1954	1955	1956	1957	1958	1959	1960	1961	1962	1963	1964
TOTAL IMMIGRANTS ADMITTED	3,197,857	170,434	208,177	237,790	321,625	326,867	253,265	260,686	265,398	271,344	283,763	306,260	292,248
Quota Immigrants (total)	1,140,479	84,175	94,098	82,232	89,310	97,178	102,153	97,657	101,373	96,104	90,319	103,036	102,844
1. Immigration & Nationality Act	1,124,863	78,053	88,016	79,617	88,825	97,084	102,077	97,651	101,352	96,074	90,305	102,995	102,814
1st preference quota: Selected immigrants of special skill or ability	30,600	77	1,429	1,776	1,946	2,992	3,941	3,518	3,385	3,460	3,313	2,288	2,475
Their spouses and children	28,676	45	1,027	1,236	1,420	2,739	3,197	3,109	3,681	3,758	3,721	2,374	2,387
Skilled agriculturists, their wives & children (1924 act)	321	321											
Parents or husbands of U.S. citizens (1924 act)	4,290	4,290											
2d, 3d, 4th preference quota: Relatives of U.S. citizens and residents	149,508	5,712	10,717	10,894	11,930	13,466	12,927	14,386	13,299	14,933	11,729	14,770	14,745
Nonpreference quota	911,468	67,608	74,843	65,711	73,529	77,887	82,030	76,638	80,987	73,923	71,542	83,563	83,207
2. Special legislation quota immigrants, chiefly displaced persons under 1948 Displaced Persons Act	15,616	6,122	6,082	2,615	485	94	76	6	21	30	14	41	30
Nonquota Immigrants (total)	2,057,378	86,259	114,079	155,558	232,315	229,689	151,112	163,029	164,025	175,240	193,444	203,224	189,404
1. Immigration & Nationality Act	1,681,285	85,015	112,854	126,135	156,808	147,243	125,591	111,341	133,087	152,382	169,346	183,283	178,200
Wives of U.S. citizens	236,980	15,916	17,145	18,504	21,244	21,794	23,517	22,620	21,621	20,012	17,316	17,590	19,701
Husbands of U.S. citizens	73,418	3,359	7,725	6,716	5,788	5,767	5,833	6,913	6,140	6,059	6,646	6,035	6,437
Children of U.S. citizens	70,896	3,268	5,819	5,662	4,710	4,798	5,970	6,869	6,454	6,480	6,354	6,981	7,531
Natives of Western Hemisphere countries	1,227,778	58,985	78,897	92,620	122,083	111,344	86,523	66,386	89,566	110,140	130,741	144,677	135,816
Their spouses and children	27,482	2,114	1,629	1,654	1,949	2,144	2,052	1,810	2,135	2,696	2,764	3,067	3,468
Persons who had been U.S. citizens	902	104	427	87	44	58	43	22	36	15	25	23	18
Ministers of religious denominations, their spouses and children	5,107	387	385	307	350	403	435	558	485	406	451	462	478

	Total												
Employees of U.S. Government abroad, their spouses and children	205	2	4	9	2	8	23	24	27	10	3	32	61
Children born abroad to resident aliens or subsequent to issuance of visa	12,117	326	358	348	412	701	926	1,228	1,458	1,411	1,495	1,611	1,843
Aliens adjusted under sec. 249, Immigrations and Nationality Act[2]	22,795							4,321	4,773	5,037	3,399	2,680	2,585
Other nonquota immigrants	3,605	554[3]	465	228	226	226	269	590	392	116	152	125	262
2. Special legislation nonquota immigrants	376,093	1,244	1,225	29,423	75,507	82,446	25,521	51,688	30,938	22,858	24,098	19,941	11,204
Displaced persons (Displaced Persons Act of 1948, nonquota)	1,030	1,030											
Orphans (act of July 29, 1953)	466	67	399										
Refugees (Refugee Relief Act of 1953)	189,021		821	29,002	75,473	82,444	1,012	198	43	9	15	3	1
Skilled sheepherders (act of Sept. 3, 1954, nonquota)	385			354	31								
Immigrants (act of Sept. 11, 1957)	61,948						24,467	24,834	6,612	3,982	1,809	213	31
Hungarian parolees (act of July 25, 1958)	30,701							25,424	5,067	122	51	20	17
Azores and Netherlands refugees (act of Sept. 2, 1958)	22,213							1,187	8,870	5,472	4,796	1,888	
Immigrants (secs. 2 and 3, act of Sept. 22, 1959)	29,337								10,314	13,255	5,488	280	
Immigrants (act of Sept. 26, 1961)	15,525										11,912	2,848	765
Other nonquota immigrants (special legislation)	412	214	5		3	2	42	45	32	18	27	12	12
Refugee and escapees (act of July 14, 1960)	6,111											2,005	4,106
Immigrants (act of Oct. 24, 1962)	18,944											12,672	6,272

[1] In 1953 figures include admissions under Immigration Act of 1924.
[2] Not reported prior to 1959.
[3] Includes 321 professors of colleges and universities, their wives and children.

Source: Senate Judiciary Committee.

TABLE 3

Immigrants, by Country of Last Permanent Residence: 1820 to 1965

[For years ending June 30. Data prior to 1906 refer to country from which aliens came. Because of boundary changes and changes in list of countries separately reported, data for certain countries not comparable throughout.]

COUNTRY	Total 146 yrs., 1820-1965	1941-1950, total	1951-1960, total	1960	1961	1962	1963	1964	1965
All countries	43,291,273	1,935,039	2,515,479	265,398	271,344	283,763	306,260	292,248	296,697
Europe	35,105,902	621,704	1,328,293	120,178	108,532	103,989	109,066	108,215	101,468
Albania	2,232	85	59	13	9	12	9	8	10
Austria [1]	285,076	24,860	67,106	2,219	1,114	944	1,526	1,311	1,743
Hungary [1]	285,076	3,469	36,637	5,166	397	400	635	649	510
Belgium	194,432	12,189	18,575	1,119	1,131	959	922	1,296	1,155
Bulgaria	66,732	375	104	20	34	37	36	261	29
Czechoslovakia	130,283	8,347	918	240	212	103	111	190	389
Denmark	356,389	5,393	10,984	1,160	902	957	1,070	970	1,088
Estonia	997	212	185	26	43	14	8	15	14
Finland	29,185	2,503	4,925	508	474	505	358	495	332
France	709,359	38,809	51,121	5,438	4,403	3,931	4,926	5,598	5,573
Germany [1]	6,845,239	226,578	477,765	29,452	25,815	21,477	24,727	24,494	22,432
Great Britain [2]	4,692,272	131,592	195,498	20,176	18,843	18,196	22,867	25,897	24,279
England	2,998,344	112,252	156,171	16,058	14,936	14,970	18,314	21,067	19,443
Scotland	802,248	16,131	32,854	3,662	3,587	2,915	4,139	4,408	4,440
Wales	93,359	3,209	2,589	247	196	181	255	283	252
Greece	506,479	8,973	47,608	3,634	3,124	4,408	4,744	3,998	3,016
Ireland [3]	4,704,251	26,967	57,332	6,918	5,738	5,118	5,746	6,055	5,187
Italy	5,041,268	57,661	185,491	13,369	18,956	20,119	16,175	12,769	10,874
Latvia	2,166	361	352	64	84	52	48	40	37
Lithuania	3,470	683	242	77	125	52	58	50	59
Luxembourg	2,372	820	684	71	42	56	52	68	85
Netherlands	343,114	14,860	52,277	8,654	7,362	6,378	4,086	2,039	2,353
Norway [1]	848,191	10,100	22,935	2,391	2,204	1,839	1,934	2,145	2,179
Poland [1]	465,200	7,571	9,985	4,216	6,254	5,660	6,785	7,097	7,093
Portugal	297,363	7,423	19,588	6,766	3,832	3,622	2,911	2,006	1,937
Romania	160,218	1,076	1,039	280	176	135	126	287	434
Spain	196,972	2,898	7,894	1,397	1,737	3,353	2,969	4,069	3,929
Sweden	1,259,905	10,665	21,697	2,462	1,670	1,760	2,056	2,196	2,413
Switzerland	333,823	10,547	17,675	1,952	1,697	1,793	1,952	2,119	2,360
Turkey in Europe	161,833	580	2,653	461	410	581	834	506	396

U.S.S.R.[1]	3,345,351	548	181	270	130	119	163	190
Yugoslavia	71,983	1,576	1,448	1,188	1,086	972	1,098	1,051
Other Europe	49,747	3,983	300	286	312	304	326	321
Asia [4]	1,202,077	31,780	21,604	19,495	20,249	23,242	21,279	20,040
China [5]	416,695	16,709	1,380	900	1,356	1,605	2,684	1,611
India	16,209	1,761	244	292	390	965	488	467
Japan	345,155	1,555	5,699	4,490	4,054	4,147	3,774	3,294
Turkey in Asia	208,050	218	5,200	4,296	4,304	307	331	365
Other Asia [4]	215,968	11,537	14,081	13,517	14,145	16,218	14,002	14,303
America	6,548,294	354,804	119,525	139,580	155,871	169,966	158,644	171,019
Canada and Newfoundland	3,798,798	171,718	46,668	47,470	44,272	50,509	51,114	50,035
Mexico	1,367,056	60,589	32,708	41,476	55,805	55,986	34,448	40,686
Central America	167,752	21,665	6,719	7,272	9,639	10,706	11,829	12,736
South America	372,813	21,831	16,494	19,095	22,550	27,759	34,891	33,757
West Indies	739,383	49,725	13,636	20,520	20,917	22,951	24,067	31,141
Other America	102,492	29,276	3,300	3,747	2,688	2,055	2,295	2,664
Africa	57,150	7,367	1,925	1,851	1,834	1,982	2,015	1,949
Australia and New Zealand	88,038	13,805	1,892	1,556	1,427	1,642	1,767	1,803
Pacific Islands [4]	22,128	5,437	248	325	144	136	88	155
All other countries	267,684	5,142	26	5	249	226	240	263

[1] 1938 to 1945, Austria included with Germany; 1899 to 1919, Poland included with Austria-Hungary, Germany, and U.S.S.R.
[2] Beginning 1952, includes data for United Kingdom not specified, formerly included in "Other Europe."
[3] Comprises Eire and Northern Ireland.
[4] Philippines included in "Other Asia" beginning 1952 and in "Pacific Islands" 1934 to 1951. Prior to 1934, recorded separately as insular travel.
[5] Beginning 1957, includes Taiwan.

Source: Dept. of Justice, Immigration and Naturalization Service; *Annual Report*.

INDEX

Index